Form and Frenzy in Swift's
TALE OF A TUB

Form and Frenzy in Swift's

TALE OF A TUB

John R. Clark
NEW YORK UNIVERSITY

CORNELL UNIVERSITY PRESS

ITHACA AND LONDON

First published 1970

Standard Book Number 8014-0551-3
Library of Congress Catalog Card Number 72-101056

PRINTED IN THE UNITED STATES OF AMERICA
BY VAIL-BALLOU PRESS, INC.

FOR ANNA

Non potest beneficium manu tangi;
res animo geritur.

Contents

. . . 'tis [Man's] reason I despise,

. . . . .

This busie, puzling, stirrer up of doubt,
That frames deep *Mysteries*, then finds 'em out;
Filling with Frantick Crowds of thinking *Fools*,
Those Reverend *Bedlams, Colledges*, and *Schools*
Borne on whose Wings, each heavy *Sot* can pierce,
The limits of the boundless Universe . . . ,

. . . . .

'Tis this exalted Pow'r, whose bus'ness lies
In *Nonsense*, and impossibilities.
This made a Whimsical *Philosopher*,
Before the spacious *World*, his *Tub* prefer,
And we have modern *Cloysterd Coxcombs*, who
Retire to think, cause they have naught to do.

—From "A Satyr against Mankind," in
*Poems by John Wilmot, Earl of Roches-
ter*, ed. Vivian de Sola Pinto (Cambridge,
Mass., 1953, by permission of Harvard
University Press and Routledge & Kegan
Paul Ltd).

Foreword

One supposes that the *Tale of a Tub* will always be a special case—composed in what Henry James would have called the "finer tone." If Swift intended, as he tells us, "to vex the world rather than divert it," he may rest in peace; for the fact is that the *Tale* and its author continue to tease us out of thought. The vexatious question for the nineteenth century was Swift himself: was he atheist, skeptic, mechanist, deist, Anglican devout, or Anglican compromised? Was he Horatian jester or Juvenalian clout? Or was he merely a gross misanthropist and jibbering madman? In the twentieth century the grand question continues to be debated, its spirit in our time tempered but hardly laid to rest.

Our century has simply turned to other matters—turned, in fact, to the *Tale of a Tub* itself. Formalist critics, seeking to discern in the *Tub* the shapely structure, have aroused a vexatious number of debates. Prominent among them is the question of persona; if Swift's work is coherent literary fiction, must not a palpable "character" who consistently speaks inhabit this *Tub?* There is *none*, say some; there is *one*, say others; there are *four*, or *five*, or *six*, still others say. This question, too, stands unresolved.

Nor has the *Tale of a Tub* profited in its literary reputation from recent studies of the history of ideas and of Neoclassical practice. A number of scholarly explorations have found the Age of Reason not so reasonable as had been once supposed. Paradoxically, in the Enlightenment, the century that exalted the epic produced no significant epics; the century that commended decorum and form produced loose sentences, loose verse satire, and loose novels about loose men and women. Another trend finds recent criticism broaching the *Tale of a Tub* by long division: Mrs. Starkman's study openly professes to treat only of the introductory pieces and the digressions, whereas Phillip Harth's deals solely with the sections of religious allegory.[1] Criticism universally concedes the *Tale of a Tub* to be a masterpiece, but criticism does not quite see why. Unaccountably, insidiously, formalism and separatism seem to be drawing together, like the theology of Swift's modern projectors, who "have discovered a gross Ignorance in the Natures of Good and Evil, and most horribly confounded the Frontiers of both." [2]

If we have been perturbed by questions about Swift's personality, the problem of his fictional persona, and the patent dichotomy of the *Tale*'s digressions and the stretches of dry, allegorical tale that splice them together, still more vexation lies in store—the question of authorship itself.

[1] Miriam Kosh Starkman, *Swift's Satire on Learning in "A Tale of a Tub"* (Princeton: Princeton University Press, 1950); Phillip Harth, *Swift and Anglican Rationalism: The Religious Background of "A Tale of a Tub"* (Chicago: University of Chicago Press, 1961).

[2] *A Discourse Concerning the Mechanical Operation of the Spirit,* in *A Tale of a Tub To which is added The Battle of the Books and the Mechanical Operation of the Spirit . . .* , ed. A. C. Guthkelch and D. Nichol Smith (2d ed.; Oxford: Clarendon Press, 1958), p. 274. Hereafter, all quotations from, and references to, specific passages in the *Tale* cite this edition. Quotations are by permission of the publisher.

Thus the cloying knife has begun to cut the soundest limb: Robert Martin Adams, reviving an eighteenth-century claim, has argued vigorously that not Jonathan Swift but Cousin Thomas Swift sired the allegorical tale of the three brothers; fully a third or more of the *Tale of a Tub*, according to this claim, is not Swift's own.[3] The "bagatelle" of vexation is too full; and we discover that not only have we succeeded in throwing out the baby with the bath water, but we must face the prospect of having to throw out the tub as well.

But in spite of all, Swift's practice upon us surmounts mere vexation. He intended his raillery, as he himself insisted, to "nettle"; yet raillery does something more; it

> Sets your Thoughts upon their Mettle:
> Gives Imagination Scope,
> Never lets your Mind elope:
> Drives out Brangling, and Contention,
> Brings in Reason and Invention.[4]

Swift's emetic art was regularly administered to purge minds of triticality, vice, and sleep. In their stead, wakened readers were encouraged to supply their own reason and imagination.

Twentieth-century criticism has responded energetically to Swift's aesthetic nettle; recent criticism of Swift and his

---

[3] "Jonathan Swift, Thomas Swift, and the Authorship of *A Tale of a Tub*," *Modern Philology*, LXIV (1967), 198–232. Edmund Curll's *A Complete Key to the Tale of a Tub* . . . (1710) had proposed this thesis of dual authorship.

[4] "An Epistle to a Lady," ll. 213–217, *The Poems of Jonathan Swift*, ed. Harold Williams (2d ed.; Oxford: Clarendon Press, 1958), II, 637. Quotations are by permission of the publisher.

work, devoted to careful reappraisal, has indeed been rea-
soned and inventive:

The current interest in the art or craft of Swift's works, the
anatomy of his masks, his rhetorical strategies, has encouraged
rather than discouraged a new engagement with his substance,
an engagement not limited to the surface. Analytical criticism
has pierced that surface and has discovered a lost, if not a new,
world.[5]

The present study is intended to be no exception; in vexation's despite, it seeks to comprehend Swift's *Tale of a Tub*
as a work of art.[6] The traditional view has been that satire
is didactic, is rhetorical—"a kind of poetry . . . invented
for the purging of our minds; in which human vices, ignorance, and errors . . . are severely reprehended." [7] Traditional criticism of this sort contends that satire is concerned, not with an end that Aristotle would have termed

[5] Milton Voigt, *Swift and the Twentieth Century* (Detroit:
Wayne State University Press, 1964), p. 164.
[6] The present study limits its attention to *A Tale of a Tub* and
attempts no analysis of its companion pieces, *The Battle of the
Books* and *The Mechanical Operation of the Spirit*. Although all
three are bound together, all "fragments," and all concerned with
Temple, Wotton, and an arrogant modernity, it is fairly well
understood that these works are deliberately disparate: a childish
(and digressive) "tale," a mock-heroic treatise, and a letter to a
friend. Swift's satire on its broadest level proposes a *reductio* of
metaphysical publishing wit: "the violent yoking together of opposites." But this functioning of the whole as a pertinent *jeu d'esprit*
does not preclude the artistic integrity of its members; and of the
three, the *Tale of a Tub* is clearly the most ambitious and most
accomplished.
[7] "A Discourse Concerning the Original and Progress of Satire,"
Essays of John Dryden, ed. W. P. Ker (New York: Russell and
Russell, 1961), II, 100.

"beauty of form," but with "the inculcation of doctrine." [8]
The striking point is that, although the vogue of the New
Criticism has directed attention to the literary virtues and
aesthetic form of all manner of specific works, satire has
too long been excluded from that feast.

Only very recently has satire commenced to obtain admission to the banquet room of art.[9] Consequently, the
purpose of the present study is to explore *A Tale of a Tub*
as a work of mimetic art. Since mimetic masterpieces display a "pattern" or "rhythm" of action, a continuity of
plot to which characters, episodes, thought, diction, and
scenes are subservient—indeed, in terms of which alone can
characters, episodes, diction, or scenes be understood at all
—we may expect in this study to discover in Swift's *Tale
of a Tub* such a rhythm or plot, or its absence. In mimetic
works, we recognize that plot or action is the crucial framework upon which all else depends—a plot whose regular
advancement raises the action to a climax and creates a totality by that action's very movement from beginning to
middle to end, ultimately communicating a large and complete feeling both to the parts of its own action and to its
audience, of a nature and singleness of kind that Aristotle,

[8] Elder Olson, "A Dialogue on Symbolism," *Critics and Criticism*,
ed. R. S. Crane (Chicago: University of Chicago Press, 1952),
pp. 589–590.
[9] In addition to the speculations of Northrop Frye, in "The Nature of Satire," *University of Toronto Quarterly*, XIV (1944),
75–89 (a version of which appears in his *Anatomy of Criticism*
[Princeton: Princeton University Press, 1957]), the reader may
consult a number of book-length studies of satire that have appeared in the last decade, such as those by James Sutherland,
Robert C. Elliott, Gilbert Highet, Alvin Kernan, Leonard Fein-
berg, and Ronald Paulson.

with reference to tragedy, calls its "power." [10] Either the *Tale* exhibits such a powerful continuity, or it does not. Examination will shortly determine whether the satiric *Tale* is a work of art, whether it is mimetic, whether there is in it a predominant single action, generating a subsequent and effective power.

The question of the presence or absence of plot, of order and form, is certainly a central question concerning *A Tale of a Tub* to be posed, carefully investigated, and answered. The perdurable *Tub*, like its ancient prototype invested by Diogenes, can withstand our kicking; and it may just happen that the *Tale of a Tub*, so long a gadfly upon the literary scene, will dramatize its own apotheosis. Perhaps, in accordance with the phrase of Alcibiades, Swift's *Tale* will prove Socratic: externally, it may appear merely an artisan's brazen and ugly Silenus figure, but when opened for inspection, its interior may reveal the artist's beautiful "images of gods." [11]

JOHN R. CLARK

New York
September 1969

[10] "Form, or synthesizing principle" (*Poetics* IX.11–12), the "wondrous" effect of a plot obeying some probable and cosmic design, is treated as an efficient power by Elder Olson, in "The Poetic Method of Aristotle: Its Powers and Limitations," *English Institute Essays, 1951*, ed. Alan S. Downer (New York: Columbia University Press, 1952), especially pp. 82 and 85; and by R. S. Crane, in *The Languages of Criticism and the Structure of Poetry* (Toronto: University of Toronto Press, 1953), p. 44 and *passim*.

[11] Plato, *Symposium* 215A–B.

Acknowledgments

I am indebted to the Horace Rackham School of Graduate Studies at The University of Michigan for three fellowships that sustained research and preparation of this book. Likewise, I am grateful to the editorial staff of Cornell University Press for their interest and kind attention and for their thoroughness and efficiency.

A version of my first chapter originally appeared as "Swift's Knaves and Fools in the Tradition: Rhetoric versus Poetic in *A Tale of a Tub*'s Section IX," in *Studies in Philology*, LXVII (October 1969); I am grateful to Ernest W. Talbert, the editor.

Finally, I want to express here my thanks to two men, scholars and friends: H. V. S. Ogden and Sheridan Baker.

PART I

Conflict in the *Tale:*
"Imagination at Cuffs
with the Senses"

I. Traditional Fools
and Knaves in Section IX

Knaves and fools divide the world.
—Proverb (1670)

One could hardly wish to deny the presence of rhetoric in the work of art; for all men—artists among them—employ rhetoric on every occasion: "All men make use, more or less, of [rhetoric and dialectic]; for to a certain extent all men attempt to discuss statements and to maintain them, to defend themselves and to attack others." [1] Nonetheless, the work of art and the rhetorical tract differ considerably; where the rhetorician seeks to persuade an audience concerning what it should think or how it should act, the artist, in Sir Philip Sidney's words, "nothing affirmeth"; he is concerned with imitation, with the creation of a complete poetic whole, "a perfect pattern." This means, in effect, that rhetoric is a "useful," where poetics is a "fine," art.

Useful art, employing nature's own machinery, aids her in her effort to realize the ideal in the world around us, so far as man's practical needs are served by furthering this purpose. Fine art sets practical needs aside; it does not seek to affect the real world, to modify the actual. By mere imagery it reveals the ideal form at which nature aims in the highest sphere of organic existence,—in the region, namely, of human life.[2]

[1] Aristotle, *Rhetoric* I.i.1, in *Rhetoric, Poetics,* trans. W. Rhys Roberts (New York: Random House, 1954), p. 19.

[2] S. H. Butcher, *Aristotle's Theory of Poetry and Fine Art* (4th ed.; New York: Dover Publications, 1951), p. 157. *Cf.* Walter J.

[3]

As Susanne Langer has argued, rhetoric is discursive, poetry presentational. For rhetoric is a *means* to creating "action" in the real world, whereas poetry is an *end* in itself, the creating of a complete and imitative action—not in the real world, but in the world of art.

Promising and eventful as the recent criticism of *A Tale of a Tub* has been, too much of it has emphasized Swift's "tactics" and his "rhetoric." [3] Such studies incline to move toward the borders of criticism rather than to its heartland. For the business of literary criticism is the study of the work of art *as* art.

The essential thing about the understanding to which the literary critic aspires is that it is understanding of literary works in their character as works of art. It is not criticism but psychology when we treat poems or novels as case-books and attempt to discover in them not the art but the personality of their authors. It is not criticism but history or sociology when we read imaginative writings for what they may tell us about the manners or thought or "spirit" of the age which produced them. It is not criticism but ethical culture when we use them

Ong, S.J., "The Province of Rhetoric and Poetic," *Modern Schoolman*, XIX (1942), 24–27.

[3] See especially John M. Bullitt, *Jonathan Swift and the Anatomy of Satire* (Cambridge, Mass.: Harvard University Press, 1953); Martin Price, *Swift's Rhetorical Art* (New Haven: Yale University Press, 1953); William B. Ewald, Jr., *The Masks of Jonathan Swift* (Oxford: Basil Blackwell, 1954); Ronald Paulson, *Theme and Structure in Swift's "Tale of a Tub"* (New Haven: Yale University Press, 1960); Charles Allen Beaumont, *Swift's Classical Rhetoric* (Athens: University of Georgia Press, 1961); Edward W. Rosenheim, Jr., *Swift and the Satirist's Art* (Chicago: University of Chicago Press, 1963); and Richard I. Cook, *Jonathan Swift as a Tory Pamphleteer* (Seattle: University of Washington Press, 1967).

primarily as means of enlarging and enriching our experience of life or of inculcating moral ideals. It is not criticism but autobiography when we content ourselves with stating our personal preferences with regard to them or the adventures of our souls in their presence. Criticism as we shall understand it is not any of these things; it is simply the disciplined consideration, at once analytical and evaluative, of literary works as works of art.[4]

The purpose of the present study is to examine the *Tale of a Tub* as a work of art. In treating the *Tale* centripetally as a single and complete work of mimetic art, we shall proceed toward a goal consciously distinct from the aim of studies which treat satire as polemic, and satire's techniques and processes as those of the orator, the magistrate, or the missionary. Let us attempt to clarify, at the outset, the approaches that distinguish the critic of rhetoric from the critic of a work of art.

I

Since the critic of rhetoric believes that the satirist's primary concern is the persuasion, reassurance, or sustenance of his audience, he conceives of the satirist's business as the manufacture (or reconditioning) and distribution of virtuous doctrine. A major difficulty at once arises from these expectations, involving the doctrine's proper shape and size.

It is correct to read every part of the *Tale* as an adaptation of one attitude: that wilful rejection of the Established Church, limited monarchy, classical literary standards, and rational

---

[4] Ronald S. Crane, "History versus Criticism in the University Study of Literature," *English Journal* (College Ed.), XXIV (1935), 654.

judgment is an act of pride, and leads to corruptions in government, religion, and learning.[5]

Such a reading may well be "correct," but unquestionably it is reductive, proposing (what the *Tale's* own modern would extol) "an universal System in a small portable Volume" (p. 125). It leaves too much about the work of art out of an accounting.

A still greater difficulty arises concerning the artist's deliverance of his doctrine: What if, after the rhetorical critic has given the work a thorough combing, no doctrine can be found? A number of critics have come to expect the satirist not only to censure folly and vice, but positively to inculcate virtue as well. With Middleton Murry, they hold that "true satire implies the condemnation of a society by reference to an ideal," [6] with such an ideal normally taking the form of social aspirations and codes—in F. R. Leavis' words, making "some kind of reference to positive standards." [7] Apparently such critics expect the reference to such standards to be open and direct, intoned rhetorically in the identifiable first-person voice of the satirist himself; they assume that the "positive standards" will at the least stick out round the edges of the satire—hard, chunky, and obvious, like a turkey bone in the throat.

Searching the *Tale of a Tub* for such positive criteria or "Augustan standards" has proved to be for many a critic a traumatic experience, for such standards often appear to be

[5] Irvin Ehrenpreis, *Swift: The Man, His Works, and the Age,* I: *Mr Swift and His Contemporaries* (Cambridge, Mass.: Harvard University Press, 1962), 202.

[6] J. Middleton Murry, *The Problem of Style* (London: Oxford University Press, 1960), p. 59.

[7] "The Irony of Swift," *Scrutiny,* II (1934), 366.

intransigently absent. It is just this elusiveness of standards in the *Tale* that has led critics frequently of late to accuse Swift of "betraying" or "trapping" his audience.[8] These claim that Swift rhetorically leads his audience to accept some clear-cut prose statement of affirmatives, only to disappoint and shock his audience by shifting ground and attacking even those positives he had appeared to sustain.

As an instance of such critical findings, we may consider those of F. R. Leavis, who in his essay "The Irony of Swift" engages to comprehend two lengthy and crucial paragraphs from the *Tale of a Tub*'s celebrated Section IX, the digression on madness. Leavis concludes that Swift in this passage deliberately betrays his readers, first coercing them to choose sides between surface (credulity, delusion, happiness) and depth (curiosity, reason, virtuoso experimentation), but for the most part leading readers to deplore depth, or curiosity, and to favor surface, or credulity. Then, in a startling climax, Swift suddenly and willfully reverses himself, admitting that those seeking after depth are "knaves," but now equally subverting admirers of surface, consigning them to the category of "fools." Fools or knaves: these are the choices. Which one is right? Leavis inquires and concludes that, for Swift, neither is, and that therefore Swift's attitude is wholly "negative." A considerable number of critics have agreed with this reasoning, some of them going so far as to urge that Swift is actually the "helpless" neurotic, attracted by credulity as well as by

[8] Consult Milton Voigt, *Swift and the Twentieth Century* (Detroit: Wayne State University Press, 1964), p. 150; the idea is developed at length by Henry W. Sams, in "Swift's Satire of the Second Person," *Journal of English Literary History*, XXVI (1959), 36–44.

curiosity, and eviscerated upon the horns of his dilemma.[9] The dilemma, however, is quite apt to be the rhetorical critic's, and not Swift's own. For the rhetorical critic is caught in a singular contradiction: first he instructs us that Swift is the rhetorician, seeking to be "*immediately* intelligible" to his audience;[10] then he informs us that Swift very unoratorically fails to communicate anything at all, immediately or otherwise.

As a matter of fact, such critics would never presume to

[9] *Scrutiny*, II (1934), 374, 375. See William Empson, *Some Versions of Pastoral* (Norfolk, Conn.: New Directions, 1960), pp. 58–60; Basil Willey, *The Eighteenth Century Background* (Boston: Beacon Press, 1961), p. 106; M. C. Bradbrook and M. G. Lloyd Thomas, *Andrew Marvell* (Cambridge: Cambridge University Press, 1940), pp. 114–117; J. C. Maxwell, "Demigods & Pickpockets: The Augustan Myth in Swift and Rousseau," *Scrutiny*, XI (1942), 34–39; D. S. Savage, "Swift," *Western Review*, XV (1950), 25–36; John Lawlor, "Radical Satire and the Realistic Novel," *Essays and Studies, 1955*, ed. D. M. Low (London: John Murray, 1955), pp. 58–75; A. E. Dyson, "Swift: The Metamorphosis of Irony," *Essays and Studies, 1958*, ed. Basil Willey (London: John Murray, 1959), pp. 53–67; Robert Martin Adams, "Swift and Kafka," *Strains of Discord* (Ithaca, N.Y.: Cornell University Press, 1958), pp. 157 ff.; David P. French, "Swift, Temple, and 'A Digression on Madness,'" *Texas Studies in Literature and Language*, V (1963), especially pp. 49–51; and Curtis C. Smith, "Metaphor Structure in Swift's *Tale of a Tub*," *Thoth*, V (1964), especially p. 26. Oswald Johnston, in "Swift and the Common Reader," *In Defense of Reading*, ed. Reuben A. Brower and Richard Poirier (New York: Dutton, 1962), pp. 174–191, extends the argument concerning Swift's "negativism" to nearly everything he wrote. Even the late Herbert Davis acknowledged Swift to be in his satires "a person of a hard-mouthed imagination, easily disposed to run away with him" (*Stella, a Gentlewoman of the Eighteenth Century* [New York: Macmillan, 1942], p. 27).

[10] James Sutherland, *A Preface to Eighteenth Century Poetry* (London: Oxford University Press, 1963), p. 103.

ask whether Oedipus or Creon is the more right in the concluding scene of *Oedipus Rex*, whether Quixote or Panza represents the "right view" of reality, whether Elizabeth Bennet or Darcy exhibits all the pride and prejudice; nor would they insist upon determining whether Milton preferred the life celebrated in "Il Penseroso" or that of "L'Allegro," or whether the classical or the Christian symbols are more correct in Joyce's *Ulysses*. This is manifestly because these critics do not really expect such narrow positives in works of art; yet they clearly do expect such overt and constricted positives in satire, in Swift's *Tale of a Tub*.

Moreover, such criticism of the *Tale* holds good *only* if Swift is understood patently to be attempting to direct wholesome rhetorical teaching into the minds of his hungry audience, *only* if Swift is prompted compulsively to appeal to standard virtuous positives, and *only* if Swift is speaking *in propria persona*. At this juncture, it becomes perfectly clear what a service Ricardo Quintana [11] and the persona critics of the past several decades have performed for Swift criticism generally, suggesting the way in which readers might extract Swift himself from his modern speaker's tangle in the *Tale of a Tub*'s multifarious Section IX. Maynard Mack, in an influential article, has demonstrated that in "formal" or "direct" satire, of the type employed by the Roman verse satirists, the first-person satirist continuously alters, shifts his pose, his stance, his very dramatized self in his work.[12] If such dramatization is common in "direct" satire, we might expect to find more complex dramatiza-

11 "Swift as a Situational Satirist," *University of Toronto Quarterly*, XVII (1948), 130–136.
12 "The Muse of Satire," *Yale Review*, XLI (1951), 80–92. Cf. Carter R. Bishop, "'Peace Is My Dear Delight,'" *West Virginia University Philological Papers*, IV (1943), 64–76.

tions in "indirect" or "fictional" satire. It is certainly apparent in the *Tale*'s digressions that a speaker (other than Swift) is present. He professes to have just been made a member of the Grub Street "Fraternity" of hack authors (p. 63) and repeatedly insists that he is "a most devoted Servant of all *Modern* forms" (p. 45) and one who, in the present work, assures his readers that he has been intent upon composing "a faithful Abstract drawn from the Universal Body of all arts and Sciences" (p. 38). The problem among recent critics has been to determine the nature of this professedly modern persona. Some maintain that here is no persona at all, but merely a careless, occasional, and partial mask of Jonathan Swift, one easily donned, as easily doffed, and seldom sustained; other critics argue that a single and consistent persona of a modern Grub Street author is present throughout the *Tale of a Tub*; and still others discover more than one character in the *Tale*—a modern present in the digressions, but perhaps a scientific virtuoso occasionally as well, and several other personae in the narrative portions of the *Tale* and in the notes.

The question of the presence or absence of a persona (or personae) in the *Tale* cannot finally be resolved at this point. What needs emphasis is precisely the fact that, at the outset of an examination of the *Tale*, one does not know whether there is a persona present or not, whereas rhetorical critics presume that there is none. Logically, we should tentatively grant that there may well be such a consistent Modern in the *Tale of a Tub* but keep in mind the equally plausible possibility that there may not.

Moreover, the rhetorical critic's assumption concerning the absence of a persona, or "character," leads to yet another and more important of his assumptions. Character in mimetic fiction is of necessity subject to, dependent upon, plot.[13] Despite the seeming contradictions and vagaries of many characters in comic and satiric plots, one should realize that one can comprehend the nature and kind of any character in a fiction by observing that character's "actions"—verbal and physical—and by studying his subservient position in the plot or narrative setting. But the rhetorical critic appears to suppose that there is in the *Tale of a Tub* no work of art, no action, no setting, no plot; instead, he appears rather arbitrarily to imagine that the whole of the *Tale*, or even its separate sections, does not represent a coherent artistic work.

If the work itself or any section had artistic coherence, the critic could not, as Leavis has done, extract a passage in the middle of the work from its context, as at the "knaves and fools" conclusion of a paragraph in the middle of Section IX, and reason about it separately. If the work does sustain mimetic continuity, what the speaker in the work has to say at any particular place about knaves and fools may well have nothing whatever to do with the author's opinions; the author is very likely to be observing that *decorum personae* in his art that has been a commonplace in the practice of Western literary tradition. Milton states the principle of dramatic decorum succinctly:

One is not to regard what the poet says, but what person in the play speaks, and what that person says; for different persons are introduced, sometimes good, sometimes bad; sometimes wise men, sometimes fools; and such words are put into their

---

[13] Aristotle, *Poetics* VI.12–13.

mouths, as it is most proper for them to speak; not such as the poet would speak, if he were to speak in his own person.[14]

One simply cannot assume that every opinion expressed in a literary work is the author's.

It might be well to remind ourselves at this point about the very nature of literary criticism. "Its approach is categorical and descriptive: it tries to *identify* a writer's work"; that is, such criticism attends to the work itself; it attempts to define, to describe, to understand the work of art. For "the academic critic's function is to add to our understanding of the writer, and this is bound to make his merits, if he has any, more obvious. To praise or blame the writer, to inflate or deflate his reputation, is not the academic critic's *primary* function at all." Such a literary critic has to bring to the work all of his wits, his humility, and his knowledge; he has to presume, however tentatively, that "the primary understanding of any work of literature has to be based on an assumption of its unity." [15]

In their critique of the *Tale of a Tub*, on the contrary,

[14] "A Defence of The People of England, in Answer to Salmasius's Defence of the King," anon. trans. of *Defensio pro Populo Anglicano*, in *The Prose Works of John Milton*, ed. J. A. St. John (London: Henry G. Bohn, 1848), I, 126. On decorum, consult John S. Coolidge, "Martin Marprelate, Marvell, and *Decorum Personae* as a Satirical Theme," *PMLA*, LXXIV (1959), 526–532. Decorum, or suitability, is the staple of classical and Renaissance criticism, and "appropriateness of character" one of its fundamental applications; see Aristotle, *Poetics* XV.1–6; Horace, *Ars Poetica* 112–118, 153–178, and 227–230; and René Bray, *La Formation de la doctrine classique en France* (Paris: Librairie Nizet, 1961), pp. 215–230.

[15] Northrop Frye, "Literary Criticism," *The Aims and Methods of Scholarship in Modern Languages and Literatures*, ed. James Thorpe (New York: Modern Language Association, 1963), pp. 61, 63.

rhetorical critics in a very real sense are not interested in literary criticism. They do not wish to understand the work of art; they wish to judge its author and the quality of his doctrine. They are interested in rhetoric, whose tactics are discursive, its "end" the creation and regulation of an audience's opinions and response.

II

Having noted the rhetorician's assumptions, it might be profitable to attempt to examine *A Tale of a Tub*'s Section IX from the literary critic's point of view, testing Section IX for art. If the *Tale* is a work of art, we shall find it decorous, dramatic, consistently coherent, with its author remaining aesthetically aloof from the speeches, scenes, and episodes unfolding within his creation.

In Section VIII, we will recall, the ostensible modern persona had deduced a "system" of the sect of Modern Aeolists, and he concluded by asserting that he had always cherished for this sect "a peculiar Honour" (p. 161). Section IX smoothly continues in this vein: the Modern urges that such "Honour" should not be palliated simply because the sect's founder, Jack, happened to be insane.

Thus it is that Section IX proceeds quite simply as a defense of, a praise of, madness, delivered in the manner of the epideictic speech—that "ceremonial oratory of display," as Aristotle terms it.[16] For, although Swift may not

---

[16] *Rhetoric* I.iii.3. That Swift was thoroughly familiar with traditional oratory is obvious; every schoolboy endured long years of such training; see Donald Lemen Clark, *John Milton at St. Paul's School: A Study of Ancient Rhetoric in English Renaissance Education* (New York: Columbia University Press, 1948), and Alice Stayert Brandenburg, "English Education and Neo-Classical Taste in the Eighteenth Century," *Modern Language Quarterly*, VIII

be the overt rhetorician given to oration, his modern persona certainly is: in Section IX he commences an encomium in praise of madness, particularly aiming to show, as such encomiastic oratory does, that madness is "worthy of praise," is "noble"; [17] and, in order to render such honor, the Modern proceeds through the appropriate and traditional oratorical divisions—*exordium, narratio, partitio, argumentatio,* and *peroratio.*[18]

Here the Modern, like Cicero's ideal orator, "beside avoiding any suspicion of a display of talent," chooses not to be "the champion of [mere] expediency," but rather the champion of "integrity"; he "urges us on the path of moral worth [by collecting] examples of our ancestors' achievements that were glorious even though involving danger, and . . . magnif[ies] the value of an undying memory with posterity." [19] His *narratio,* or postulate, simply urges that

(1947), 174–193. That Swift also employed such oratory (to his own ends) in his satires is likewise apparent; see, for instance, Charles Allen Beaumont, "Swift's Classical Rhetoric in 'A Modest Proposal,'" *Georgia Review,* XIV (1960), 307–317, and Lamarr Stephens, "'A Digression in Praise of Digressions' as a Classical Oration: Rhetorical Satire in Section VII of Swift's *A Tale of a Tub,*" *Tulane Studies in English,* XIII (1963), 41–49. I owe a considerable debt, in these pages treating of the Modern's oration, to the thorough study by Henry Knight Miller, "The Paradoxical Encomium with Special Reference to Its Vogue in England, 1600–1800," *Modern Philology,* LIII (1956), 145–178.

[17] Aristotle, *Rhetoric* I.iii.3, I.ix.1–13.

[18] Raymond L. Irwin, "The Classical Speech Divisions," *Quarterly Journal of Speech,* XXV (1939), 212–213. Such terminology varies among different authors; I have largely relied upon Cicero's *De oratore* II.lxxviii.315–lxxxi.333.

[19] *De oratore* II.lxxxii.334–335, in *De oratore,* ed. and trans. E. W. Sutton and H. Rackham, Loeb Classical Library (Cambridge, Mass.: Harvard University Press, 1948), I, 451–452.

"the greatest Actions that have been performed in the World" are directly owing to madness (p. 162). In his brief *partitio*, he announces that his *argumentatio* will produce great examples in which madness is responsible for (1) "the Establishment of New Empires by Conquest," (2) "the Advance and Progress of New Schemes in Philosophy," and (3) "the contriving, as well as the propagating of New Religions" (p. 162). All these "proofs" or "confirmations" make the traditional appeals to the noble ancestry of madness, as well as present a respectable analysis of the company madness keeps—proofs, that is, which make the usual appeals to genesis, tradition, and association.[20] The oration advances regularly enough, the orator citing two examples under each of the three announced heads: Henry IV and Louis XIV; Epicurus and Descartes; Jack of Leyden and (presumably) brother Jack, founder of Aeolism. Thus far, the modern persona is fulfilling the promise of parts of his oration's title—"A Digression concerning the Original, the Use, and Improvement of Madness, in a Commonwealth"—to demonstrate "the Original" (vapors) and "the Use" (in politics, philosophy, and religion) of madness.

In the crucial eighth and ninth paragraphs, the Modern proceeds further to demonstrate "the Use" of madness: madness, or delusion, is in fact the *only* source of happiness; all mankind must make a choice between madness and

[20] Theodore C. Burgess, in *Epideictic Literature* (Chicago: University of Chicago Press, 1902), especially pp. 157–166, discusses typical "Universal Lines of Argument" or "commonplaces" an orator employs in praising a person. Under the general heading *genos* are subdivisions for the praise of the subject's ancestors (*progonoi*), parents (*pateres*), race (*ethos*), and youth, upbringing, and companions (*anatrophe*).

a sort of caviling curiosity; and even those who elect the latter come to discover their error (p. 173). He concludes this portion of his oration resoundingly, asserting that madness is entirely superior to sanity, to reason, and to science. Its superiority is that of a "fool" among "knaves."

The knave in the case is a tricky and deceitful fellow simply because he is not "tranquil," "serene," and "peaceful"; his "curiosity" leads him to uncover the ugly and the unpleasant, to the endorsement of "the Art of exposing weak Sides, and publishing Infirmities" (p. 172), as well as to "unmasking" (a practice never accepted as "fair usage" in art or in life—p. 173). From the perfectly regular viewpoint of the Modern, who is praising insanity, the knave's deceit consists wholly in his favoring unnatural exploration, in preferring experiments and anatomies, in discovering a world of flaws and imperfections. The fool (in French, *fou* or *fol*), on the other hand, is the madman, or "natural"; he is naturally favored in an oration which is a celebration and defense of himself.

Having demonstrated the "Original" and the "Use" of madness, the Modern in the remainder of his oration (sounding increasingly like the modern "projector") proposes the refinement of madness—its "Improvement in a Commonwealth." The madmen of the nation are to be turned loose from Bedlam, are to occupy the choice seats in society and secure the reins of government.

In context, Section IX is a deliberate praise of folly, candidly presenting the confirmation of foolishness and the refutation of its opposite, knavery. It is difficult to understand how the rhetorical critic could have wondered which "side"—that of fools or of knaves—could possibly be "correct."

III

Nevertheless, it might still be objected that one is wrong to isolate both "credulity" and "curiosity" from the life that adheres to the "common forms." A reader might insist that Swift sanctions a credulity which is synonymous with shallow adherence to the "common forms" of the Anglican Church and of a genteel and questionably enlightened upper class. Such a reader would argue that Swift in the *Tale of a Tub* betrays—often helplessly—the selfsame credulous shallowness that he would endorse; the reader might feel that this is so because Swift, no very bright thinker, had nothing better than "surfaces" and "forms" to offer in the place of fanatic curiosity and an indifferent scientific determinism.

The reply must be that Swift is not at all equivalent to his committed persona. We shall discover that, unlike the Modern in Section IX who is devoted to credulity, Swift stands broadly aloof from the positions of either the curious or the credulous man.

In Section IX, we will remember, the sane mind is distinctly devoid of credulity and curiosity. For the sane mind, "in its natural Position and State of Serenity" (p. 171), chooses, elects to pass its life in adherence to the "common forms," which compose "the pattern of human learning"—the vast accumulation of value and experience that distinguishes the historical sense and, indeed, that renders any sort of civilization possible. We cannot enough emphasize the idea of the mind's "natural" position, and the concept that the sane mind elects, or chooses, such a pattern, permitting itself to be "instructed" by it. Such a mind is marked by decision and self-possession.

In sharp contrast, credulous man and curious are equally emblematic of an "unnatural" state. In both, the mind is overcome (this is its *harmartia*) by an *idée fixe;* in both, "a Man's Fancy gets *astride* on his Reason" (p. 171), and such minds cease to retain self-possession, becoming themselves possessed. Throughout the Restoration and the Age of Reason, Englishmen, mindful of the enthusiastic excesses of the Puritan Civil Wars, feared every expression of "fancy" and "spirit"—feared any mind overthrown, inhabited by spirits and devils. It was commonplace in the period to warn against inspiration: "Beware *what Spirit* rages in your breast; / *For ten inspir'd ten thousand are Possest.*" [21]

Swift's credulous and curious men *are* so possessed. In the context of Section IX's wit, both the credulous man and the curious "conceive it in [their] Power, to reduce the Notions of all Mankind, exactly to the same Length, and Breadth, and Height of [their] own" (p. 166). This conception is clearly not Swift's own; but it is the endeavor of the credulous and curious. They both would attempt to measure the world by themselves, *qui ratione sua disturbant moenia mundi;* [22] in this crazed undertaking they both appear to choose either tranquil Epicurean delusion or an ultimately unsatisfactory materialistic or virtuoso experimental-

[21] Wentworth Dillon, Earl of Roscommon, "An Essay on Translated Verse" (1684), in *Critical Essays of the Seventeenth Century,* ed. J. E. Spingarn (Bloomington: Indiana University Press, 1957), II, 306; quoted by permission of Indiana University Press and Oxford University Press.

[22] Jonathan Swift, "Thoughts on Religion," *The Prose Works of Jonathan Swift,* ed. Herbert Davis, 14 vols. (Oxford: Basil Blackwell, 1939–1968), IX, 261; hereafter cited as *Prose Works.* Quotations are by permission of the publisher.

ism. Yet in reality they are minds violently possessed—by vapors from we know not where, if you will, but possessed all the same—by the determination to measure the world by themselves. Ignorant and unaware of the "common forms" or of existence itself outside their own minds, they, forsake God, religion, politics, tradition, and learning. They evidence instead a monolithic reliance either upon their own senses or upon their immediate private imaginings.

Such an egocentric ambition explains why, in Section IX, Swift's modern persona, himself a veritable archetype of "Sufficiency," [23] intends to deduce a system that can so easily contradict every opinion save his own, and why his system emphasizes at bottom a local and private "something Individual in human Minds" (p. 162). It explains why "great actions" (upon which the Modern expends so much time) are repeatedly attributed to the isolated individual— Henry IV, Louis XIV, Epicurus, Cartesius, Wotton, Jack, and, to be sure, the Modern himself. For the modern persona, mad and solitary in his garret, is concerned only with the actions and the ideas of "Single Men" (p. 162), single men concerned with themselves alone. Both credulous and curious men are withdrawn into singularity—where they sleep and dream or engage in private occult study, poring over data amassed from brief forays into the external world, whence they have obtained information from visions and anatomies.

As Ian Watt has observed, "From the Renaissance on-

[23] Consult the discussion of sufficiency (a term favored by Sir William Temple) in Paulson's *Theme and Structure in Swift's "Tale,"* especially pp. 92–93.

wards, there was a growing tendency for individual experience to replace collective tradition," [24] culminating, as we
know, in the victory of romantic singularity and economic
individualism in the nineteenth century. Restoration and
eighteenth-century men fought the good fight against this
encroaching "freedom"; poets and practical men alike were
repeatedly reminded that they should "hate *minuteness*, and
[be] afraid of *singularity*." [25] Traditional Restoration criticism continually warns against the private, the singular;
these are equated with the perverse.

In framing a Character for Tragedy, a Poet is not to leave his
reason, and blindly abandon himself to follow fancy, for then
his fancy might be monstrous, might be singular, and please no
body's *maggot* but his own; but reason is to be his guide, reason is common to all people, and can never carry him from
what is Natural.[26]

Swift, unlike his modern credulous and curious men, partic-
ipates in this tradition that opposes enthusiastic fancy and
the private maggot.

Moreover, there is decisive evidence that the credulous
and curious men do not express Swift's own views. This becomes clear when we examine the tradition of the seven-

[24] *The Rise of the Novel* (Berkeley and Los Angeles: University
of California Press, 1957), p. 60.

[25] Anthony Ashley Cooper, Third Earl of Shaftesbury, Treatise
II of *Characteristics of Men, Manners, Opinions, Times* (1711),
quoted in Watt, *Rise of the Novel*, p. 16. On the distrust of singu-
larity, see Scott Elledge, "The Background and Development in
English Criticism of the Theories of Generality and Particularity,"
PMLA, LXII (1947), 147–182.

[26] Thomas Rymer, "The tragedies of the Last Age Consider'd . . ." (1678), *Critical Essays of the Seventeenth Century*, II,
192.

teenth-century genre of the "character." The "humor character," with his singular and pronounced foible, had been popular in English drama since the time of Jonson. He is descended from Menandrian comedy's highly conventionalized characterizations, such as those of the cunning slave, the kindly matron, the fawning parasite, the *miser amor*, the *miles gloriosus*.[27]

The humor character has a still older life in tradition; in the *Nicomachean Ethics*, Aristotle explored at length a number of "settled dispositions" of mind that produced in men an excess or defect in some moral virtue. In treating of such error-ridden extremes, Aristotle created illustrative characters such as the buffoon, the vain man, the profligate, the paltry man, the niggard.[28] In the work of Aristotle's disciple Theophrastus, examples of excesses and defects of virtue are presented more "humorously," at greater length, in bolder colors. His portrayals of exemplary excesses and defects include such pairs of characters as the complaisant man and the surly, the buffoon and the boor, the *alazon* and *eiron*, the coward and the bully.[29]

[27] Jonson expresses his conception of the humor character well in Asper's eighth speech of the Prologue to "Every Man out of His Humour" (1598). In the Prologue to *Heauton Timorumenon* (ll. 37-39), Terence had listed some prominent character types: the "servos currens, iratus senex, edax parasitus, sycophanta autem inpudens, avarus leno." For delineation of sixteen such character types, see Marvin T. Herrick, "Comic Theory in the Sixteenth Century," *Illinois Studies in Language and Literature*, XXXIV (Urbana: University of Illinois Press, 1950), pp. 147-173.

[28] *The Nicomachean Ethics*, ed. and trans. H. Rackham, Loeb Classical Library (Cambridge, Mass.: Harvard University Press, 1947), pp. 249, 227, 181, 213, 201-203.

[29] "The Characters of Theophrastus," ed. and trans. J. M. Edmonds, in *The Characters of Theophrastus; Herodes, Cercidas, and*

As is well known, Elizabethans—Joseph Hall, Sir William Cornwallis the Younger, John Earle, Sir Thomas Overbury—recommenced the tradition of such satiric character-writing, which continued to be popular throughout the seventeenth century. We soon discover that during this period no humorous affectation or excess was more popularly characterized than that "curiosity" in pedants, antiquaries, and similar Baconian collectors of the type ridiculed long ago in Lucian's "Ignorant Book Collector" (*Adversus indoctum*). Later in the seventeenth century, with the growth of the Royal Society and inductive science, this collector is more specifically embodied as the Sir Nicholas Gimcrack of Thomas Shadwell's play, *The Virtuoso* (1676), and Addison's "virtuoso" who in his will leaves to his associate his "rat's testicles, and Whale's pizzle," and to his son his "monsters, both wet and dry." [30]

Caught in this satiric tide, the curious virtuoso is laughed at for fully a century. Marston deals with several characters named Curio; Pope utilizes a Curio in his epistle "To Mr. Addison," as does Swift in the *Discourse of the Contests and Dissentions . . . in Athens and Rome;* and such a virtuoso is, properly, as Gwendolen Murphy labels him, "The Curious Man." Thomas Adams (fl. 1612–1653) in his

the Greek Choliambic Poets, Loeb Classical Library (Cambridge, Mass.: Harvard University Press, 1946), pp. 50–53, 76–79, 68–71, 48–51, 98–103, 40–43, 104–109, 52–57.

[30] Joseph Addison, *The Tatler*, No. 216, in *The Tatler, The Guardian* (London: Henry G. Bohn, 1852), I, 394. Addison's virtuoso is still named Sir Nicholas Gimcrack, a name that had won renown in Shadwell's play. For surveys of such satire, see C. S. Duncan, "The Scientist as a Comic Type," *Modern Philology*, XIV (1916), 281–291, and especially Walter E. Houghton, Jr., "The English Virtuoso in the Seventeenth Century," *Journal of the History of Ideas*, III (1942), 51–73, 190–219.

"character" well portrays the type: "If this *Itching* curiositie take him in the Cephalica veine, and possesse the understanding part, he mootes more questions in an houre then the seven *Wise men* could resolve in seven yeeres." His curiosity regularly exceeds any prudence or self-restraint:

He hath a greater desire to know where Hell is, then to scape it. . . . For want of correcting the garden of his inventions, the weedes choke the herbes; and he suffers the skimme of his braine to boile into the broth. He is a dangerous Prognosticator, and propounds desperate riddles.

Such a meddler, Adams adds, is driven to study mystical emblems, adores astrology, and engages in Popish plots; for he is overpowered by vapors, overcome by *humorem in cerebro, in corde tumorem, rumorem in linguae* ("humor in the brain, tumor in the heart, rumors on the tongue").[31]

On the other hand, the credulous man is equally popular in the "characters" of the tradition. He is the ironic *ingénu*

[31] "The Curious Man," in *A Cabinet of Characters,* ed. Gwendolen Murphy (London: Oxford University Press, 1925), pp. 54–56. Curiosity was originally designated Disease 17 by Adams in "The Itch, or the Busy-body," in *The Soules Sicknesse: A Discourse Divine, Morall, and Physical,* published in *The Workes of Tho: Adams . . .* (London: John Grismand, 1630), pp. 472–473. See Thomas Lodge's portrait of "Curiositie" in his *Wits Miserie, and the Worlds Madness . . .* (1596), in *The Complete Works of Thomas Lodge* (New York: Russell and Russell, 1963), IV, 17–19; and the several attacks upon "curyosyte" in Sebastian Brant's *The Ship of Fools,* trans. Alexander Barclay (1509), ed. J. H. Jamieson (London: Henry Sotheran, 1874), I, 19–23, 129–132, 176, II, 18–22. Many a classical author had inveighed against idle curiosity in antiquity; see R. Joly, "Curiositas," *L'Antiquité Classique,* XXX (1961), 33–44. "Curiosity" was considered in the Renaissance one of the gravest sins and the cause of Adam's fall; see Howard Schultz, *Milton and Forbidden Knowledge* (New York: Modern Language Association, 1955), especially pp. 1–74.

or witless naïf treated in Nigel Wireker's *Speculum Stultorum*, Friedrich Dedekind's *Grobianus*, Thomas Dekker's *Guls Hornbook*, Voltaire's *Candide*, and is represented by all those silly praisers of folly who can be traced back in one strand to the Middle Ages.[32] Alexander Barclay is severe with such "Foles of lyght credence"; such a gull

> . . . is lyght myndyd, and voyde of all prudence
> Whiche alway is wont, without aduysement
> To all vayne talys sone to gyue credence
> Aplyenge his erys thereto.

Barclay holds the credulous man precisely as guilty as the "tale berers": "They ar as lewde that wyll the same byleue." [33]

Furthermore, the Old Testament makes little or no distinction between the fool and the knave, both alike being sinners; [34] nor was such a distinction always maintained in the late Middle Ages and early Renaissance.[35] Samuel Butler transfixes fool and knave together:

[32] Consult Barbara Swain, *Fools and Folly: During the Middle Ages and the Renaissance* (New York: Columbia University Press, 1932), especially pp. 10–26.

[33] Brant, *Ship of Fools*, II, 214, ll. 1–4, 215, l. 21.

[34] In Proverbs the fool is a blabber and lazy (9:13, 10:5, 10:14, 13:16, 14:15, 17:24, 19:15), but he is kin to the "talebearer" of 11:13. Fools and knaves merge in 12:15: "The way of a fool is right in his own eyes." Traditionally, fools and knaves were equally sinners, for ignorance is understood as criminal negligence, as in Leviticus 5:17.

[35] "The first thing to be remembered is that the words 'fool' and 'knave' were constantly coupled together, but not always in quite the same way; for sometimes they were treated as synonyms, sometimes emphasis was laid on the distinction between them" (Enid Welsford, *The Fool: His Social and Literary History* [New York: Farrar and Rinehart, 1936], pp. 236–237).

Doubtless the pleasure is as great
Of being cheated, as to cheat;
As lookers-on feel most delight,
That least perceive a juggler's slight,
And still the less they understand,
The more th'admire his slight of hand.[36]

Bacon argues precisely this point: Fool and knave alike are dangerous. The "foulest" "vice or disease of learning," Bacon asserts, is

that which doth destroy the essential form of knowledge, which is nothing but a representation of truth. . . . This vice therefore brancheth itself into two sorts; delight in deceiving, and aptness to be deceived; imposture and credulity; which, although they appear to be of a diverse nature, the one seeming to proceed of cunning, and the other of simplicity, yet certainly they do for the most part concur: for as the verse noteth,
    Percontatorem fugito, nam garrulus idem est,
an inquisitive man is a prattler, so upon the like reason a credulous man is a deceiver.[37]

Although the twin vices of curiosity and credulity may be akin, they are nonetheless the twin poles, respectively, of excess and defect discussed in Aristotle's ethical analysis. Unlike the fool or knave, the wise, the prudent man sustains a balance, a mean, that these others lack: "A wise man

[36] *Hudibras*, II, iii, 1–5.
[37] *The Advancement of Learning, The Works of Francis Bacon* . . . , ed. James Spedding, Robert Leslie Ellis, and Douglas Denon Heath (Boston: Taggard and Thompson, 1861–1864), VI, 125. The Latin verse is from Horace's *Epistles* I.xviii.69. Earlier (VI, 117), Bacon had explained *all* "vanities in studies" by attempting to define "vain": men are vain who are "either credulous or curious."

is neither governed, nor seeks to govern others: he wants reason—only and always—to be governor." [38]

Thomas Hobbes, working with these commonplace ideas, distinguishes two extreme states of mind, sensuality and fancifulness. First, he analyzes the extremity of "sensual man." "The appetite of sensual or bodily delight" in such a man causes him to seek "pleasures of sense, which only please for the present," leading him to ignore honor or future events and goals, until he becomes progressively less diligent, less curious, less sensible, withdrawing into himself with a totally inert lassitude common to many a psychotic. Such a state of withdrawal Hobbes calls "dulness."

The contrasting state, Hobbes explains, is revealed by the man who turns utterly outward in his interests, who literally appears to take flight from himself. He reveals "the *quick ranging* of mind . . . , which is joined with *curiosity* of comparing the things that come into the mind, one with another: in which comparison, a man delighteth himself either with finding unexpected *similitude* of things, otherwise much unlike, in which men place the excellency of *fancy*." In excess, such a mind betrays a still further "*mobility* in the spirits" that Hobbes designates "levity."

An example hereof is in them that in the midst of any serious discourse, have their minds diverted to every little jest or witty observation; which maketh them depart from their discourse by a parenthesis, and from that parenthesis by another till at length they either lose themselves, or make their narration like a dream, or some studied nonsense. The passions from whence this proceedeth, is *curiosity*, but with *too much equality* and

[38] Jean de La Bruyère, *Les Caractères ou les moeurs de ce Siècle* . . . , ed. G. Mongrédien (Paris: Editions Garnier Frères, [1954]), p. 132.

indifference: for when all things make equal impression and delight, they equally throng to be expressed.

The final triumph of any humor character's *idée fixe* Hobbes understands as the mind's "principal defect"—either a soaring flight outside the self or a dejected submersion within: "that which men call *madness*, which appeareth to be nothing else but some *imagination* of some such *predominancy* above the *rest*, that we have *no passion but from it*; and this conception is nothing else but excessive vain glory, or vain dejection." [39]

For our purposes, the most revealing presentation of the twin faults of curiosity and credulity occurs in Samuel Butler's "characters" of "A Credulous Man" and "A Curious Man." Butler's curious man is unconcerned with the utility of any goal, but rather seeks rarity and "stores up Trifles."

He admires subtleties above all Things, because the more subtle they are, the nearer they are to nothing; and values no Art but that which is spun so thin, that it is of no Use at all. He had rather have an iron Chain hung about the Neck of a Flea, than an Alderman's of Go[l]d, and *Homer's* Iliades in a Nutshel than *Alexander's* Cabinet. . . . he so much affects Singularity, that rather than follow the Fashion, that is used by the rest of the World, he will wear dissenting Cloaths with odd fantastic Devices to distinguish himself from others, like Marks set upon Cattle.

Such a curious man "is wonderfully taken with abstruse Knowledge, and had rather hand to Truth with a Pair of

[39] *Human Nature, or the Fundamental Elements of Policy* (1640), *The English Works of Thomas Hobbes of Malmesbury*, ed. Sir William Molesworth (London: John Bohn, 1839–1845), IV, 55–57; *cf. Leviathan*, I, xi. John Locke offers a brief but similar analysis of madmen and "naturals" in *Essay Concerning Human Understanding* (1690), II, xi, 13.

Tongs wrapt up in Mysteries and Hieroglyphics, than touch it with his hands, or see it plainly demonstrated to his Senses." He is dedicated to "Study upon Things that are never to be known"; and his studies ultimately lead him to visionary pursuit of the "Philosopher's Stone and universal Medicine." [40]

At the opposite extreme is Butler's "Credulous Man," the supergull who actually tempts others to deceive him. "He is the same thing to a lyar, as a thief is to a receiver," and is, in fact, more blameworthy than the liar, "for if it were not for easy believers, liars would be at a loss." Above all, he is tranquil in his ignorance:

His faith is of a very strong constitution, that will swallow and digest anything, how crude, raw, and unwholesome so ever it be. . . . He finds most delight in believing strange things, and the stranger they are, the easier they pass with him; but never regards those that are plain and feasible, for every man can believe such.[41]

During the seventeenth century, jests and "characters" about such credulous and curious men were quite common;[42] and Swift knew well enough the tradition of humors and "characters" we have been exploring.[43] Swift

[40] "A Curious Man," *Characters and Passages from Note-Books*, ed. A. R. Waller (Cambridge: Cambridge University Press, 1908), pp. 66–67.

[41] "A Credulous Man," *Characters and Passages*, pp. 212–213.

[42] Chester Noyes Greenough, in *A Bibliography of the Theophrastan Character with Several Portrait Characters*, ed. J. Milton French (Cambridge, Mass.: Harvard University Press, 1947), lists "characters" of Curio and curiosity (pp. 11, 21, 26, 210, 216, 227), and of Credulo and credulity (pp. 95, 190, 272).

[43] Swift records that he had read Theophrastus in 1697 (*Tale*, pp. lvi–lvii). "The tradition of the Theophrastan character had for Swift's age defined moral types; the drama had created its humor

naturally understood the excess of curiosity and the defect
of credulity exactly as Aristotle had understood them—as
defections from temperance and intellectual prudence.

Surely, too, the reader familiar with the *Tale of a Tub*
will have observed the similarity between Swift's digressive
narrator and Hobbes's wondering, curious wit who loses
himself within a series of parentheses.[44] The reader will
also have noted the similarity in subject matter and language between Swift's modern speaker and the curious and
credulous characters of the tradition: their discussions of
such matters as "the skime" of the curious man's brain,
which tends to "boile into the broth";[45] their joint interest
in "*Homer*'s Iliades in a Nutshel";[46] their proud penchant

characters and given them the further trappings of a social position" (Price, *Swift's Rhetorical Art*, p. 63). On Swift's own repeated use of the satiric, *ad hominem* "character," 1710–1714, see
Richard I. Cook, "Swift's Polemical Characters," *Discourse*, VI
(1962–1963), 30–48.

[44] Just as Hobbes's digressive man departs from his discourse into
a parenthesis, and from that into another, until he lose himself, so
the *Tale*'s Modern—no mean digresser by any standard—claims,
"I have known some Authors inclose Digressions in one another,
like a Nest of Boxes" (p. 124).

[45] "There is a Brain that will endure but one *Scumming:* Let the
Owner gather it with Discretion, and manage his little Stock with
Husbandry: but of all things, let him beware of bringing it under
the *Lash* of his *Betters;* because, That will make it all bubble up into
Impertinence, and he will find no new Supply: Wit, without knowledge, being a Sort of *Cream*, which gathers in a Night to the Top,
and by a skilful Hand, may be soon *whipt* into *Froth;* but once
scumm'd away, what appears underneath will be fit for nothing,
but to be thrown to the Hogs" (*Battle of the Books, Tale*, pp. 215–
216).

[46] "I HAVE sometimes *heard* of an *Iliad* in a Nut-shell; but it hath
been my Fortune to have much oftner *seen* a *Nut-shell* in an *Iliad*"
(*Tale*, p. 143). The expression was all but proverbial; consult

for asking "more questions in an houre then the seven *Wise men* could resolve in seven yeeres"; [47] their devotion to "Study upon Things that are never to be known"; [48] their fondness for propagating riddles, their addiction to astrology, and their susceptibility to vapors. Like these seventeenth-century characters, Swift's moderns love mysteries, fashions, and dissenting "Cloaths;" delight in "Hieroglyphics," in alchemy and the *Philosopher's Stone.*" Swift knew well these traditions mocking credulity and curiosity.

IV

Though Swift knew these traditions well, Swift's modern teller of the *Tale* does not: all finely unaware, the persona argues that a mere "mobility of spirits" causes madness *both* in curious and credulous men. In a handsome anticlimax that enjoys developing the images of ghosts haunting an empty manse, Swift's Modern, full of singularity, contradicts the age-old classical tradition of excess and defect, arguing that the two deviations from prudence are the same. In his own private system, he deduces that

every *Species* [of madness] proceeds from a Redundancy of Vapour. . . . Now, it usually happens, that these active Spirits,

Wilma L. Tague, "Stephen Gosson and 'Homer's Iliades in a Nutte Shell,' " *Notes and Queries*, CCV (1960), 372–373.

[47] "It were to be wisht, and I do here humbly propose for an Experiment, that every Prince in *Christendom* will take seven of the *deepest Scholars* in his Dominions, and shut them up close for *seven* Years, in *seven* Chambers, with a Command to write *seven* ample Commentaries on this comprehensive Discourse" (*Tale*, p. 185). This was a popular comic reduction of the Septuagint legend.

[48] The typical curious schemer in philosophy, according to the modern persona, takes it into his head "to advance new Systems with such an eager Zeal, in things agreed on all hands impossible to be known" (p. 166).

getting Possession of the Brain, resemble those that haunt waste and empty Dwellings, which for want of Business, either vanish and carry away a Piece of the House, or else stay at home and fling it all out of the Windows. By which are mystically display'd the two principal Branches of *Madness*, and which some Philosophers not considering so well as I, have mistook to be different in their Causes, overhastily assigning the first to Deficiency, and the other to Redundance [p. 174].

In this passage, although the modern persona himself is unable to recognize them, we encounter precise examples of excess and of defect from that virtue which would adhere to the "common forms." In the modern world, credulous and curious men alike deviate from nature, from normalcy.

On one hand, in religion, politics, and deductive philosophy, those men who adhere to credulity are governed by private visions of the moment: their projects and dreams are, for them, reality; and they ultimately recommend actions and attempt to win proselytes only to prove themselves. They have no sense whatever of a larger responsibility to the state, to ethics, to God or to man. They simply begin and end their motions in themselves. The project to free madmen from Bedlam in the *Tale*'s Section IX (pp. 174–179) is but a bright central signal of the irresponsibility of the credulous man's personal notions, a sign of the threat such men constitute to organized society, religion, and learning. Like Anne Hutchinson and the Antinomians of America, they are solipsists, relying for candle power upon a single, private "inner light."

On the other hand, the curious man, the anatomist or virtuoso who plumbs the depths of all things, likewise seeks a personal pleasure: he is the Cartesian observer, who satisfies himself about the world by measuring it from his own single point of view, from within the confines of a cramped cranium. He is ultimately depressed and deluded by his practice, because a thoroughgoing materialism will ultimately exclude the observer himself: only atoms and void will remain—and nothing at all can ever be induced from these.[49]

Both groups—the credulous and the curious—if they did not function privately, individually, and in isolation, would experience in a more unified society "a mighty Level in the Felicity and Enjoyments of Mortal Men" (p. 172). But Renaissance individualism at its extremity leads to a terrible and isolating subjectivism, whether it be the credulity of Cartesian egoism, the naïveté of fanatic enthusiasm's mysterious beliefs, the gullible idealism of Hobbesian absolute monarchy, the utopianism of the Roundhead Commonwealth, or whether it be the curiosity of Epicurean atomism and effete pleasure-seeking, the investigating itch of alchemists and Royal Society scientists, the historical and rational investigations of deistic theologians.

However, it is not simply, as Kathleen Williams urges, that Swift would exhort us to steer between credulity and curiosity, as between some Scylla and Charybdis of the mind, to a utopian—or an Anglican—compromise.[50] For in an amusing way, the modern persona is, this once, quite correct in his postulates: he is certainly right that both

[49] This point is made by Alfred North Whitehead, in *Science and the Modern World* (New York: New American Library, 1948), pp. 44–45; acceptance of the Cartesian dualism of mind and matter even eliminates the possibility of induction.

[50] *Jonathan Swift and the Age of Compromise* (Lawrence: University of Kansas Press, 1958), p. 134. Miss Williams postulates that Swift endorses a "mean" everywhere in his writing and thinking; in Section IX it is a mean between reason and passion.

types are abnormal—deviations from the norm of moral virtue. At their very heart, the credulous and the curious man function alike—dependent upon a basic subjectivism and selfishness that spread both in the mind and in the state like a stain. This is why the phrases "for the Universal Improvement of Mankind" (p. 1) and for "the good of my Country" (p. 96), both of them frequently repeated throughout the *Tale of a Tub*, are so patently ridiculous. Credulous and curious man alike are ignorant; what they ignore is precisely that social and moral sense of responsibility to something outside themselves embodied in the more classic view of man.

> What weight of ancient witness can prevail,
> If private reason hold the public scale? [51]

What, indeed? The modern eccentrics are utterly devoid of virtue, of thought, of action, of patriotism, and of a sense of civic duty. Not for them the ancient maxim *Salus populi suprema est lex* ("The people's well-being is the supreme law"); [52] neither do they heed traditional concepts of *sophrosyne*, of balance, of ideal harmony. Nor are they controlled by the most elementary prudence, a prudence that, Aristotle believed, "calculate[s] well with a view to attaining some particular end of value." [53]

Instead, both credulous and curious men live for the present moment, concerned with yesterday's dissection or with this morning's trope or the midday vision. For both, immediate and unweighed experience takes precedence over all the traditions of the past—of history, of custom, of Scripture.

[51] John Dryden, "The Hind and the Panther," Part I, ll. 62–63.
[52] Cicero, *De Legibus* III.iii.8.
[53] *Nicomachean Ethics* VI.v.2, p. 337.

Nevertheless, despite the seeming brotherhood of credulity and curiosity, these two still remain isolated, the poles of Cartesian dualism: mind and matter. Descartes's famous *Cogito, ergo sum* in the seventeenth century had isolated at a stroke the observer from the observation, *res cogitans* from *res extensa*, the perceiving subject from the external object. The result in philosophy was to allow, and eventually to insist upon, man's inability accurately to observe an "outside" world (if there be one), ultimately isolating from each other the Cartesian egoist and the mechanical world, just as Swift's credulous egoist is divorced from his curious scientist.

The mind kicked out of doors into the enormous bin of quanta, of mass, and of motion; the mind turned inward upon itself and left alone, allowed, like the cannibal, to feed —these movements are truly what gave the brain, toward the end of the seventeenth century, its "unlucky shake." Like so many ghosts, the humors of the curious man utterly vanished, turning his attention outward and carrying his mind, as it were, out of doors; while the spirits of the credulous man caused him, like the dead in Bryant's poem, to be vacantly soothed by an unfaltering trust, and to wrap the drapery of his couch about him and lie down to pleasant dreams.

Thus have we surveyed the tacit and suggestive meanings of the credulous and the curious man in the *Tale of a Tub*'s Section IX—tacit and suggestive because Swift himself makes no statement. Rather, Swift is artistic, dramatic; he has created and shaped the modern persona, as well as the contentious credulity and curiosity, like little tubs and has embarked them upon their own sea of dramatic action. Swift himself sustains an artistic aloofness, consistently retains aesthetic distance. That is the important point which must again be emphasized: in Section IX of the *Tale of a Tub* the modern persona is certainly committed to the defense of credulity and to the tactics of rhetoric; but Swift is not. Swift is not at all the rhetorical advocate either of curiosity or of credulity, as a number of critics seem to believe. Nor is Swift the idle or the confused orator, teasing his audience when he should be delivering virtuous doctrine. As an artist, rather, Swift stands well aloof from the actions of the drama taking place upon his stage.

2. Agon and Icarus: The Split Levels of Allegory

... geminas opifex libravit in alas
ipse suum corpus, motaque pependit in aura.
　Instruit et natum, "Medio" que "ut limite curras,
Icare," ait, "moneo, ne, si demissior ibis,
unda gravet pennas, si celsior, ignis adurat:
inter utrumque vola."

—OVID

(. . . the artificer balanced his body on twin wings, and hung in the blowing breeze. He instructs his son, saying, "In order to course in the middle way, Icarus, I warn you that if you fly too low, the water will oppress your wings, if too high, the sun will burn them: fly in between.")

Study of Section IX indicates that rhetorical critics were perhaps misdirected when they inquired whether the *Tale*'s audience should prefer credulity or curiosity, and which of two positions—knavery or folly—Swift himself preferred. A more significant and provocative question may be, Which position—credulity or curiosity—does the modern persona endorse?

A simple answer is not easily obtained. For although the Modern is defending and even praising credulity throughout his oration, he is nevertheless patently employing the curious man's tactics of meticulous analysis and his scien-

[37]

tific habit of scrutinizing objects external to himself. Reviewing the vocabulary, the images, and the topics recurring in the traditional "characters" of the curious and the credulous man, we perceive that the modern persona embodies striking traits of *both*.

Like the credulous man whom he defends, this Modern reveals a simple-minded belief in every manner of strange and fantastic theory or report: his own credulity permits him to embrace Aeolism, to sanction the dangerous enthusiasm of Jack as well as the militant knavery of Peter, to endorse the project of freeing madmen fom Bedlam, to worship Grub Street and all modernity. He believes, in sum, his own manifestly incredible schemes. Like the fool of the tradition, he is a prattler, telling all he knows. Or again, like Hobbes's "sensual" man, who withdraws increasingly into himself and his dreams until his "dulness" devolves into madness, the modern persona is equally mad, withdrawn into the private world of his own garret.

Yet the modern persona is likewise an exemplar of the traditional curious man. He is highly susceptible to the flights of his own fancy; he loves "dissenting Cloaths," and engagement in mystery—in alchemically dark knowledge, in the hieroglyphics of types, allegories, and metaphysical conceits. He loves to "study upon Things that are never to be Known," to propound riddles, and to manufacture "more questions in an houre then the seven *Wise men* could resolve in seven yeeres." The Modern is, in short, distracted from self-knowledge by his curiosity, his interest in tales, theories concerning vapors, and scientific anatomies. And, of course, he is the victim of the curious man's devotion to digression. As Hobbes had noted,

In the midst of any serious discourse, [he has his] mind . . . diverted to every little jest or witty observation; which maketh [him] depart from [his] discourse by a parenthesis, and from that parenthesis by another till at length [he] either lose[s] [himself], or make[s] [his] narration like a dream.

Increasingly we recognize in the *Tale of a Tub*'s Modern the qualities of curious *and* credulous man; in him such qualities are at times contrapuntally juxtaposed and at times fused together.

Although it is true that credulity and curiosity may well be found together in an individual, we must remember that, in Section IX, the Modern himself conceived of these qualities as diametrically opposed. For him, the curious man was the aloof and reasoning virtuoso and scientific collector, whose attention was directed outside himself, objectively, whereas the credulous man was dreamer and fool, given to imaginings and to mysteries, whose attention was directed entirely inward, subjectively. The *Tale of a Tub*'s composition would seem to bear the Modern out, revealing a sustained contention between credulity and curiosity, whereby curious tale is repeatedly juxtaposed with credulous digression; whereby, even within a given paragraph, flights of fancy are contrasted with spates of scientific analysis; whereby speculation is at cuffs with empirical fact.

Naturally, critics in the past have observed the presence of such contradictory elements and the role they play in the *Tale*. Ricardo Quintana comments:

We are to observe . . . how two dominant motifs run through the *Tale*, and how their development in opposition to one another forms the basic compositional pattern. We are driven back and forth between two modes of experience: creation, imaginative construction, the wild flight of fancy; dissection, analysis. In symbolic terms, the contrast is between the outside and the inside.[1]

Such opposition of "two dominant motifs" is particularly manifest in the contest between credulity and curiosity. In the operation throughout the *Tale* of these two terms we discern rudiments of the traditional *protagonist* and *antagonist*, necessary parties to any struggle or debate. The hostility of tale to digression, of science to fabrication, of Peter to Jack, despite the fact that the extremes are at times joined together, constitutes the vital controversy of the *Tale*. Such controversy between credulity and curiosity dramatizes an elemental conflict.

If we are correct in following Aristotle and attributing so much importance to plot,[2] we can understand very well that no plot, no extended work of art, is possible without such elemental conflict, such an agon or debate; for no progress in a temporal narrative, in a train of thought, in the development of a mood, would be possible without the pressures of opposition. This opposition, William Blake contends, exists in the realm of ethics: unity within the soul is dependent upon diversity. "Without Contraries is no progression. Attraction and Repulsion, Reason and Energy, Love and Hate, are necessary to Human existence."[3] This

[1] *Swift: An Introduction* (London: Oxford University Press, 1955), pp. 64–65.

[2] An important discussion of plot in Aristotelian terms is R. S. Crane's "The Concept of Plot and the Plot of *Tom Jones*," *Critics and Criticism* (Chicago: University of Chicago Press, 1952), pp. 616–647. See also Marvin Mudrick, "Character and Event in Fiction," *Yale Review*, L (1961), 202–218.

[3] "The Marriage of Heaven and Hell," *The Poetical Works of William Blake*, ed. John Sampson (London: Oxford University Press, 1914), p. 248; quoted by permission of the publisher.

necessary contention is expressed, in metaphysics, by Hegelian dialectic, where *synthesis* is made dependent upon the interaction of *thesis* and *antithesis;* and it is implied, in the realm of aesthetics, when Aristotle urges that there cannot be an artistic ending without an attendant beginning and middle, what he implies when he posits that there cannot be katharsis of emotions without the previous and full exercise of those selfsame emotions—without, indeed, the previous conflict of the discordant emotions of pity and fear. "Conflict" in literary criticism has become a reputable term for delineating that part of the plot which creates the increasing complication that is necessary before plot can be simplified and completed by resolution or denouement.

Conflict or agon is fundamental to the work of art. In a work like Swift's *Tale of a Tub,* where there is, it would seem, but a single voice present, conflict will be less apparent than in a work of overt action, where two men quarrel or engage in physical combat. Yet conflict in such a work as the *Tale* is apparent, nevertheless. In order to discern the structure, function, and meaning of the *Tale's* artistic plot, we must first locate and define the nature of its conflict.

I

We have sought to demonstrate that the modern persona in Section IX seeks to frame an orderly oration in praise of folly. Yet the reader of Section IX is hardly left with the dominant impression of having encountered an orderly mock oration. Swift's humor everywhere conflicts with, undermines, the seriousness that the Modern would ostensibly maintain. Punster that he is,[4] Swift frequently obtrudes

[4] Consult George P. Mayhew, "Jonathan Swift's Games with Language" (Ph.D. diss., Harvard University, 1953).

plays upon words that foist havoc upon the orderly business of the oration. In Section VIII he had already played upon such words as "wind" and "aeolism," exploiting the root meaning of the word "spirit." In Section IX, he further treats of such topics as spirit, winds, ghosts, humors, and vapors, while introducing a discussion of the term "fool" (derived from Latin, *follis*, bag or bellows). All such windy terms are now brought together in the service of madness, the author even utilizing medical terms like the swelling "bag," the "orgasm," and the *fistula in ano*.

In addition to this punning, there are, within the framework of the jocoserious oration, many further disturbances of continuity and seriousness, which appear isolated and insignificant at first perhaps, but which become increasingly observable and insistent. Slowly Swift assembles every manner of excursus and reversal that agitate the surface of the oration.

For one thing, the epideictic declamation becomes forensic without warning: the modern speaker suddenly recommends the release of the Bedlam insane as politically expedient, for the "universal benefit" of the commonwealth. The ceremonial oration, which is, "properly speaking, concerned with the *present*, since all men praise or blame in view of the state of things existing at the time," changes purpose, since "the political orator aims at establishing the expediency or the harmfulness of a proposed course of action" [5] in the *future*. And of course this new recommendation, to let madmen *out* of Bedlam (p. 175), conflicts amusingly with the Modern's assertion in the Preface that the *Tale of a Tub* was written to save the commonwealth from the present "wits" of the land, at least until "a large

[5] Aristotle, *Rhetoric* I.iii.4, 5.

Academy [could be] erected, capable of containing [them]" (p. 41).

The oration is further undermined by the speaker's cheerful admission that he himself is mad. An orator is normally to be admired for his disinterested praise or advice (appealing as he does to utility, to the good of the state, to justice, to honor); [6] here, the descent of the oration into confession emphasizes the Modern's private "interest"; and in this revelation of his dishonesty, of his incapacity to achieve detachment from his subject, he becomes kin to Dionysus discoursing in praise of wine, Phalaris praising tyranny, Erasmus' fool endorsing folly, or a modern lauding modernity.

The Modern's encomium is vitiated still further by its tendency to dissolve into nigglings of the kind found in the scholastic treatise. Bacon had proposed that

the Empirical philosophers are like to pismires; they only lay up and use their store. The Rationalists are like to spiders; they spin all out of their own bowels. But give me a philosopher, who like the bee, hath a middle faculty, gathering from abroad, but digesting that which is gathered by his own virtue.[7]

The Modern resembles Bacon's spider, manufacturing cobweb problems. At the same time, we witness the most hu-

---

[6] *Rhetoric* I.iii.5. The Modern had stated earlier, promising to do "Justice" and "Honour" to Aeolism, "I think it one of the greatest, and best of humane Actions, to remove Prejudices, and place Things in their truest and fairest Light; which I boldly undertake without any Regards of my own" (p. 161).

[7] "Apothegms New and Old," *The Works of Francis Bacon . . .* , ed. James Spedding, Robert Leslie Ellis, and Douglas Denon Heath, (Boston: Taggard and Thompson, 1861–1864), XIII, 404. Bacon's more renowned figure of the spider and the bee appears in *The Advancement of Learning*, VI, 122.

morous spectacle of a modern—committed of necessity to endorsing all things modern—who nevertheless adopts the ancient theory of vapors as the cause of madness.[8] Such a thesis favoring vapors also conflicts with and even alters the tone of the oration; for it is expounded in a style increasingly logical and occult, scholastically attempting a proof: its subject matter is no longer concerned with praise; its tone is distinctly unoratorical.

Finally, the conclusion of this argument in favor of the vapors theory begs the question:

The Reader will, I am sure, agree with me in the Conclusion; that if the *Moderns* mean by *Madness*, only a Disturbance or Transposition of the Brain, by Force of certain *Vapours* issuing up from the lower Faculties; Then has this *Madness* been the Parent of all those mighty Revolutions, that have happened in *Empire*, in *Philosophy*, and in *Religion* [pp. 170–171].

At the outset, the central thesis, that madness is caused by vapors, had been *assumed* (p. 163) and certain "examples" given; now, in a *post hoc* reversal, it is supposed that the examples have proved the theory.

The confusion at this point in the oration is due as well to the modern persona's militant scientific materialism: all can be explained, he assures us, by the existence of solid, of

[8] The theory of "vapors" and the four humors, originating in antiquity (Hippocrates, Empedocles), was still common in Swift's day; consult the useful survey of seventeenth-century medical theses in Lily B. Campbell, *Shakespeare's Tragic Heroes: Slaves of Passion* (New York: Barnes and Noble, 1963), pp. 68–83. Concerning Swift's employment of writings of Henry More and Robert Burton in his vapors analysis in the *Tale*'s Section IX, see Phillip Harth, *Swift and Anglican Rationalism: The Religious Background of "A Tale of a Tub"* (Chicago: University of Chicago Press, 1961), pp. 103–116.

concrete vapors; madness and vapors, in fact, are equivalent. The Modern (like many a seventeenth-century virtuoso) does not care, as he repeatedly affirms, for final
causes: "It is of no import, where the Fire was kindled, if
the Vapor has once got up into the Brain" (pp. 162–163).
As we know, seventeenth-century science differed from
classical and medieval philosophy in its methodology and
purpose—a difference that E. A. Burtt reviews effectively:

Medieval philosophy, attempting to solve the ultimate *why* of
events instead of their immediate *how*, and thus stressing the
principle of final causality (for the answer to such a question
could only be given in terms of purpose or use), had had its
appropriate conception of God. Here was the teleological hierarchy of the Aristotelian forms, all heading up in God or Pure
Form, with man intermediate in reality and importance between him and the material world. The final *why* of events in
the latter could be explained mainly in terms of their use to
man; the final *why* of human activities in terms of the eternal
quest for union with God. Now, with the superstructure from
man up banished from the primary realm, which for Galileo is
identified with material atoms in their mathematical relations,
the *how* of events being the sole object of exact study, there
had appeared no place for final causality whatsoever. The real
world is simply a succession of atomic motions in mathematical
continuity. Under these circumstances causality could only be
intelligibly lodged in the motions of the atoms themselves,
everything that happens being regarded as the effect solely of
mathematical changes in these material elements.[9]

The scientist, in short, directs his attention, not to the final
cause, but to efficient causes. But the modern persona is

[9] *The Metaphysical Foundations of Modern Physical Science* (2d
ed., rev.; London: Routledge and Kegan Paul, 1959), pp. 89–90.

more narrow still; he ignores even efficient causes, focusing his attention upon material causes alone. He is reduced in Section IX to conjecture concerning efficient causes; his sole interest is in the material cause, in the fact that vapor itself is some kind of matter. Where the schoolman had asked *why*, and the scientist *how*, the Modern is reduced to putting the pygmy question *what*.

Perhaps vapor is caused, he conjectures, by dietary revolutions, by alterations in quantities of education, by the influence of quanta of air, by variations in the soil (p. 162); or perhaps vapor is due to the machinations of the liver, of the spleen, of the genitals. His very concern with the physical nature of his causes ultimately reduces him to searching for the material cause (perhaps soil or liver) of the material cause (vapors) of madness. Farther he cannot go—or perhaps not so far: he finally avoids all decision by manufacturing a lacuna in his text (p. 170). At best he generally appears to adopt the myopic thesis that all events occur by "chance," "luck," or "fortune," but this is a thesis which, subject to his inveterate materialism, increasingly assumes the features of the ancient Epicurean atomistic determinism that prescribes "the accidental Approach and Collision of certain Circumstances" (p. 162). He becomes that paradoxical creature, an Epicurean modern, and can cope with naught but material causes.

Nevertheless, with all his absurdity and narrowness, the Modern has captured something of the flavor of the scientific dilemma; for as Whitehead observes, in assessing the achievement of seventeenth-century science, "One unsolved problem of thought, so far as it derives from this period, is to be formulated thus: Given configurations of matter with locomotion in space as assigned by physical laws,

to account for living organisms." [10] Exactly so; what the
modern persona leaves out of account is creation, organisms, and, more particularly, Pope's famous "proper study
of mankind"—man. By omitting these, as Swift well
knows, the Modern is running directly counter to the main-
stream of Western tradition, a tradition which a little later
Samuel Johnson could still ringingly defend: "Nature is
not the object of human judgment; for it is in vain to judge
where we cannot alter." In his "Life of Milton," Johnson
amplifies this point:

It was [Socrates'] labour to turn philosophy from the study of
nature to speculations upon life; but the innovators whom I
oppose are turning off attention from life to nature. They seem
to think that we are placed here to watch the growth of plants,
or the motions of the stars. Socrates was rather of opinion, that
what we had to learn was, how to do good, and avoid evil. . . .
The first requisite is the religious and moral knowledge of right
and wrong.[11]

The Modern knows nothing of this tradition. And he encounters still more disruptions of his intentions. If he cannot in his materialism cope with the efficient or final cause
of vapors, neither can he explain vapors' "effects." He understands that such vapors produce a variety of effects
upon different brains, leading to a considerable "numerical
difference" in the behavior of madmen—some setting out
with armies to make conquests, some turning feverishly to
philosophy, some embracing cant. But how or why, he cannot say. Indeed, the Modern, struggling with just this ques-

[10] Alfred North Whitehead, *Science and the Modern World*
(New York: New American Library, 1948), pp. 41-42.
[11] *Lives of the English Poets* (London: J. M. Dent, 1925), II, 233;
I, 63.

tion, is reduced to what is perhaps the most helpless hiatus in his treatise; and in perpetrating the gap, Swift produces one of his finest puns. "Hic multa desiderantur" (p. 170) marks the hiatus, in accordance with editorial usage, asserting, "Here much is missing." Yet the words, in the most literal sense, baldly expose the inadequacy of the Modern's materialistic philosophy, which can account for nothing: "Here much is to be desired."

II

Not only an oration and a scientific materialism are observed, in Section IX, to trip and fall. Everywhere in that section the Modern endures the self-defeat of his every intention. Somehow, even within a pair of sentences, intentions go wrong. Thus, at one celebrated point, when the modern persona argues against experimental curiosity, against reason, he insists that reason arrives always "officiously with Tools for cutting, and opening, and mangling, and piercing, offering to demonstrate, that [qualities in bodies] are not of the same consistence quite thro' " (p. 173). He continues, his indignation against reason and incisive anatomies mounting, until he commences a peroration: "I do here think fit to inform the Reader, that in such Conclusions as these, Reason is certainly in the Right" (p. 173). The reader is abruptly halted, surprised at the sudden reversal: reason, somehow upon the instant, is now in the right! But a second reversal immediately follows, overturning the inversion again: reason is, after all, in the wrong; for the Modern continues, "and that in most Corporeal Beings, which have fallen under my Cognizance, the *Outside* hath been infinitely preferable to the *In*" (p. 173). This rapid series of peripeties serves to emphasize the central dilemma the modern persona is acting out: the use of reason to anatomize, to condemn reason.

We should observe as well, in this passage, the impertinent serenity of the Modern's insistent egoism, as in the phrase, "I do here think fit to inform the Reader." Similarly, a few sentences earlier, we note his use of "I" with the same aggressive complacency. If it were not for deception and false lights and the tinsel of surfaces, he argues there, all mankind would be forced to a "mighty level" of felicity.

If this were seriously considered by the World, AS I HAVE A CERTAIN REASON TO SUSPECT IT HARDLY WILL; Men would no longer reckon among their high Points of Wisdom, the Art of exposing weak Sides, and publishing Infirmities; an Employment IN MY OPINION, neither better nor worse than that of *Unmasking*, WHICH I THINK, has never been allowed fair Usage, either in the *World* or the *Play-House* [pp. 172–173].

The Modern's prose, already copious and tortuous with lengthy sentences, and punctuated by numerous minor clauses and deviations from the languid track, is further complicated by the standard egoistic insertions (here capitalized). As a result, the turns of this prose are misleading; its meanings seem to be struggling to escape the reader altogether. Hence, in addition to the vague reference of the opening *this*,[12] there is the obscurantist verbiage of the balanced "neither better nor worse," while the "allowed" near the end for a moment threatens a double meaning: either (1) unmasking has at no time been considered fair by the

---

[12] The vagueness of the demonstrative pronoun here is apparently deliberate: presumably it refers to the infelicity of the world without fog and varnish, introduced two sentences earlier.

world, or (2) unmasking has never been given a chance, never been given a fair opportunity.[13]

We notice, as well, here and elsewhere, how often conventional clichés and trite expressions—abundant in the Modern's prose at all times—manage to muddy and confuse meaning. Thus, after explaining that when a man's "Fancy gets *astride* on [a man's] Reason," *then* a man prefers delusion, he asserts, "nor is Mankind so much to blame in his Choice, thus determining him" (pp. 171–172)—*as if* the vapor-ridden madman had a choice. The immediate contiguity of the words "choice" and "determining" becomes one more silly and amusing violence committed against the passage's sense. Similarly, after asserting that all mankind helplessly, even naturally, prefers delusion, he inserts a hackneyed phrase that controverts his meaning: He starts to suggest what would happen if mankind would consider how poor and meager is the world of base actuality *without* delusions, then adds, "as I have a certain Reason to suspect it hardly will." At a stroke, his assertion that men *always* espouse delusion is destroyed.

Indeed, when we attempt to read Section IX with seriousness, we are impressed by the flux of constantly conflicting words and phrases that seem not so much to come from the mind and pen of the modern persona but rather to take on a vital and even fortuitous life of their own, like so

---

[13] Consult the entry "Allow" in Samuel Johnson, *A Dictionary of the English Language* . . . , 2 vols. (London, 1757), I, Rr. Definitions 1 through 4 (to admit, to grant, to permit, to authorize) all could give either meaning in the passage under consideration. Definition 5 ("to give to") is more like the second reading. The earlier meaning of "allow" (as in "he is allowed a fool"), a meaning generally accepted in Swift's day, was slowly being replaced by the more common meaning of the word today—"to permit."

many Democritean atoms spilling about, by chance, in the void.

At every level, Section IX demonstrates a dichotomy of intentions, meanings, and conclusions. No single wave of sense seems to be started but that an undertow directly opposed rushes in, diverting that sense and often washing it completely away. What can it be but comedy that permits these currents of self-defeating shifts in format, intention, logic, and sense which accumulate beneath the surface of the modern persona's a priori argument? In Section IX, the Modern in his arguments, his procedures, his statements can be depended upon to go awry, to lose control.

III

We have seen how the modern persona in Section IX tends to wade cheerfully into a stream of self-confident thought, only to be overborne—somehow losing control of the organization, structure, language, and sense of his prose. We shall find that this conflict is not at all restricted to Section IX; its pattern of attempt and retreat, undertaking and defeat, occurs again and again throughout the *Tale of a Tub*. Such a repetitive pattern, moreover, bears the characteristics of what may be called the Icarian, or crazy metaphorical, flight:

> Whilst a *State-Pylot* would Charybdis shun,
> What boots-it, if on *Scylla* he must run?
> 'Twixt two Extreams, let *Vertue* keep her Throne,
> The *Golden Mean* to Statesmen's rarely known.
> With *Icarus* on waxen Plumes they flye,
> And soar a pitch, for their weak wings too high,
> 'Till they come rumbling headlong from the skie.[14]

[14] Anon., *The Sentiments: A Poem To The Earl of Danby In The Tower, By a Person of Quality* (London: James Vade, 1679),

The *locus classicus* in the *Tale* for such collapsing Icarian flying is one the Modern himself attempts:

AND, whereas the mind of Man, when he gives the Spur and Bridle to his Thoughts, doth never stop, but naturally sallies out into both extreams of High and Low, of Good and Evil; his first Flight of Fancy, commonly transports Him to Idea's of what is most Perfect, finished, and exalted; till having soared out of his own Reach and Sight, not well perceiving how near the Frontiers of Height and Depth, border upon each other; With the same Course and Wing, he falls down plum into the lowest Bottom of Things [pp. 157–158].

Here is the pattern of the Icarian flight: not only is its course being described, but also Swift's Modern, apparently unconsciously, in his prose is mimetically realizing that self-same course. At this point, the author himself, with high diction and the prolonged figure, is still mounting up-

p. 6, ll. 85–91. Icarus became an emblem of pride's fall in antiquity; note Horace's observation about any poet who might dare attempt to rival Pindar: "Pindarum quisquis studet aemulari, / . . . caeratis ope Daedalea / nititur pennis, vitreo daturus / nomina ponto" (Whoever, with waxen wings and Daedalus' help, attempts to emulate Pindar, will surely give his name to the glassy sea—*Odes* IV.ii.1–4). In the Renaissance, Icarus continued emblematic of arrogant curiosity and intellectual pride; consult John W. Ashton, "The Fall of Icarus," *Renaissance Studies in Honor of Hardin Craig*, ed. Baldwin Maxwell *et al.* (dedicatory issue of *Philological Quarterly*, XX [1941], 345–351), and Harry Levin, *The Overreacher: A Study of Christopher Marlowe* (Cambridge, Mass.: Harvard University Press, 1952), frontispiece, Appendix A, and especially pp. 159–165. Critics have discussed in different terms the silly flights in the *Tale of a Tub*. See, for example, Martin Price, *Swift's Rhetorical Art* (New Haven: Yale University Press, 1953), pp. 75–95; Philip Pinkus. "The Nature of the Satire in *A Tale of a Tub*" (Ph.D. diss., University of Michigan, 1956), p. 39 and *passim;* and Ronald Paulson, *Theme and Structure in Swift's "Tale of a Tub"* (New Haven: Yale University Press, 1960), pp. 30–31, 52–65.

ward. Even at this early stage of his flight, however, there is a comically ominous foreshadowing in the wild mixing of metaphors—the horse and bridle with bird and wing and with geography and frontier—of the flight's unfortunate end.[15] Still, it is early in the flight, and the unwary Modern continues his ascent.

After this point, however, the Modern's own mind, as he describes the broken flight, as if by sympathy begins to be weighted by the accumulation of metaphors and analogies, until his own flight is sadly impeded, "like one who travels the *East* into the *West;* or like a strait Line drawn by its own Length into a Circle."

Whether a Tincture of Malice in our Natures, makes us fond of furnishing every bright Idea with its Reverse; Or, whether Reason reflecting upon the Sum of Things, can, like the Sun, serve only to enlighten one half of the Globe, leaving the other half, by Necessity, under Shade and Darkness: Or, whether Fancy, flying up to the imagination of what is Highest and Best, becomes overshot, and spent, and weary, and suddenly falls like a dead Bird of Paradise to the Ground.

Then the soaring flight, after faltering, falls, in a resounding anticlimax: "Or, whether after all these *Metaphysical* Conjectures, I have not entirely missed the true Reason" (p. 158).[16] The motion and countermotion of the Modern's metaphor and his prose are expensive, their circularity

---

[15] The winged horse is, doubtless, Pegasus; but it is not the inspiring steed that falls, but rather a Bellerophon, a Phaethon, or an Icarus. And his launching out in several directions simultaneously is unaccountably amphibious.

[16] *Cf.* Burton's figure of the long-winged hawk, *Anatomy of Melancholy*, II,ii,3. Swift's parody is compared with Burton's passage by Kathleen Williams, in *Jonathan Swift and the Age of Compromise* (Lawrence: University of Kansas Press, 1958), p. 16.

wasteful. Like the example the Modern cites of Louis XIV, who "amused himself to take and lose Towns; beat Armies, and be beaten" (p. 165), such a ceaseless series of Icarian flights appears in almost every passage in *A Tale of a Tub*. Like the Aeolists in their ceremonies, the *Tale's* thought and style rehearse a seeming intaking of the "spirit," an applying of the bellows to the breeches, the subsequent enormous expansion, and a final disemboguement to depletion.

Not only are such Icarian motions cyclic and self-exhausting, but also, in spite of their drollery, they are for the reader disturbing, confounding. As though climbing the grand ladder, that second "Oratorical Machine," upon which orators mount aloft to "oblige their Audience in the agreeable Delivery . . . [and even] the whole World," the *Tale* and its teller mount their series of machines and metaphors; and, just as the orators mount in fact the hangman's platform, where they deliver their notable speech, only to descend again—with a noose about their necks (pp. 58–59) —so does the modern persona's confounding vigor frequently appear nothing less than suicidal: "Since my *Vein* is once opened, I am content to exhaust it all at a Running" (p. 184).

First, within the shortest phrases, the Modern involves himself in ambiguous expressions and in contradictions of terms. He represents occult or "dark" authors as the "*true illuminated*" (p. 186); or he finds the Aeolist *Coelum Empyræum* none other than Σκοτία, the land of darkness (p. 155). He speaks of "the intervals of a long Peace" (p. 39).[17] He praises pulpit orators for their "Common places

[17] A series of spaces between a single peace is an absurdity. Yet the jest is manifest: peace was neither regular nor prevalent. Note

equally new and eloquent" (p. 52). And he speaks of descending "to the very *bottom* of all the *Sublime*" (p. 44), of time's dispatching "to unavoidable Death" all "immortal Productions" and *"never-dying* Works" (p. 33), of poor Henry IV who "tried in vain the Poet's never-failing Receipt" (p. 164). The Modern's military metaphor grows comically ambiguous when he speaks of those wits and projects that appear to threaten the government: "the Danger hourly increasing, by new Levies of Wits all appointed . . . with Pen, Ink, and Paper which may at an hours Warning be drawn out into Pamphlets, and other *Offensive* Weapons, ready for immediate *Execution*" (pp. 39–40—italics mine). He speaks, not of a discovery or a work, but of an "Attempt" as being "useful" (p. 67); and he blandly observes that one orator speaks "with his last *moving* and *standing* Piece of Rhetorick" (p. 131).

In like manner, the Modern's longer passages of praise and defense cultivate this habit of reversal, the words controverting the original intention. The Modern asks, Does Time dare to argue that because contemporary works are not to be found in the future, they therefore never existed? What has become of them? the Modern questions: "Are they sunk in the Abyss of Things? 'Tis certain, that in their own Nature they were *light* enough to swim upon the Surface for all Eternity" (p. 32). Again, in offering three concluding wise maxims that might serve readers as guides "to distinguish a *True Modern Critick* from a Pretender," he delivers himself thus:

THE first is, That *Criticism*, contrary to all other Faculties of the Intellect, is ever held the truest and best, when it is the very

the allusion later in the *Tale* to "Times so turbulent and unquiet as these" (p. 208).

first Result of the *Critick*'s Mind: As Fowlers reckon the first aim for the surest, and seldom fail of missing the Mark, if they stay for a Second [p. 103].[18]

At first glance, a reader understands (perhaps) that fowlers who maintain that their first shot must be accurate would naturally feel, since with the first shot the startled bird would have flown, that the second shot would almost always miss the mark. Yet the tortuous prose of this simile manages itself to miss the mark. The word "shot" never appears, although it is understood; in the passage, therefore, too much emphasis is made to rest upon the word "aim." More important, the curious double negative—the "failing of missing" the mark—undermines the intended sense; for here, contrary to all normal usage, "failure" is associated with the successful hitting of the mark, whereas, the passage implies, failure to hit the mark would be "success." This double negative is further compounded by the proximity of the negative qualifier "seldom." Most important, the casual use of the coordinating conjunction "and," linking the elements of the compound predicate of the simple clause in this simile, avoids the salient introduction of subordination, which would show cause and effect. As a result of such haphazard coordination, the final "if" clause can easily be taken to modify the first verb of the clause as well as the second, so that we have the confounding read-

---

[18] Swift's figure echoes a common paradoxical distortion of the archer; Mulgrave thus claims that Horace's mild satires are more effective than Juvenal's railing: "As men aim rightest when they shoot in jest" (John Sheffield, Earl of Mulgrave, and John Dryden. "An Essay upon Satire" [1679], *Poems on Affairs of State: Augustan Satirical Verse, 1660–1714*, I: *1660–1678*, ed. George de F. Lord [New Haven: Yale University Press, 1963], p. 402, l. 20; quoted by permission of the publisher).

ing: "As Fowlers reckon the first aim for the surest . . . if they stay for a Second." [19]

With such frequent "mythologizing," analogizing, and ornamenting, the Modern's figures and types regularly manage to befuddle meaning. When he writes of a Grand Committee, formed to prevent present wits from "pick[ing] Holes in the weak sides of Religion and Government," we observe that such a committee appears to admit that religion and government do have "weak sides"; ideas whose meanings conflict are brought infelicitously together. This said Grand Committee continues in its deliberations, reflecting:

Sea-men have a Custom when they meet a *Whale*, to fling him out an empty *Tub*, by way of Amusement, to divert him from laying violent Hands upon the Ship. This Parable was immediately mythologiz'd: The *Whale* was interpreted to be *Hobs*'s *Leviathan*, which tosses and plays with all other Schemes of Religion and Government, whereof a great many are hollow, and dry, and empty, and noisy, and wooden, and given to Rotation. This is the *Leviathan* from whence the terrible Wits of our Age are said to borrow their Weapons. The *Ship* in danger, is easily understood to be its old Antitype the *Commonwealth*. But, how to analyze the *Tub*, was a Matter of difficulty; when after long Enquiry and Debate, the literal Meaning was preserved: And it was decreed, that in order to prevent these *Leviathans* from tossing and sporting with the *Commonwealth*, (which of it self is too apt to fluctuate) they should be diverted from that Game by a *Tale of a Tub* [pp. 40–41].

[19] This last reading was common; editions 2–5 of the *Tale* supply a "stay not" in this passage (p. 103, n. 3). There are further complications, for in the phrase "fail of missing," the preposition is ambiguous.

From the outset, this attempt to "mythologize" the sea-
men's actual practice creaks and groans with resistance.
The passage itself represents an amusing reversal of normative allegorizing, since here the seamen's real, traditional, and
lowly practice is fictionalized, converted into monstrously
significant allegory. Within the passage, the committee
makes the whale out to be Hobbes's *Leviathan*, a work
which is in fact a "scheme" dangerous to liberal government. But soon the tubs are identified as "*other* schemes of
Religion and Government," so that dangerous schemes appear to be both the attacking whale and the defensive mea-
sures; whales and tubs alike are menacing to the ship of
state. All such schemes, as if they had become a host of
whales, are now to be diverted by a single tub, the present
Tale of a Tub.

The present *Tale of a Tub*, like the previous tubs, by association is acknowledged to be "hollow, and dry, and
empty, and noisy, and wooden, and given to Rotation." As
a matter of fact, the *Tale of a Tub* in the course of its
many pages proves to be all these; and, finally, in the *Tale*'s
ninth section, when its projector proposes to set madmen
free, the *Tale* overtly becomes in earnest but another
scheme of religion and government. Seen in this light,
whales, tubs, and even the Grand Committee itself are all so
many schemers, dangerous to government; and the reader
finds himself in perilous and confusing waters.

Once again, the progress of the narrative, the ready col-
loquialism (notice that the whale is to lay violent "hands"
upon the ship of state), and the confident tone all conflict
with the long, loose sentences, with the numerous capitals
and italics, and with the shifting analogies themselves. In
the press, among so much verbiage, emphasis, and allegori-

zation, meaning itself, inundated, tends to sink from sight. And, overall, in this passage, the Icarian pattern of flight and reversal is again effected, for that Grand Committee's determination to allegorize every feature of the sailors' practice finally breaks down: after long contemplation upon the tub, the committee at last surrenders and lamely agrees to accept its "literal Meaning."

Such inversion and confusion tend to visit all the Modern's long passages of accumulated metaphors. In a famous paragraph, for instance, the persona tells us that modern authors justly complain about their audience, whose superficiality prevents it from "inspect[ing] beyond the Surface and the Rind of Things";

. . . whereas, *Wisdom* is a *Fox*, who after long hunting, will at last cost you the Pains to dig out: 'Tis a *Cheese*, which by how much the richer, has the thicker, the homelier, and the courser Coat; and whereof to a judicious Palate, the *Maggots* are the best. 'Tis a *Sack-Posset*, wherein the deeper you go, you will find it the sweeter. *Wisdom* is a *Hen*, whose *Cackling* we must value and consider, because it is attended with an *Egg;* But then, lastly, 'tis a *Nut*, which unless you chuse with Judgment, may cost you a Tooth, and pay you with nothing but a *Worm* [p. 66].

Wisdom is hidden, often in a coarse, unassuming jacket; it is heady, intoxicating; but—and here the figure begins to turn—we value most the signs of its decay; and, finally, wisdom is noisy and overt, valued for something beyond itself to which it gives birth; and that something of value beneath the rind, after all the pains of the journey, is in reality valueless, offensive.[20] The hidden, internal wisdom of

[20] That wisdom is at once desirable and worthless, even dangerous, is but one further application of the Janus-faced qualities of

the early analogies suddenly becomes external in the metaphor of the hen's egg; or wisdom is of value until, with the hen, wisdom itself becomes noisy and superficial, with something beneath wisdom that is more important; and, at last, this something beneath proves to be a worm. Once again the metaphor has risen, become complicated in Icarian flight, finally reversed itself, and fallen to the ground.

Like Jack, the modern persona believes "that the *Wise Man was his own* Lanthorn" (p. 192). And, like Jack, whenever he "would shut his Eyes as he walked along the Streets, [he invariably would] bounce his Head against a Post, or fall into the Kennel (as he seldom missed either to do one or both)" (p. 192). The tale of the broken flight is an old story; it is told, for instance, by Agrippa of the astronomer Anaximenes, "who one day going out a little later than ordinary to look upon the Sky, while he was gazing among the Stars, ne're minding the scituation of the place, fell into a Ditch." [21] Moreover, the modern persona him-

curiosity and credulity, inimical and mutually exclusive virtues that somehow must both be obtained. Throughout the *Tale*, first one, then the other is elevated and preferred; a distinct and conclusive choice is never confirmed.

[21] Henry Cornelius Agrippa, *The Vanity of Arts and Sciences . . .* , trans. Roger L'Estrange (?) (London: Samuel Speed, 1676), pp. 86–87. Agrippa errs; the story is told by Anaximenes about Thales; see Plato, *Theaetetus* 174A and Diogenes Laertius' "Life of Anaximenes." *Cf.* biblical versions of such falls: Matt. 15:14 and Luke 6:39. Swift delighted in such capitulations and descents into the kennel; see *Tale*, pp. 276 and 289; and recall the typical Laputan, who without flapper and bladder is virtually helpless: "always so wrapped up in Cogitation, that he is in manifest Danger of falling down every Precipice and bouncing his Head against every Post; and in the streets, of jostling others, or being jostled himself, into the Kennel" (*Gulliver's Travels*, III, ii, *Prose Works*, XI, 144).

self appears to acknowledge that he dwells in an Icarian world. He accepts that it is in the nature of things that writers and writings will "hourly start up" (pp. 148, 182–183), but that, completing the Icarian pattern, they "will grow quite out of date and relish" (p. 43) and that *"the Memorial of them [will be] lost among Men"* (pp. 34–35). He assumes that there is in the course of events the pattern of rise and return, just as he acknowledges that "a strait Line [will be] drawn by its own Length into a Circle" (p. 158) and just as he explains that most Wit "is observ'd to run much upon a Line, and ever in a Circle" (p. 61). He is regularly "confident to have included and exhausted all that Human Imagination can *Rise* or *Fall* to" (p. 129). In his search for and flying after invention (p. 209), the modern persona verifies what Pope's Martinus Scriblerus later more weightily demonstrates:

that there is an Art of Sinking in Poetry. Is there not an Architecture of Vaults and Cellars, as well as of lofty Domes and Pyramids? Is there not as much skill and labour in making Dikes, as in raising Mounts? Is there not an Art of Diving as well as of Flying? [22]

Indeed there is.

This recurrent Icarian pattern governing the Modern's prose discloses not only the conflict when height and depth are brought repeatedly into proximity, but also another and more paradoxical conflict with the reader's expectations when height and depth are no longer juxtaposed but merged together and ultimately united. Just as the modern mind inevitably discovers "how near [are] the Frontiers of

[22] "Peri Bathous, or, Of the Art of Sinking in Poetry," *The Works of Alexander Pope, Esq.* . . . , ed. William Warburton; VI: *Miscellaneous Pieces in Prose and Verse* (London, 1751), 204.

Height and Depth" (pp. 157–158), just as the modern projectors "have discovered a gross Ignorance in the Natures of Good and Evil, and most horribly confounded the Frontiers of both" (p. 274), so does the madman freed from Bedlam become most sane and the historian of the tale of the three brothers become identical with the blatant Grub Street author of the digressions. Most important, once the modern persona has abandoned any value system, there are brought together in his single personality the Icarian "up" of the imagination and the "down" of virtuoso science that create the sense and nonsense of so many passages in the *Tale of a Tub* and ultimately bring together the diverse subjects and styles of digressions and tale. Thus, many diverse subjects and tones in the *Tale* are repeatedly and paradoxically united, precisely in the way that in Section IX, the modern persona managed to reconcile within himself traits of fools and of knaves.

The Icarian is the grand bathetic archetype which the Modern employs and which the *Tale of a Tub* as a whole sustains: each time a rise is initiated, peripety ensures a decline and a return to rest; then a new rise commences, only in its turn to subside. Such a repetitive pattern [23] is constantly circular, committed indefinitely to recurrence, just as the *Tale* itself is committed to the endless multiplication of story followed by digression, story followed by digression. The modern persona's speeches, topics, metaphors—everything he does—are like the members of the dissenting congregation:

several Hundreds link'd together in a circular Chain, with every Man a Pair of Bellows applied to his Neighbour's Breech,

---

[23] *Cf.* Price, *Swift's Rhetorical Art*, pp. 91–93, employing Kenneth Burke's conception of "repetitive form."

by which they blow up each other to the Shape and Size of a
Tun. . . . When . . . they were grown sufficiently replete, they
would immediately . . . disembogue for the Publick Good [p.
153].

Each piece of wit serves to blow up its neighbor, every one
of them growing to a tun: not only the Modern, but his
every particle of wit, then, is its own lanthorn, its own bil-
lowing and battered tub.

IV

Perhaps the greatest and most persistent single figure
used throughout the *Tale of a Tub* to represent the conflict
of rising and falling, of surface and depth, is that of allegory itself. For allegorizing is a fine double-edged method
that permits "levels" of meaning. In allegory, as in no other
literary form, the levels of meaning—surface and depth—
are successfully united.

I have been prevailed on, after much importunity from my
Friends, to travel in a compleat and laborious Dissertation upon
the prime Productions of our Society [i.e., Grub Street], which
besides their beautiful Externals for the Gratification of superficial Readers, have darkly and deeply couched under them,
the most finished and refined Systems of all Sciences and Arts
[pp. 66-67].[24]

[24] Ironically, the Modern's defense of allegory here is traditional;
cf. Sir John Harington's "A Brief Apology for Poetry," *Elizabethan
Critical Essays,* ed. G. Gregory Smith (London: Oxford University
Press, 1957), II, especially pp. 200-203. It was likewise traditional to
read Homeric epics as allegorical, discovering in them, as George
Chapman does, all arts presented and explained. See especially
Joshua McClennen, *On the Meaning and Function of Allegory in
the English Renaissance, University of Michigan Contributions in
Modern Philology,* No. 6 (1947), pp. 1-38; and Donald Lemen
Clark, *Rhetoric and Poetry in the Renaissance* (New York: Colum-

Accordingly, the Modern, as when he introduces the allegorical figures of the three "oratorical machines," always avers that his figures are "a great Mystery, being a Type, a Sign, an Emblem, a Shadow, a Symbol, bearing analogy" (p. 61) to almost anything.

Moreover, the modern persona manages paradoxically to contain these levels of surface and depth *within himself*. At one extreme, the Modern with his allegories is like Jack and the Aeolists,

whose converting Imaginations dispose them to reduce all Things into Types; who can make *Shadows*, no thanks to the Sun; and then mold them into Substances, no thanks to Philosophy; whose peculiar Talent lies in fixing Tropes and Allegories to the *Letter*, and refining what is Literal into Figure and Mystery [pp. 189–190].

At the opposite pole, the modern persona is more the scientist, the projector, the virtuoso Democritean materialist, whose concern is with *bulk* and *subject* and *body* in every case. He has "dissected the Carcass of *Human Nature*, and

bia University Press, 1922), pp. 139–161. As McClennen and Clark point out, although a few men, like Sidney and Jonson, sought to draw criticism away from an almost medieval adoration of allegory and its "hidden layers" of instruction, popular conceptions of allegory hardly changed at all between 1550 and 1650. In Swift's own day, John Hughes and Sir Richard Blackmore still piously claimed for allegory that it is written for the honor of one's country, that it surprises and gratifies the reader's curiosity, that it fosters clarity and "clothes" a moral. Consult Blackmore's "Preface to Prince Arthur" (1695), *Critical Essays of the Seventeenth Century*, ed. J. E. Spingarn (Bloomington: Indiana University Press, 1957), III, 241, and Hughes's "On Allegorical Poetry" (1715), *Critical Essays of the Eighteenth Century: 1700–1725*, ed. Willard H. Durham (New Haven: Yale University Press, 1915), pp. 86–104, especially pp. 99–100.

read many useful Lectures upon the several Parts, both *Containing* and *Contained;* till at last it *smelt* so strong, I could preserve it no longer" (p. 123). He is, in this physical role, the anatomist, concerned with the "numerical Difference in the Brain" (p. 170), with experiments inspecting the flayed woman and the carcass of the beau (p. 173); the careful historian who has thoroughly checked his sources (p. 189); the writer preoccupied with his collections (p. 148), with prefaces (p. 45), with commonplace books (pp. 54, 209). When these two aspects—physical scientist and imaginative visionary—are successfully united within himself, the Modern is attaching airy metaphors and fables (p. 66) to base machines: "deducing Similitudes, Allusions, and Applications, very Surprising, Agreeable, and Apposite, from the *Pudenda* of either sex" (p. 147), or contriving meticulous analysis of a grand type, as when oracular Aeolism (in Section VIII) is redacted, dissected, and displayed.

In spite of the Modern's tendency to mix credulity and curiosity, surface and depth, into a kind of discordant harmony, there has always been an inclination on the part of critics examining the *Tale* to elect one of the two extremes and to favor it, or to believe that Swift favored it. Thus Gordon McKenzie recognizes the conflict between surface and depth, and he believes Swift is endorsing the surface of the Church, the surface of the visionary, revealing "a desire on [Swift's] part to save the surface, even though what is underneath may have decayed."[25] On the other hand, Paul Fussell concedes that eighteenth-century writers forcefully attack the naturalistic and the materialistic, yet he be-

[25] "Swift: Reason and Some of Its Consequences," *Five Studies in English,* University of California Publications in English, VIII (Berkeley: University of California Press, 1940), p. 122.

lieves they feel a "vast spiritual embarrassment implicit in the idea of a wholly naturalistic 'unaccomodated' man" that is revealed by their protesting too much. Fussell maintains that they harbor a secret and terrible attraction to materialism or depth, for he notes that these humanists do "participat[e] . . . in a Newtonian, Lockian, naturalistic view of things." Especially, "Swift, for one, constantly betrays his predicament by his instinctively materialistic images, which suggest his debt to Newtonian physics and optics." [26]

Long ago H. M. Dargan came much nearer to a resolution of the seeming dichotomy of surface and depth. He noted that a "sartorism," what Emile Pons later was to label *l'esthétomorphisme*, predominates in the *Tale*, with its emphasis upon surface and outer garments. He realized that the knaves-and-fools climax in Section IX appears to be a peripety, finally making fools of clothes fanciers. Provocatively Dargan accounted for this reversal by recognizing "an intellectual current running counter to the imaginative sweep of the allegory." Yet, perspicacious as his observation was, Dargan felt that this double motion in Section IX, creating an enervated Sargasso, was to be accounted for by assuming that Swift "played" with his subject, for he cites with approval Leslie Stephen's comment that Swift was "playing with paradoxes." [27] No one would seriously question the assertion that Swift was "playful"; his works are full to abundance with incisive wit and comic

[26] "The Frailty of Lemuel Gulliver," *Essays in Literary History Presented to J. Milton French*, ed. Rudolph Kirk and C. F. Main (New Brunswick, N.J.: Rutgers University Press, 1960), p. 122.

[27] H. M. Dargan, "The Nature of Allegory as Used by Swift," *Studies in Philology*, XIII (1916), 166–167. See Leslie Stephen, *Swift* (New York: Fowle, [1905]), p. 40.

genius—for which he is famous. But one might well question an examination of the *Tale*'s serious artistry that is resolved by implying that playfulness in itself is the work's end or purpose.

A much more balanced view of the problem, which would explain the interplay between surface and depth, is Edwin Honig's comment upon the procedure in Swift's *Mechanical Operation of the Spirit*, a procedure that Honig believes represents the play of "double irony":

The substance of the [virtuoso's, the persona's] "discovery" is that religious enthusiasm in principle and practice is not of a spiritual but "of a corporeal nature." But the discourse itself is a two-pronged weapon. For in satirizing the extreme forms of puritan irrationality, Swift assumes the role of a virtuoso for whom everything is scientifically determined.

Thus is a delusive enthusiasm at war with a base materialism. "Therein," Honig concludes, "he uses one extreme as a foil to destroy and be destroyed by the opposite extreme." [28] Honig's view approaches most closely the findings of the present chapter concerning the *Tale*'s conflict. Not only are the Puritan religious fanatic and the fanciful Grub Street poetaster reduced by science to a low "profund," but also the meticulous historian and the anatomical scientist, in their turn, are revealed to be dreamers and fanciful fliers, men yearning toward posterity, men helplessly optimistic in their fantasies of completing the book of universal knowledge.

Because the modern persona is both the material scientist

[28] "Notes on Satire in Swift and Jonson," *New Mexico Quarterly Review*, XVIII (1948), 158. An equally fine, related study is James L. Calderwood's "Structural Parody in Swift's Fragment," *Modern Language Quarterly*, XXIII (1962), 243–253.

and the airy visionary, he is virtually severed in two; and these two sides of the Modern—his flight and his fall, his poetry and his prosaism, his creative digressions and his toneless history, his science and his religion—exemplify his excess and his defect, his foolishness and his knavery. These sides are mutually exclusive and, when brought together, mutually destructive. Study of conflict in the *Tale of a Tub* reveals that the struggle continues everywhere in the Modern's "world," but that the central struggle is mimetically acted out most vigorously within the schizophrenic Modern himself. Torn from within, he becomes his own battered and sinking tub.

But how does it happen that the Modern is at war with himself? How does it happen that he endures, to use a term that C. S. Lewis has revived, a permanent *psychomachia?* We do know that the modern of 1660–1700 came from a world of faction and dissent, a world of excess and defect in human conduct. In religion, for instance, men had disbanded into two extremes; the Roundheads and the Cavaliers created a Civil War out of the irreconcilable poles of their opposition. And thereafter, High Church Nonjurors and rigorous Anglicans continued to be opposed to Dissenters and Scotch Presbyterians.[29] Similarly, in politics, the victory of Parliament in 1689 merely confirmed party faction; the newly formed Whigs and Tories grew increas-

[29] John Ryerson Maybee, "Anglicans and Nonconformists, 1679–1704. A Study in the Background of Swift's *A Tale of a Tub*" (Ph.D. diss., Princeton University, 1942), esp. pp. 133–191, 203, 247. Consult also the thorough political analysis of 1697–1702 in Ellis' Introduction to Swift's *A Discourse of the Contests and Dissentions Between the Nobles and the Commons in Athens and Rome,* ed. Frank H. Ellis (Oxford: Clarendon Press, 1967), pp. 1–79.

ingly hostile to one another.[30] In London's literary and journalistic circles, the rise of publishers and printers encouraged not only vast numbers of carping invective poems, satires, and religious and political pamphlets, but also a market full, as never before, of panegyrics and adulatory pamphlets heavy with overpraise.[31] Against these trends toward extremes of opposition in the latter half of the century, few voices were raised; Halifax had, in his "Character of a Trimmer" (1688), appealed to Englishmen to become "trimmers," to elect "a wise Mean" that would balance *"Madmen, in two Extreams."*[32] Such pleas had gone largely unheeded.

Most important, this era had witnessed the growth of a new type of allegory. The revolt of the Renaissance and Reformation against medieval authority led to the rejection of the scholastic discrimination of four levels of meaning in allegorical exegesis—literal, allegorical, anagogical, tropological—based upon tradition and authority. In its stead, the

[30] *The Oxford History of England,* ed. Sir George Clark; X: *The Later Stuarts* (Oxford: Clarendon Press, 1955), 101–102. Sir Lewis Namier long ago made clear that party divisions were not absolute, but that nonetheless strong divisions, tensions, and factions were developing; see Robert Walcott, "The Idea of Party in the Writing of Later Stuart History," *Journal of British Studies,* I (1962), 54–61.

[31] Cecil A. Moore, "Whig Panegyric Verse: A Phase of Sentimentalism," *Backgrounds of English Literature: 1700–1760* (Minneapolis: University of Minnesota Press, 1953), pp. 104–144. The tradition is traced in Thomas Henry Cain's "The Poem of Compliment in the English Renaissance" (Ph.D. diss., University of Wisconsin, 1959).

[32] *The Complete Works of George Savile, First Marquess of Halifax,* ed. Walter Raleigh (Oxford: Clarendon Press, 1912), pp. 54, 47. Appeals to an Aristotelian "mean" are common in the period.

individual after the Reformation, rejecting authority, turns inward, finding authority for interpretation within the self:

It is the consequences of the loss of authority that mark the real changes for Biblical exegesis, and for allegory generally. For the distinction between Biblical interpretation and literary interpretation . . . —so carefully preserved throughout the Middle Ages—ceases to exist.

The individual more and more is thrown upon himself and his private resources; each private person is left to rely upon his own "common sense and individual experience": he is given a new "associative freedom to allegorize." In fact, only "an elaborate and diverse series of rationalizations" permits "freedom of private interpretation [to be] given a new claim to validity and in this way individual readings escape, to some extent, the charge of being idly ingenious." [33] Such a revolutionary pattern of private "freedom" had become an established tradition with the Puritans of the seventeenth century.

What such ingenious freedom led to in fact was greater emphasis upon individuality, upon association, upon invention. Swift opposes this trend; he disapproves when he finds "St. Paul's allegories, and other figures of Grecian eloquence, converted by divines into articles of faith"; [34] and he deplores the general popularity of private allegorizing, which he calls "refining"—where any meaning whatsoever might be privately invented, since it now depended "upon

---

[33] Abraham Bezanker, "An Introduction to the Problem of Allegory in Literary Criticism" (Ph.D. diss., University of Michigan, 1955), pp. 184–186, 2, 209–210; quoted by permission of the author.

[34] "Thoughts on Religion," *The Prose Works of Jonathan Swift*, ed. Herbert Davis, 14 vols. (Oxford: Basil Blackwell, 1939–1968), IX, 262.

the Caprice of every Coxcomb; who, because Words are the Cloathing of our Thoughts, cuts them out, and shapes them as he pleases, and changes them oftner than his Dress." [35] Like Swift, serious members of the Anglican church and the Royal Society attempted to combat such new freedom; Samuel Parker, for instance, in 1666 complained:

Now to Discourse of the Natures of Things in Metaphors and Allegories is nothing else but to sport and trifle with empty words, because these Schemes do not express the Natures of Things, but only their Similitudes and Resemblances, for Metaphors are only words, which properly signifying one thing, are apply'd to signifie another by reason of some Resemblance between them. When therefore any thing is express'd by a Metaphor or Allegory, the thing it self is not expressed, but only some similitude observ'd or made by Fancy.[36]

Nevertheless, the seventeenth century was conquered by the individualists and the allegorizers, those "single men" of the *Tale of a Tub*'s Section IX like Peter, Jack, Louis XIV, and Descartes. Religious fanatics read Scripture as they chose, devising their own meanings; men selected the political faction they preferred, proliferating pamphlets to justify their choice; philosophers constructed systems at will; and Royal Society scientists conducted scrupulous experiments upon minutiae as they chose, frequently reading into them all manner of allegorical meanings and universal laws.

[35] *The Tatler*, No. 230, *Prose Works*, II, 176.
[36] *A Free and Impartial Censure of the Platonick Philosophy* (Oxford, 1666), p. 75; quoted by George Williamson, "The Restoration Revolt against Enthusiasm," *Studies in Philology*, XXX (1933), 593.

These trends *were* the conflicts and the tensions in the air during the Modern's period, and he—and his "world" —embody them fully: they *were* that "Carcass of *Humane Nature*, and [its] *Parts*, both *Containing* and *Contained*" (p. 123). For the world of the *Tale of a Tub* is a world of private allegory and refining metaphor; it is therefore proper that its very existence be dependent upon conflict, upon "metamorphosis."

V

But how can one repeatedly refer to this mélange, to these contending dichotomies in *A Tale of a Tub*, as constituting a world? Precisely because it is not the Modern alone who is infected with credulity and curiosity, with religion and science, with fancy and logic; everyone is. Peter, for one, is engaged in credulously following every current fashion; he comes to believe his own posturings and inventions. Yet, at the same time, Peter is also the curious master of "projects" and occult readings of his Father's will. Jack, too, is given to inventions and creations, but he is still more the believer in every manner of fantasy; the credulity of his "inner light" leads him to fall into the kennel; but his curiosity permits him to "explain," to allegorize, the meaning of that kennel and his fall.

Moreover, consideration of the maker of the footnotes and the dedication—the bookseller or his scholiast [37]— shows that he, precisely like the modern persona in the *Tale* proper, is maddeningly various and protean. Often, he

[37] At times (see *Tale*, p. 187, note on *Bythus* and *Sigè*) the annotator sounds like the naïve bookseller himself. But it is usually asserted that *"a judicious Friend"* (p. 260) or *"several Gentlemen"* (p. 20) have helped with or have devised the notes.

simply gives helpful notes on occult points (as on pp. 78 and 85 and *passim*), or supplies dates (in the margin, p. 69); but at other times he makes it perfectly clear that his author is a satirist (p. 30) and that the annotator knows it and even agrees with the attitudes toward the subjects being satirized; yet at still other times he chastises the book's author for making silly comments (p. 170) or arraigns him for being "so severe a Censurer of others" (p. 42). At times the bookseller overreads the meanings of the tale's allegory (p. 86), and at times he displays a remarkable occult knowledge (p. 165, on Paracelsus and *zibeta occidentalis*), while at still other times he insists that he is absolutely ignorant of what a passage can possibly mean (pp. 159, 179). He, too, can be contradictory: at one point he barely recalls Thomas Vaughan's existence (p. 127) but at another appears quite familiar with Vaughan's writings (p. 187). Moreover, the bookseller is a master of curiosity—in his collection of dedications, in his exact calculation of the effect on the sale of books of "two Principal Things, . . . the *Bulk*, and the *Subject*" (p. 206), and in his scientific footnotes and nice annotations. Yet he is a credulous fool when he—and later, the poor William Wotton, B.D., as well—is drawn, in making notes and explications, into the vortex of allegories and hidden meanings in the *Tale of a Tub*.

Thus such a world, where every member is both curious and credulous, is "well compact." This is why so much of the *Tale* is so full of fanciful images, metaphorical flights, and allegorical emblems: the parable of the leviathan (p. 40), the figure of the pusher in the crowd (p. 46) and of the three oratorical machines (p. 56), the reading of the "Hind and the Panther" and the ballad of Tommy Potts as

significant allegories (p. 69), the elaborate clothes philosophy (p. 76), the analysis of hieroglyphics in works alluding
to ancient critics (pp. 97–98), the catalogue of Peter's projects and inventions and their meanings (p. 105 and *passim*)
and the later listing of Jack's projects and inventions (p.
190 and *passim*), the investigation into the origin and meaning of Aeolism (Section VIII), and the cultivation of an
original system that will explain madness (Section IX). Yet
the *Tale of a Tub* is likewise dominated by an impulse to
scientific meticulousness, by attempts to measure, to weigh,
and to analyze: the study of dedications (pp. 23–24) and
prefaces (p. 45), the construction of a learned argument to
"prove" the existence of contemporary writers (pp.
33–38), the composition of the *Tale of a Tub* itself as a
"scheme" to institute civil quiet (pp. 39–41), the manufacture of a system of stage machines (p. 56), the investigation
into the nature of digressions (Section VII), the anatomy
of Aeolism (Section VIII), and the learned explication of
madness (Section IX). Even the tale of the three brothers
itself is presented to us as a learned and accurate retelling
of an ancient story.

The whole of *A Tale of a Tub* is in fact constructed so
as to give the reader a portion of credulous tale followed
by a portion of curious digression. But the two cannot be
kept separate; as we have noted, very often the "surface"
of statement is complicated by a "depth" of invention and
dark meaning; and similarly, poetic and metaphysical invention is very often delivered in the scientific vocabulary of
the virtuoso. At such times there is achieved a tenuous coa-
lition of reason and fancy, with each of the members pull-
ing in its own direction.

Despite such frequent uneasy conjunctions of surface

and depth, the modern persona struggles to keep them separate and undiluted:

I have found a very strange, new and important Discovery;
That the Publick Good of Mankind is performed by two
Ways, *Instruction,* and *Diversion.* . . . However, . . . I have
attempted carrying the Point in all its Heights; and accordingly
throughout this Divine Treatise, have skilfully kneaded up both
together with a *Layer* of *Utile* and a *Layer of Dulce* [p. 124].

In one sense, the Modern's digressions are what he affirms
them to be, rich dark conceits filled with allegorical meaning; they are the very high point, as it were, of depth. Concerning his digressions, he recommends that "every Prince
in *Christendom* will take seven of the *deepest Scholars* in
his Dominions, and shut them up close for *seven* Years, in
seven Chambers, with a Command to write *seven* ample
Commentaries on this comprehensive Discourse" (p. 185).
Here the modern persona is the perfect "dark" author, a
prophet, inventor, and allegorist. On the other hand, the
narrative "tale" of the three brothers is treated only as a
simple tale, only as surface. Commencing as it does with
the conventional "once-upon-a-time" formula and with a series of traditional encounters with "dragons," and overfull
of narrated "Accidents, Turns, and Adventures, both New,
Agreeable, and Surprising" (p. 204), and taken, exactly as
medieval romances were taken, from an ancient
"author," [38] the narrative is everywhere treated as a literal
story of brothers and fashions.

[38] E.g., in the *Tale:* "HERE the Story says" (p. 74); "(says my
Author)" (p. 115); "I shall therefore be extreamly careful and exact
in recounting such material Passages of this Nature, as I have been
able to collect, either from undoubted tradition, or indefatigable
Reading" (p. 189); and *passim.*

Yet the central and shocking point here—and it is one of the finest ironies of Swift's book—is that the wise, scientific, and allegorical modern persona appears wholly ignorant of the fact that his tale is, clearly, an allegory of the history of Christianity. The *Tale of a Tub*'s final irony, its final touchstone of conflict, is the utter topsy-turviness of credulity and curiosity. For the Modern treats his digressions as allegories filled with depth and significant meaning when they represent shallow surface, while he treats his tale as pure and literal surface when it in fact represents allegorical depth. Insofar as the Modern believes the literalness of his own tale, he is indeed the supreme example of the credulous "fool." Insofar as, from avarice and vanity, he consciously would persuade his readers that his digressions contain deep and useful meanings, he is clearly the curious and calculating "knave." Here credulity and curiosity, surface and depth, draw conclusively together: the Modern author of Restoration Grub Street and the people of his world *are* business-hungry, money-seeking, and lying knaves—whenever they can possibly manage to be so. Yet in matters of tradition and of sense, of knowledge and of true insight, such moderns are utterly, helplessly, and fantastically fools.

Knavery and foolishness, the discordant terms of the *Tale*'s conflict, are separate; and yet they meet together in the persona of the *Tale*. The combining of the two aspects in the modern persona is like the discordant harmony that ironically conjoins knavish Peter and foolish Jack, the two religious leaders who had sought above all else to be unlike:

For, the Phrenzy and the Spleen of both, having the same Foundation, we may look upon them as two Pair of Compasses, equally extended, and the fixed Foot of each, remaining in the same Center; which, tho' moving contrary Ways at first, will be sure to encounter somewhere or other in the Circumference [p. 199].

This marriage in the *Tale of a Tub* of fool and knave ultimately renders, the reader must feel, a piece of poetic justice. Seen in the light of tradition, their integration is nicely appropriate. For just as Peter and Jack deserve to be associated because of their machinations, their gullibility, and their vanity, so the fool and the knave of a long tradition had been indentified. In Solomon's Proverbs, fool and knave are indistinguishable, folly and vice together accommodated by the single term "fool." Fool and knave alike in biblical tradition are proud, aggressive, and boastful; both are prattlers and talebearers; both are self-reliant "single" men, who trouble their own houses; both are considered deceitful to others, while they themselves love to be deceived.[39] Fool and knave in Proverbs are curious *and* credulous.[40] Swift, in the *Tale of a Tub*, suggestively recurs to this older tradition [41] and in doing so mounts the

[39] Prov. 14:16, 15:21, 16:5, 25:14, 27:1; 10:14, 11:13, 13:3, 20:19, 26:22, 29:11; 11:29, 12:15, 26:16; 10:23, 12:6, 28:10; 20:17.

[40] Prov. 17:24: "Wisdom is before him that hath understanding: but the eyes of the fool are in the ends of the earth"; 14:15: "The simple believeth every word: but the prudent man looketh well to his going."

[41] Swift himself thought fools and knaves, though not identical, very closely allied; he honored them on consecutive days: "Without question, the holiday which Swift most enjoyed celebrating, and the one which furnished his ironic nature the most sport was the ancient public Feast of All Fools, April Fools' Day. In Swift's private calendar, however, it sometimes seems to have been followed, appropriately enough, by All Knaves' Day, April second"

finest comic irony upon the boards of his dramatic house: knave and fool in the *Tale*, for all their insistent conflict, appear at the last, like Donne's famous pair of compasses, men whose sphere and whose circularity are the same.

This *mixtus*, this wavering, this ground swell of backward and forward jostling and confusion that pattern the *Tale of a Tub*'s conflict among the parts of its singular organization reflect exactly the subjective impasse in the modern persona himself, between knave and fool, with fool turning knave and knave metamorphosing into fool—all before our eyes. With a vengeance is "Imagination at Cuffs with the Senses" (p. 171), for this is the central and continual conflict that we discover in the *Tale*.

In addition to the deep undercurrent of significant meaning that Swift implies in this work, we must observe the considerable skill Swift reveals in perpetuating this artistic conflict; the sheer profusion of his reversals and the careful juxtaposing and patterning of folly and knavery appear not to demonstrate the "hat[red] for human life at large" [42] or the "loathing of the bestiality of human beings" [43] that critics have so often tended to find in his work; nor is it true in the *Tale* that Swift "bitterly concludes" anything at all in his own person. By mimesis, rather, Swift has merely set in motion an artistic dance of two elusive combatants, fool and knave. His artistic handling of this conflict appears to be homogeneous, widely imaginative, and, above all,

(George P. Mayhew, "Swift's Bickerstaff Hoax as an April Fools' Joke," *Modern Philology*, LXI [1964], 271).

[42] Introduction, *The Portable Swift*, ed. Carl Van Doren (New York: Viking Press, 1948), p. 6.

[43] M. C. Bradbrook and M. G. Lloyd Thomas, *Andrew Marvell* (Cambridge: Cambridge University Press, 1940), p. 115.

consistently brilliant literary comedy. The fierce and farci-
cal agon of these contending voices of folly and vice indeed constitutes the very motion and direction of the *Tale
of a Tub* itself.

PART II

Plot: The Creation of Satiric Action

3. Ancients and Moderns: The Context and Occasion of the *Tale*

Nostre France est plaine d'une infinité d'Homères, de Virgiles, d'Euripides, de Sénecques, de Ménandres, de Térences, d'Anacréons, de Tibulles, de Pindares, d'Horaces, de Démosthènes, de Cicérons françoys, et bref en quelque manière d'écrire que ce soit, la France pour le jourd'huy ne doit rien à l'antiquité des Grecz, ni des Latins: O France heureuse!

—JACQUES TAHUREAU (1555)

(Our France is full of an infinite number of Homers, Virgils, Euripideses, Senecas, Menanders, Terences, Anacreons, Tibulluses, Pindars, Horaces, Demostheneses, French Ciceros, and, in short, whatever the manner of writing may be, France today owes nothing to the antiquity of Greece and Rome: Oh, happy France!)

We have discovered in *A Tale of a Tub* relentless, comical, and continuous war between fools and knaves. But what does this internal conflict mean? What is the point behind it? We wish to comprehend the necessary cause of this struggle between credulity and curiosity, of "Imagination at Cuffs with the Senses," that portrays the modern persona a schizophrenic, at war with himself. Conflict or agon lies at the heart of a work of art's action; such overt contest represents in any literary work the very stuff of which plot is made. But plot itself is the containing and controlling form of all else in the work:

The most important of [the constituent elements of a work] is the arrangement of the incidents of the plot; for [a literary work] is not the portrayal of men (as such), but of action, of life. . . . Men are the certain kinds of individuals they are as a result of their character; but they become happy or miserable as a result of their actions. . . . Therefore, the incidents and plot constitute the end of [the literary work], and the end is the greatest thing of all.[1]

"For the critic, therefore, the form of the plot is a first principle, which he must grasp as clearly as possible for any work he proposes to examine before he can deal adequately with the questions raised by its parts."[2] What internal principle or principles of plot govern conflict in the *Tale of a Tub?* And how does such an internal principle utilize the *Tale's* conflict, rendering it a meaningful part of a comprehensive whole?

We may well ask if there is any formal structure, any typical action, any internal principles that organize fictional satires generally. Alvin Kernan has observed: "The most striking quality of satire is the absence of plot. We seem at the conclusion of satire to be always at very nearly the same point where we began." Kernan is quite right in suggesting that plots in satire are oversimplified, monstrous, perhaps even seemingly static; but I do not believe we can assert that satire is plotless, that "constant movement without change forms the basis of satire."[3] Satiric plots too

[1] Aristotle, *Poetics* VI.9–10, *The Poetics of Aristotle*, trans. Preston H. Epps (Chapel Hill: University of North Carolina Press, 1942), p. 13.

[2] R. S. Crane, "The Concept of Plot and the Plot of *Tom Jones*," *Critics and Criticism* (Chicago: University of Chicago Press, 1952), p. 622.

[3] *The Cankered Muse: Satire of the English Renaissance* (New Haven: Yale University Press, 1959), pp. 30, 33.

often do have a typical and discernible motion that transcends stasis or flux. Philip Pinkus is surely more accurate when he notes that satire controverts the action of traditional romance; in satire, the heroic St. George is ignominiously defeated by his dragon; in satire, it is the evil dragon who wins the terrified princess and lives "unhappily ever after."

Ultimately every satire creates a world of madness, an upsidedown world where evil is good and the traditional principles of order, harmony and reason are overturned, where there is no centre, no abiding values—only emptiness or brutality and words full of sound and fury.[4]

The satirist dramatizes the defeat of virtue and the necessary and consequent effect of such a defeat: the triumph of folly and vice.

"Let there be darkness," the satirist postulates, and Aristophanes' wrong logic, Juvenal's gluttons and foreigners, Jonson's alchemists, Pope's dunces, Huxley's brave new utopians, Nathanael West's Hollywood locusts, and Dr. Strangelove's vicious and infernal bombs commence to reign triumphant. "Let there be Folly," the satirist postulates, and Aristophanes' old women, Horace's bore, Rabelais's Panurge, Dryden's MacFlecknoe, Philip Wylie's mothers—and, of course, Erasmus' Folly herself—commence to tumble into an easy (and ugly) Paradise.

[4] "Satire and St. George," *Queen's Quarterly*, LXX (1963), 31, 37. For further discussion of the patterning of satiric plots, see Anna Lydia Motto and John R. Clark, *"Per iter tenebricosum:* The *Mythos* of Juvenal 3," *Transactions of the American Philological Association*, XCVI (1965), 267–276; and Philip Pinkus, "The New Satire of Augustan England," *University of Toronto Quarterly*, XXXVIII (1969), 136–158.

Thus, in answer to the question, "What is the procedure of satiric creation?" it is not strikingly new—but it is necessary—to assert that satire is the mimesis of the paradox of virtue's demise; that satire operates by means of artistic negation. I use the expression "artistic negation"—at first seemingly an oxymoron—because the satirist is no misanthropic negator. Like any artist, rather, he is a creator. The pattern of his plot is a creative vehicle, and the good satiric craftsman can no more be thought to endorse the negation of virtue than Shakespeare can be thought to endorse the violent action of an Othello or the violent inaction of a Hamlet.

We can cast further light upon satiric procedure by referring to terminology from another realm: that of Platonic and Hegelian dialectic, the renowned process of *thesis, antithesis,* and *synthesis*. In satire, the vital role in the action is significantly given to antithesis, which of course, derives its meaning from its opposition to thesis and which marks the negative boundary outside which the stuff for synthesis cannot be selected. Antithesis designates an extreme of locus and direction, which, although of no extraordinary importance in itself, is real enough, and without which there can be no synthesis at all. It is similar to that process in science's experimental method whereby not only must the hypothesis under consideration be made to account for all the concrete facts at hand, but crucially, by negative and skeptical analysis, it must be determined that *no other* hypothesis can similarly account for the selfsame facts.[5]

[5] Joseph Turner, "Is There a Scientific Method?" *Science,* CXXVI (Sept. 6, 1957), 431. See Mill's discussion of the "method of difference in experimental induction," in *John Stuart Mill's Philosophy of Scientific Method,* ed. Ernest Nagel (New York: Hafner, 1950), especially pp. 211, 214–216. Such methodical skepticism is traditional in British empiricism.

Without this negative, this skeptical, proceeding, no valid scientific conclusions can be obtained.

In like manner, the pattern, or "rhythm," of tragedy is understood dialectically by Francis Fergusson and Kenneth Burke as *poiema, pathema, mathema:* that is to say, as a movement from purpose, through passion (or suffering), to new perception.[6] In terms of this analysis, satire isolates and explores passion. Emphasizing negation and suffering, satire by nature is akin to Polonius' practice:

> Your bait of falsehood takes this carp of truth:
> And thus do we of wisdom and of reach,
> With windlasses and with assays of bias,
> By indirections find directions out.[7]

In fictional satire, such a procedure is devoted wholly to the phase of suffering, or passion; here satire constitutes the flames of the bruising but purifying purgatorial (or, more properly, infernal) fire. In essence, the satiric negative action is the hero's (and the audience's) kathartic ordeal—never itself producing katharsis, but the stimulus that makes katharsis necessary.

Fictional satire immerses one in that necessary mental state akin to the "dark night of the soul" of mysticism, or to the Inferno of Dante, or to the wilderness of the Jews—by means of which the superior mystical union with God or the discovery of the Promised Land can at all be

---

[6] Kenneth Burke, "Ritual Drama as 'Hub,'" *The Philosophy of Literary Form* (rev., abr. ed.; New York: Vintage Books, 1957), pp. 87–113, and *A Grammar of Motives* (New York: Braziller, 1955), pp. 262–274; Francis Fergusson, *The Idea of a Theater* (New York: Doubleday, 1953), esp. p. 31.

[7] *Hamlet*, II.i.63–66.

achieved. Yet the winning of Paradise must take place *outside* the borders of satire; for satire's action is set solely in Hell; its plot enacts the winning of Hell itself.

This is why it has been frequently (and justly) asserted that satire "is the completion of the logical process known as the *reductio ad absurdum,* and that is not designed to hold one in perpetual captivity, but to bring one to the point at which one can escape from an incorrect procedure." [8] For the satiric action brings one to the "point" of katharsis, to the point at which one wishes to escape—but only to that point; any further step must be taken after the satire has been read and put aside. "Satire reminds one that certain things are not worth while. It draws one to consider time wasted." [9]

What is important is not simply naming *reductio ad absurdum* and noting its relationship to logical procedure, but regarding it as a formal, a structural framework that organizes individual works of satiric art into coherent wholes. Whereas for the scientist *reductio* is an intensive and necessary phase of a larger methodology, for the satirist *reductio* is the totality of his work. Therefore it is important to consider *reductio ad absurdum* as the pattern of the plot employed by the satirist. Like the mathematician or the experimental scientist or the logician, the satirist postulates an absurd thesis [10]—expressed by an absurd mode of behavior, a fatuous goal, or a series of ignorant tenets—then he constructs a plot which permits such a postulatum freely to ex-

[8] Northrop Frye, "The Nature of Satire," *University of Toronto Quarterly*, XIV (1944), 89.

[9] Ezra Pound, "The Serious Artist," *Literary Essays of Ezra Pound*, ed. T. S. Eliot (Norfolk, Conn.: New Directions, 1954), p. 45.

[10] A thesis that is itself the antithesis of a common opinion.

tend its absurdity—serenely, with an intrepid logic that obeys probability and necessity [11]—to its uttermost conclusion. "Grant Aristophanes his premises, and his logic is ruthlessly consistent" [12] has often enough been observed about the unfolding of many a satiric action.

Yet the satiric artist, *unlike* the mathematician, the experimental scientist, or the logician, does not heed only the "utility" of the operation, in order that he may move on to other business. Rather, the satirist positively takes his inspiration from cultivating such absurd postulates in the making of his plot—and it is plot that is the rich crop he harvests from the original hypotheses he planted in the soil. His postulates have generated the satiric action: the artistic creation of the "downward path to wisdom."

Unlike those other theorists, furthermore, the satirist halts everywhere along the road to his goal in hell, occupies himself with musing, conducts business, founds cities, cultivates gardens, arranges shrubs and hedges, adjusts clouds, manipulates even the very pebbles of the land. For the fictional satirist is not interested in the mere discovery of a world, but in a world's creation. *Fiat lux* are the words initiating that creation, and if he is an artist of stature, he will see to it that his creation is good.

Because he is concerned with such creation, the satiric artist renders moral decisions, delivers pious truths, makes positive discursive statements no more frequently than does any other serious artist.

[11] There is no paradox here; just as Aristotle recommended tragedy's imitating "probable impossibilities," so in satire the improbable is imitated consistently, decorously; that is, satire is the mimesis of "probable improbabilities."

[12] Aristophanes, *The Clouds*, trans. William Arrowsmith (Ann Arbor: University of Michigan Press, 1962), Introduction, p. 3.

Literature presents, not an affirmation or a repudiation of facts, but a series of hypothetical possibilities. The appearance of a ghost in *Hamlet* does not owe its dramatic appeal to the question whether ghosts exist or not, or whether Shakespeare or his audience thought they did. Shakespeare's only postulate is, "let there be a ghost in *Hamlet*." In this the poet resembles the mathematician rather than his verbal colleagues in history and science.[13]

Indeed, since the satirist regularly imposes an invariable and single thesis, his work, more than that in any other fictional mode, appears most closely related to the operations of the mathematician. "There is a Trick in Arithmetique by giving a false Number, to find out a true one. So there is no way to come nearer to Truth then by Fable [*sic*] Allegories and apologues that have not truth at all in them." [14]

In every fictional satire, there appears close beneath the surface a clear and simple set of artistic postulates that govern the artist's hypothetical creation. The satirist is a creator, and his first law, like that in any genesis, is *Fiat lux*. But since he is a satirist, an imitator and parodist of the negative, all his subsequent laws are those of faulty, of antithetic, creation: *Fiat nox*. The satirist ever hypothecates an inverted nature, a stunted soil as the setting of his creation, where

> Realms shift their place, and Ocean turns to land.
> Here gay Description Ægypt glads with show'rs,

[13] Northrop Frye, "Levels of Meaning in Literature," *Kenyon Review*, XII (1950), 249.

[14] Samuel Butler, *Characters and Passages from Note-Books*, ed. A. R. Waller (Cambridge: Cambridge University Press, 1908), p. 443.

Or gives to Zembla fruits, to Barca flow'rs;
Glitt'ring with ice here hoary hills are seen,
There painted vallies of eternal green,
In cold December fragrant chaplets blow,
And heavy harvests nod beneath the snow.[15]

He postulates a world, as in *Candide,* where kings have
been deposed, where war and quake are regnant, where
syphilis alone is pregnant. He devises a barren ground governed by an impotent lord—whether it be the waste land of
Mr. Eliot, the Land of Torelore in *Aucassin et Nicolette,*
or Neapolitan Italy in the *Satyricon* of Petronius. There
may be the hint of the coming of a cleansing rain—but in
the satiric climate, that rain can never fall.

By postulating a further series of laws as dogma and
coercing them into operation, the satirist is able to "solve"
his equation; pragmatically he is able to demonstrate the inability of these postulated laws to create a healthy world.
In this sense satiric form "tries on" the postulates of select,
restrictive dogma; the distorted, unilluminated world that
results is simply allowed to prosper. Viewing the *Tale of a
Tub* as such a satire, we can comprehend more fully the
negative fiats legislated there—where a modern author
writes and writes, until his pen falls, his ideas evaporate,
and his notes disappear. We can more readily understand
the function of the disturbing conflict persisting throughout the *Tale* between surface and depth, credulity and curiosity, that is finally left "open"—falling abruptly to an inconclusive conclusion that forbids katharsis, the long con-

---

[15] *Dunciad,* I, 72–78, in *The Poems of Alexander Pope,* one-vol.
ed. of the Twickenham text, ed. John Butt (New Haven: Yale
University Press, 1963), p. 724. Quotations are by permission of
Yale University Press and Methuen & Co. Ltd., London.

flict hardly resolved by a temporizing *non liquet*, an exasperating *desunt nonnulla*.

I

But what exactly are the laws made to operate in *A Tale of a Tub?* What laws govern the operation of its kingdom, laws that, like Newton's law of motion, ultimately marshal and compel the atoms and the void of its world? In answering this question, we must agree, I believe, with Mrs. Starkman, who finds the *Tale*'s pertinence "within the large and comprehensive boundaries of the Ancients and Moderns controversy." [16] We find John Forster voicing the same opinion as long ago as 1875:

Proper significance has never, by any of his biographers or critics, been given to the fact, that corruptions of religion and the abuses of learning handled in the *Tale of a Tub* are but the continued pursuit [as in the *Battle of the Books*], in another form, of the controversy between the claims of the ancients and moderns.[17]

Obvious as the point may seem upon a first perusal—that Swift entered the quarrel to champion the ancients and to expose the moderns—nevertheless, it is important to understand that there is a strong and sometimes subtle current of critical opinion opposed to the concept.

From the very outset, William Wotton himself directed attention elsewhere, away from the ancients-and-moderns controversy.

[16] Miriam Kosh Starkman, *Swift's Satire on Learning in "A Tale of a Tub"* (Princeton: Princeton University Press, 1950), pp. xviii–xix.

[17] *The Life of Jonathan Swift (1667–1711)* (London: John Murray, 1875), p. 95.

For, believe me, Sir, what concerns us [i.e., Wotton, Bentley, and the modern party], is much the innocentest part of the Book, tending chiefly to make Men laugh for half an Hour, after which it leaves no farther Effects behind it. . . . But the rest of the Book which does not relate to us, is of so irreligious a nature, is so crude a Banter upon all that is esteemed as Sacred among all Sects and Religions among Men [as to be the central concern].[18]

Rigault makes a similar claim. For him, it is not irreligion but the *ad hominem* nature of the quarrel in England which is most important; and for him this personal quibbling undermines the salience of the quarrel itself:

The history of the *querelle* of ancients and moderns in England is merely a digression, a scuffle conducted outside the proper boundaries of the battlefield and covered by a dust so thick that witnesses of the struggle confuse even the identity of the combatants. One mistakes ancients for moderns, and moderns for ancients; the confusion is general, and Swift may justly laugh at the whole affair.[19]

The idea that Swift was volatile and indiscriminate, that he was a general railer, not necessarily concerned with the battle, is confirmed by Emile Pons, who argues that "the question of principle, vital to the champions of France, important to Wotton and seemingly so to Temple, left Swift indifferent." [20] Modifying this attitude but slightly, Ricardo Quintana suggests, concerning "the relative merits of

[18] *A Defense of the Reflections upon Ancient and Modern Learning* (1705), quoted in *Tale*, pp. 316–317.

[19] H. Rigault, *Oeuvres complètes;* I: *Histoire de la querelle des anciens et des modernes* (Paris: Librairie de L. Hachette, 1859), 353.

[20] *Swift: Les Années de Jeunesse et le "Conte du Tonneau"* (Paris: Librairie Istra, 1925), p. 267.

the ancients and moderns": "To the philosophic questions which were here involved Swift was supremely indifferent; it was enough that Temple had been attacked." [21] Such an interpretation is yet again expressed by Irvin Ehrenpreis, who feels that Swift "was wholeheartedly borrowing the standards of a small, powerful group." Moreover, "Swift's tone suggests the cocksure arrogance of one who has taken over wholesale the opinions of others." After all, Ehrenpreis argues, "Swift felt no inclination to limit his literary taste to ancient works"; in his satire in the *Tale*, "Swift may be said to have borrowed his emotion." [22]

Yet all of this criticism is conjectural: its implication is that Swift was a man who had a satiric talent, in the way that Zeus was possessed of thunderbolts; that he could very easily be lured into the use of this talent without integrity, conviction, or serious moral responsibility. Such a view is, one supposes, perfectly legitimate as an opinion—one chosen from among several that are equally plausible—so long as it is understood to be nothing more than an opinion. But this view has prospered; it has been too often reproduced, as if it were a certainty. One step further, and a critic could suggest that Swift was not only divorced from the issues of the quarrel, but helpless in the face of them. Actually, it has been proposed that Swift was incapable of defending the ancients, as he intended:

And yet—and yet Swift himself, in his own best work, was far more of a modern than an ancient. Compared with those of

[21] *The Mind and Art of Jonathan Swift* (London: Methuen, 1936), p. 77.

[22] *Swift: The Man, His Works, and the Age*, I: *Mr Swift and His Contemporaries* (Cambridge, Mass.: Harvard University Press, 1962), 214, 206, 193, 209.

Boileau and of Pope, his satires are boldly original, owing relatively little to his satiric predecessors; and sometimes, like his own spider, they are marked by "an over-weening Pride, which feeding and engendering on itself, turns all into Excrement and Venom." [23]

One critic goes so far as to intimate that Swift remains, in *The Battle of the Books* and in the *Tale*, aloof from both sides, critical of ancients *and* moderns: "Swift is attacking extremes, whether they are Modern or Ancient, because extremes represent unreason." In the *Tale*, this critic argues, Swift "uses" the ancients-and-moderns controversy for his own very different didactic purposes.[24]

This last opinion seems very wide of the mark. I am perfectly willing to admit that I can only guess what Swift's intention or degree of sincerity was in his artistic work, but I believe that such conjecture is largely beside the point. The purpose of the present chapter, rather, is to demonstrate that the satiric "occasion" for the *Tale of a Tub* was indeed the ancients-and-moderns controversy and to establish that the work's procedures and its meaning are sharply clarified by a knowledge of the controversy. Yet let it be said—emphatically—that the *Tale's* content should reveal an internal artistic continuity transcending any mere catering to the opinions of William Temple, any mere opportunism or artistic helplessness, or any particular instances of cantankerous *ad hominem* name-calling. If the *Tale of a Tub* is to reveal itself as a coherent work of art, then the

[23] Gilbert Highet, *The Classical Tradition: Greek and Roman Influences on Western Literature* (New York: Oxford University Press, 1949), p. 286.

[24] Philip Pinkus, "Swift and the Ancients-Moderns Controversy," *University of Toronto Quarterly*, XXIX (1959), 50, 55–56, 52.

ancients-and-moderns controversy of the 1690's in England must be understood as the work's occasion only, not as the work's tyrannous cause. "Obviously what makes any great satirist is much less the occasion for scoffing than the disposition to scoff; for the true satirist, opportunity, so far from knocking only once, knocks all day long." [25] The occasion is merely the means to an end; ultimately the true work of art will have to bend and transform all extraneous and external subject matter, rendering it subservient to the work's own internal principles.

Nonetheless, the ancients-and-moderns controversy *is* the *Tale*'s occasion; their relationship is crucially important; and it is too seldom that the central point concerning the *Tale* is tersely and openly stated: "The Hack's great heresy is his advocacy of the 'modern's' principle that Man, independent of the past, can progress without help from the Ancients, or from anyone else." [26] This point needs stating —openly and emphatically. More important, this point requires demonstration, revealing how this "satiric occasion" is related to, made subservient to, and ultimately integrated with, the aesthetic demands necessary to shape them into a single work of art. Let us examine, first, the quarrel of ancients and moderns, the better to comprehend how many of its nuances and ideas come to play an important role in Swift's *Tale of a Tub*.

II

Swift, we know, while in Sir William Temple's employ during the 1690's, found himself by chance, as it were,

[25] Louis Kronenberger, "Byron's Don Juan," *The Republic of Letters* (New York: Knopf, 1955), p. 149.

[26] S. A. Golden, review of Ronald Paulson's *Theme and Structure in Swift's "Tale of a Tub,"* in *Criticism*, III (1961), 255.

plunged into the local outburst of the famous and continuing *querelle* of the ancients and moderns.[27] In their pride, "moderns," particularly in France, violently rejected the classical past—even in the realm of the arts—and elevated themselves, men living in the age of Louis le Grand, above the ancients of Greco-Roman tradition. In England, on the other hand, most phases of the quarrel since the time of Bacon had been less turbulent, Baconians often merely arguing the moderns' superiority in the sciences. In 1690, Sir William Temple, prompted by excessive "modern" claims of Frenchmen like Charles Perrault and Bernard de Fontenelle,[28] countered by offering general praise of the

[27] Properly speaking, the "battle" of ancients and moderns commenced at the very outset of the Renaissance; see Hans Baron, "The *Querelle* of the Ancients and the Moderns as a Problem for Renaissance Scholarship," *Journal of the History of Ideas*, XX (1959), 3–22. In fact, as E. R. Curtius observes, such a battle is a recurrent phenomenon in *all* ages. See Curtius' *European Literature and the Latin Middle Ages*, trans. Willard R. Trask (New York: Pantheon Books, 1953), pp. 251–255; and J. F. D'Alton's "Ancients v. Moderns," *Roman Literary Theory and Criticism* (New York: Russell and Russell, 1962), pp. 266–353. The battle in France is best treated by Rigault, in *Histoire de la querelle des anciens et des modernes*, and by Hubert Gillot, in *La Querelle des anciens et des modernes en France* (Paris: Librairie Ancienne, 1914). No equivalent account of the *querelle* in England is so thorough; but consult Richard Foster Jones, "The Background of the *Battle of the Books*," *Washington University Studies*, Humanistic Series, VII (1920), 99–162, and his *Ancients and Moderns: A Study of the Background of the Battle of the Books* (St. Louis: Washington University Press, 1936). A useful brief survey and bibliography of the battle in England during the 1690's may be found in A. Guthkelch's edition of *"The Battle of the Books," by Jonathan Swift, with selections from the Literature of the Phalaris Controversy* (London: Chatto and Windus, 1908).

[28] Temple originally cited an English work and a French for excessively praising modernity: Thomas Burnet's *Theory of the*

ancients.[29] Thereupon, English moderns like William Wotton (1694) and Richard Bentley (1697) generated an intellectual storm when they attacked Temple's gentlemanly rambling essay. However gentle and reserved Wotton's own learned and inordinately lengthy response to Temple's essay was, arguing for modern supremacy in the sciences alone, it was nevertheless enough to ignite once again local English skirmishing on the subject. I shall deal here with that general "battle" in the 1690's only insofar as it contributes directly to our establishing the "laws" governing Swift's satiric land in the *Tale of a Tub*.

In their debate with the ancients, the moderns may be said to have followed two procedures; these are very well summarized in *The Battle of the Books* by Swift, who pictures the ancients as occupying the larger and higher of two hilltops on Parnassus. The moderns demand

either that the *Antients* would please to remove themselves and their Effects down to the lower Summity, which the *Moderns* would graciously surrender to them, and to advance in their Place; or else, that the said *Antients* will give leave to the *Moderns* to come with Shovels and Mattocks, and level the said Hill, as low as they shall think it convenient [p. 220].

Earth (1684, 1690) and Fontenelle's *Entretiens sur la pluralité des mondes* (1686). On Burnet's work, see Ernest Tuveson, "Swift and the World-Makers," *Journal of the History of Ideas*, XI (1950), 54–74. The most important works affecting the English quarrel, however, were Fontenelle's *Digression sur les anciens et les modernes* (originally included in his *Poésies pastorales*, 1688) and Charles Perrault's *Paralèlle des anciens et des modernes . . .* (1688).

[29] "An Essay Upon the Ancient and Modern Learning" (1690), *Sir William Temple's Essays "On Ancient and Modern Learning" and "On Poetry,"* ed. J. E. Spingarn (Oxford: Clarendon Press, 1909), pp. 1–42.

The moderns, in other words, occupy themselves either
(1) with their own elevation or (2) with an appropriate
leveling of the reputations of the ancients. For purposes of
order, we shall deal with each of these separately, commencing with the moderns' attempts in the 1690's to elevate
modernity.

One such means of elevation was the appeal to "soils"
and "climates." William Wotton argues that Greece and
Rome had greater orators simply because the climate or soil
there was rich and varied enough to produce such seed. The
modern commonwealth, however, has neither encouraged
nor required oratory; hence there are not such great
orators.[30] Fontenelle likewise appeals to climatic variations,
asserting that differing soils produce differing ideas. But
Fontenelle, as is his wont, commences to round upon himself: despite variations such as these, human minds are
more pliable, more adaptable than plants upon their soils. In
a final reversal, he insists—in an argument that seems
"good" to himself, and he so praises it—that the climates of
Greece, Rome and modern France are actually very like;
thus, these nations' cultures and men would be "perfectly
equal." [31]

Not only does climate or soil vary from age to age, but
the "humor" of each age is also unlike; thus Wotton explains that the modern humor leads men to suspect oratory

[30] William Wotton, *Reflections upon Ancient and Modern
Learning* (London: Peter Buck, 1694), p. 38.

[31] [Bernard Le Bovier de] Fontenelle, "Digression sur les anciens
et les modernes," *Entretiens sur la pluralité des mondes, Digression
sur les anciens et les modernes,* ed. Robert Shackleton (Oxford:
Clarendon Press, 1955), pp. 162–163. Quotations are by permission
of the publisher.

as a mode of trickery: "Hence it will follow, that the present Age with the same Advantages, under the same Circumstances, might produce a *Demosthenes*, a *Cicero*, a *Horace*, or a *Virgil;* which, for any thing hitherto said to the contrary, seems to be very probable." [32] Fontenelle appeals to vaporous humors of another sort—to the famous Cartesian *esprits animaux;* [33] since such "spirits," like the humors, are similar and all but identical in every period of history, Fontenelle can urge that ancients and moderns (by laws of physics) are likewise similar and nearly identical. Differences among men, he asserts, are caused only by a variety of permutations and combinations of such spirits in their material liaisons in various human brains. In effect, this means that Fontenelle is proposing, in the Epicurean manner, that differences among men, differences between ancients and moderns, are due wholly to "chance." Fontenelle expands this argument, explaining that a Cicero or a Livy *could be* produced in modern times, but chance and "customs" and "fortune" often prevent their reappearance and, as with Gray's "mute, inglorious Miltons," their ripening and coming of age. [34]

Wotton also appeals to the effects of sheer chance; repeatedly he asserts that, after all, the ancients "had an advantage by being born first." In comparing languages, he points out that the variety of multisyllabic words in ancient Greek is merely a "lucky Accident"; it is merely chance

[32] Wotton, *Reflections*, p. 39.

[33] On the "animal spirits," see "Les Passions de L'Ame," especially Part I, Section xxxiv, *Oeuvres de Descartes*, ed. Charles Adam and Paul Tannery (Paris: Léopold Cerf, 1909), XI, 354–355.

[34] Fontenelle, "Digression," pp. 161–162, 170.

and hazard that place moderns with their far different "Mother-Tongues" at a disadvantage.[35]

As a result, Wotton and Fontenelle find that all ages could have produced the *same* great men but for the fact that ages vary according to soil, humor, and chance. Nevertheless, the equality of ancients and moderns is maintained; for in Wotton's and Fontenelle's day, attempting "to find out the motions of the Heavens and to calculate the Distances of the Stars" replaces writing "like *Cicero* and *Virgil*." Both tasks are equal; both offer the same difficulty.[36] Any clear system of values is here kicked downstairs, an egalitarian relativism established in its stead. Yet a victory of modern values is nonetheless smuggled into the attic. Many critics of modern virtuosi object that poring over musty scholia and glossaries and the comparison of variant readings in ancient texts is only drudgery; but Wotton counters this charge by asserting that the genius of modern editors *exceeds* the genius of the ancient authors they edit:

For, whoever will be at the pains to reflect upon the vast Extent of the various Knowledge which such Men as those I named before have gathered together, which they were able to produce to such excellent Purposes in their Writings, must confess that their *Genius*'s were little, if at all, inferior to their *Memories;* those among them, especially, who have busied themselves in restoring corrupted Places of Ancient Authors. There are Thousands of Corrections and Censures upon Authors to be found in the Annotations of Modern Critics, which required more Fineness of Thought, and Happiness of Invention, than,

[35] *Reflections,* pp. 24, 25.
[36] *Reflections,* p. 24.

perhaps, Twenty such Volumes as those were, upon which these very Criticisms were made.[37]

Ages and men are equal in talents and capacities, but the sevententh century, with its pedants and virtuosi, is "more equal."

Wotton also seeks to define the essence of modern virtues. In discussing historians, he selects Philip Comines (c. 1445–1511) as exemplar. In spite of the fact that he lived in a "barbarous Age" and had "no Learning," as a historian Comines is superior to Polybius and comparable to Livy and Tacitus. What is admirable in Comines, Wotton explains, is his masculine style and the "peculiar Air of Impartiality" apparent throughout his work. Particularly praised is his work's magnitude and the author's verbosity: "though diffuse, yet not tedious; even his Repetitions, which are not overfrequent, are diverting: His Digressions are wise, proper, and instructing." [38] Elsewhere, in spite of this praise of the untutored and the digressive, Wotton, like other moderns, handsomely acclaims modern abridgments of books; with digests and outlines moderns may learn faster.[39] The "efficient" saving of time is a modern prepossession. On the other hand, Wotton, like all British empiricists, condemns "hypothesizing" of the kind employed by Hobbes, Gassendi, and Descartes, and extolls "theorizing" —the inductive method which endorses the slow and painful accumulation of particles of knowledge.[40] He has noth-

[37] *Reflections*, pp. 317–318.

[38] *Reflections*, p. 43.

[39] *Reflections*, p. 338. His recommendations are traditional in Baconian induction.

[40] *Reflections*, p. 244; he distinguishes here between the Baconian inductive (or experimental) and the Cartesian deductive (or rational) methods.

ing but praise to bestow upon those modern "learned Men, who . . . have, rather than not contribute their Proportion towards the Advancement of Knowledge, spent a World of Time, Pains and Cost, in examining the Excrescencies of all the Parts of Trees, Shrubs, and Herbs, in observing the critical Times of the Changes of all sorts of Caterpillars and Maggots." [41] Yet despite his admiration for such a slavish and meticulous methodology, Wotton esteems liberty perhaps above all else:

It is Liberty alone which inspires Men with Lofty Thoughts, and elevates their Souls to a higher Pitch than Rules of Art can direct. Books of Rhetorick make Men Copious and Methodical; but they alone can never infuse that true Enthusiastick Rage which Liberty breaths into their Souls who enjoy it: And which, guided by a Sedate Judgment, will carry Men further than the greatest Industry and the quickest Parts can go without it. [42]

But, in spite of all this adulation of liberty and human nobility, something compels these moderns to espouse the theory of an implacable determinism governing man and history:

The comparison just made of men of all centuries with a single man can be applied to the whole question of the ancients and moderns. A sound, cultivated mind is, so to speak, composed of all the intellects of preceding centuries; it is surely not a mind nurtured only in the present. Thus, this general man, who has lived from the beginning of the world to the present time, has passed through an infancy in which he was preoccupied solely with life's necessities, through a childhood successfully preoccupied with affairs of the imagination (such as rhetoric and

[41] *Reflections*, p. 270.
[42] *Reflections*, p. 37.

poetry), although it was also a period in which he began to reason, though with less soundness than passion. Now he is in the age of vigorous manhood, in which he reasons with more force and possesses more enlightenment than ever.

At this point, the metaphoric comparison of all history with the life of a single man becomes embarrassingly awkward; it leads one to expect that henceforward that single life will inevitably age, decay, and die—a demise Fontenelle cannot intend or allow. Accordingly, after eloquently mounting this figure and expounding it, he must abruptly alter its course: "I am forced to insist that this man will never grow old." Historical man, after arriving at the present "Âge de virilité," will never grow older or decay; "that is to say, to abandon the allegory, that men will never degenerate, and that the sound ideas of all good minds will in successive generations be added each to the others." [43] The "allegory" suffers the Icarian strains and wobbling that beset Swift's own persona in the *Tale;* and it discovers further difficulties. Historical man's coming of age, his arrival at full manhood, is remarkably sudden, according to Fontenelle. After thousands of years in a lingering childhood, Descartes has taught him *in that very century* the secret and the method of reasoning; all real advances in civilization will shortly ensue.[44]

Wotton and the Royal Society virtuosi (however much they disagree about method) agree with this conception of civilization's sudden, miraculous, and modern advancement.

---

[43] "Digression," pp. 171, 172. Comparison of the ages of history with periods in the life of a single man has long been popular. For an early instance of this analogy, see Lucius Florus, *Epitome* I. intro. 4–5.

[44] "Digression," pp. 166–167.

Wotton asserts—"without Vanity"—that if so many scholars continue entering the fields of natural and mathematical
study, "the next Age will not find very much Work of this
Kind to do." [45] With this view, moderns are elevated to a
pitch where they threaten to discover literally everything
that is to be known.

On the other side of the modernist program, arguments
are put forward which seek to "level" the ancients and
their high seat upon Parnassus hill. Fontenelle depreciates
the ancients, for instance, by sophistically arguing that it is
easy to be an inventor or founder, but difficult to improve
upon an invention thereafter:

Truly, to add to original discoveries often requires more effort
of intellect than was necessary to make the discoveries in the
first place; but also, it is much easier to make this effort. For
one already has a clear view of these discoveries when one has
them before one's eyes; we have conceptions borrowed from
others added to our own, and if we surpass the original inventor, it is he himself who has helped us to surpass him.[46]

Living in the early ages of the world, the ancients, Wotton
adds, were really quite like "children," and it might therefore even be questioned whether they were inventors of
anything at all:

He that has only a Moral Persuasion of the Truth of any Proposition . . . cannot so properly be esteemed the Inventor . . .

[45] *Reflections*, p. 348.

[46] Digression," p. 165; his words paraphrase the long popular
figure comparing moderns to dwarfs standing upon the shoulders
of gigantic ancients. See Foster E. Guyer, "The Dwarf on the
Giant's Shoulders," *Modern Language Notes*, XLV (1930), 398–
402; and the Shandean satiric spoof by Robert K. Merton, *On the
Shoulders of Giants* (New York: Free Press, 1965).

of that Proposition, as another man, who, though he lived many Ages after, brings such evidences of its Certainty, as are sufficient to convince all competent Judges.[47]

Bayle, in his renowned *Dictionary*, makes a similar point. Although modern works are virtually filled with quotations and borrowings from the ancients, the moderns deserve credit for originality, since each modern work as a whole is fashioned into a complete and creative "system" in a way that ancient writings never were. We borrow from the ancients, but we nevertheless remain original—perhaps even without owing a debt.

An "infinity" of modern ideas might appear to have been "dérobées aux Anciens," Bayle concedes, but it is not so:

Doubtless, if one compares the ancients with the moderns in terms of isolated thoughts and *sententiae*, one will easily be convinced that the advantage does not lie with the moderns. For I do not believe that in this century anyone has thought anything great and refined that one has not already observed in books of the ancients. The most sublime conceptions of metaphysics and ethics that we admire in some moderns are to be found in the books of the ancient philosophers. Thus, in order to arrange it so that our century can presume to superiority, it is necessary to compare each complete work with another complete work. For who can doubt that a work of beauty nonetheless yields to another work's beauty if its parts are weak and more numerous and gross than the weak spots of other works? Who can doubt, even if M. Descartes had discovered all parts of his system in the books of the ancients, that he deserves more admiration than they, since he knew how to

[47] *Reflections*, pp. 11–12, 89.

fit together all the scattered pieces and form a methodical system of material which had been without coherence? [48]

Moderns question even the acknowledged debts to the ancients.

In fact, this very questioning of obvious contributions of the ancients introduces a repeated and paradoxical theme in Wotton's book: after all, whatever the ancients have postulated or discovered has *since* been found out. Here the definite location in time of ancients and moderns and the very nature of time itself begin to be destroyed. At one point, Wotton urges that it will be of "mighty use to prove, That the Ancients cannot be supposed to have known many of the most eminent Modern Discoveries." He notes that Galen in the *De Usu Partium* "does not discourse as if he were acquainted with Modern discoveries." And he argues that

> though the noble Discoveries of these latter Ages might possibly be found in *Hippocrates, Aristotle,* and *Galen,* yet, since no interpreters could ever find them there, till they had been discovered anew by Modern Physicians, who followed Nature as their guide, these late Discoverers have an equal right to the Glory due to such Discoveries, as the Ancients could possibly have.[49]

This confusion of times and inventors is enhanced by the very relativity accorded the term "modern." Fontenelle, ex-

[48] Pierre Bayle, *Dictionnaire historique et critique* (1697), 5 vols. (5th ed.; Amsterdam: P. Brunel *et al.,* 1740), II, 215a. Bayle's *Dictionnaire* is itself an exemplary "modern" production, devoted to a miscellany of collections, curiosities, digressions; the content of the footnotes far exceeds the amount of matter in the text.

[49] *Reflections,* pp. 192, 210, 297. Cf. p. 322.

ploiting a paradox abducted from Horace, reminds his readers that the Romans were moderns in comparison with the Greeks, and he observes that we must not therefore idealize the ancients; we must treat them as moderns. We moderns are better and more enlightened precisely because we are enriched by moderns of the past.[50]

Wotton is harsher still on the ancients. Sir William Temple in his original essay defending antiquity urges that learning had come from those "who were Ancients to those that are Ancient to us."[51] Wotton dryly summarizes Temple's point thus:

That those whom we call Ancients, are Moderns, if compared to those who are ancienter than they: And that there were vast Lakes of Learning in *Egypt, Chaldea,* and *China;* where it stagnated for many Ages, till the *Greeks* brought Buckets, and drew it out.

Wotton's reply to this argument is a ringing rebuttal: *"Where are the Books and Monuments wherein these Treasures were deposited for so many Ages?"* And he concludes that they did not exist, *because they are not now to be found.*[52] Modern materialism here seizes a powerful rod: if works and remnants of works by the ancients are no longer physically present and measurable, we may question whether they ever existed at all.

The sheer confusion of the terms "ancient" and "mod-

[50] "Digression," pp. 168, 170. See Horace, *Epistles* II.i.34–92.

[51] "Essay Upon the Ancient and Modern Learning," p. 15. Reverence for aged tradition is commonplace in classical and biblical antiquity. For the idea that Egypt housed a vast wisdom far more ancient than Greece's, see Herodotus, *Histories* II, and Plato, *Timaeus* 22B–C.

[52] *Reflections,* p. 81; *cf.* Temple's "Essay," pp. 4, 9–14.

ern" that we have been exploring takes a new turn: the existence of antiquity is challenged. This annihilating of antiquity is most strikingly achieved in the 1697 edition of Wotton's *Reflections*. Perhaps Temple's most renowned single assertion in his essay of 1690 defending antiquity are these sentences:

It may, perhaps, be further affirmed in Favour of the Ancients, that the oldest Books we have are still in their kind the best. The two most ancient that I know of in Prose, among those we call prophane Authors, are *Æsop*'s Fables and *Phalaris*'s Epistles, both living near the same time.[53]

To the second edition of Wotton's work, in 1697, was attached Richard Bentley's famous "Dissertation," which Wotton (with understatement) said would prove "a considerable Point in the Controversie." For Bentley's treatise established with cumbersome scholarly precision the spuriousness of the works of Aesop and Phalaris.[54]

Here was the apex of the arguments seeking to "level" the ancients. There could be no higher pitch, no more bold emprise—and Swift saw distinctly the humor at the heart of the matter. It is not only that, in the words of the epic "historian" of *The Battle of the Books*, "as for any Obligations they [the moderns] owed to the *Antients*, they renounced them all" (p. 227); but it is also, and more outrageously, the fact that "our Illustrious *Moderns*" have entirely "eclipsed the weak glimmering Lights of the *An-*

[53] "Essay," pp. 34–35.
[54] *Reflections upon Ancient and Modern Learning . . . With A Dissertation upon the Epistles of Phalaris, Themistocles, Socrates, Euripides; &c. and Aesop's Fables By Dr. Bentley* (London: Peter Buck, 1698), p. 6. Bentley argues the spuriousness of the Pharlaris letters (pp. 11–78) and of Aesop's fables (pp. 134–152).

tients, and turned them out of the Road of all fashionable Commerce, to a degree, that our choice Town-Wits of most refined Accomplishments, are in grave Dispute, whether there have been ever any *Antients* or no" (pp. 124–125). Here is the modern's case in the 1690's against antiquity. Such a case is clearly the satirist's "occasion"— and thereby hangs the *Tale.*

III

To such a case Swift responds fully, with a series of postulates legislating into existence an author and a world in the *Tale of a Tub* that are modern par excellence. Its landscape is dedicated to "soil" and "climate" and "spirits," its world devoted to "humors" in brains and to "chance" and "accidents" in affairs. All the "adventures" of the three brothers are recorded expansively, with a "World of Time, Pains and Cost," in the flat, mechanical tone of the scrupulous virtuoso. The narrator traces all "Accidents, Turns, and Adventures" (p. 204) that befall his characters with deterministic exactitude. The words of the persona himself are accidental, "being like Seed, which, however scattered at random, when they light upon fruitful Ground, will multiply far beyond either the Hopes or Imagination of the Sower" (p. 186). Accident accounts for the "wide compass" (p. 188) that the modern persona's writing zigzaggedly travels. Chance explains the arrangement of the parts of the work, whereby any "judicious Reader" may take any one of the digressions and "remove it into any other Corner he pleases" (p. 149).

Swift responds to the arguments of men like Wotton and Fontenelle by postulating a world where commentary and commonplace do surpass original composition: in the *Tale of a Tub*, narrative *is* overwhelmed by digression. Swift responds by postulating a modern author in a world committed to commentaries. The modern author's own concern has been with "Annotations upon several Dozens" of texts —upon "Tom Thumb," *Dr. Faustus*, "Whittington and His Cat," *The Hind and the Panther*, and "The Wise Men of Gotham" (pp. 68–69). Appropriately, even the persona's writing is heavily annotated by his bookseller, by "several Gentlemen" (p. 20), by Denis Lambin (p. 73), by William Wotton, B.D.—and, of course, will continue to be annotated by all later editors. In keeping with this perpetual habit of annotation, the modern persona naturally recommends that future ages write "*seven* ample Commentaries" upon his own work (p. 185). They have. For modern virtuosi always seek "an Opportunity to introduce [their] Collections" (p. 148), and their writings literally consist of "Abstracts, Summaries, Compendiums, Extracts, Collections, Medulla's, Excerpta quaedam's, Florilegia's *and the like*" (p. 127).

Swift responds by legislating a modern world where "liberty" is transcendent: "Now, . . . by the Liberty and Encouragement of the Press, I am grown absolute Master of the Occasions and Opportunities, to expose the Talents I have acquired" (p. 210). Such a fervor for "liberal" invention and innovation obtains in this world that it amounts to rage. Moderns favor a "freedom" in the commonwealth associated with the Civil War; for them, such freedom is associated with Cromwell's rule, a period "under the *Dominion of Grace*" (p. 201). Modern liberty in this fictional world extends to the privilege of making free with the ancients, a freedom of the moment that resembles strictest despotism: "I here think fit to lay hold on that great and honourable Privilege of being the *Last Writer;* I claim an absolute Authority in Right, as the *freshest Modern*, which gives me a Despotick Power over all Authors before me" (p. 130). Commentators possess this same liberty in determining the *meanings* of texts they survey; they insist upon discovering "Meanings, that the Authors themselves, perhaps, never conceived, and yet may very justly be allowed the Lawful Parents of them" (p. 186). Everywhere in *A Tale of a Tub*, in fact, becoming as pervasive as gas, liberty of thought, of image, of metaphor, of flight, of fall, of anatomy, of digression increasingly extends its sway.

By far the most extreme argument put forth by Wotton and Fontenelle was one that began to obscure the differences between ancients and moderns themselves—that displaced and confounded antiquity and modernity, that usurped antiquity into modernity, or that doubted antiquity's very existence. Swift responded with postulates in kind: "As for any Obligations they owed to the *Antients*, [the *Moderns*] renounced them all" (p. 227). Here is the crux of Swift's imitative world: throughout the *Tale of a Tub*, antiquity is significantly conspicuous by its absence. At times, modernity literally extends its borders, consuming antiquity entirely: moderns are superior as moderns, but moderns are also ancients, are everywhere the world's only authorities. This is the oft-repeated and re-enacted jest at the center of the *Tale of a Tub*'s hypothetical world.

Thus, Swift's modern persona proves that the "very Art of *Criticism*" is ancient, and *not* "wholly *Modern*"; yet he can only prove the critic's antiquity "thro' the Assistance of our Noble *Moderns;* whose most edifying Volumes I turn indefatigably over Night and Day," because it is the moderns who

have proved beyond contradiction, that the very finest Things
delivered of old, have been long since invented, and brought to
Light by much later Pens, and that the noblest Discoveries
those *Antients* ever made, of Art or of Nature, have all been
produced by the transcending Genius of the present Age.
Which clearly shews, how little Merit those *Antients* can justly
pretend to; and takes off that blind Admiration paid them by
Men in a Corner, who have the Unhappiness of conversing too
little with *present Things* [pp. 96–97].

The wavering back and forth between ancients and moderns in this passage results almost in their muddled and
hopeless fusion. Caught in that web, the reader cannot help
forgetting that the persona's original intention was to con-
fer dignity upon criticism by proving its antiquity—against
the blind counterassertions of many moderns.

Such confusion blossoms everywhere in the *Tale of a
Tub's* world: ancients simply cannot be distinguished from
moderns. The modern persona placidly speaks of "an establish'd Custom of our newest Authors" (p. 132) or "the
very newest, and consequently the most Orthodox Refiners"
(p. 44); or he can confirm that the "*Antients* [in using satire or panegyric, do so] in Imitation of their *Masters* the
Moderns" (p. 97). At one point, the modern historian of
the tale cites a "very ancient Author" as source for his information about a king—but that king, we discover, is none
other than the very contemporary Louis XIV (p. 165).

Such confusion of ancients and moderns is most fully realized in the three brothers of the allegorical tale. The
brothers, we know, are moderns, town wits of Restoration
London (pp. 74–75), contemporaries who yet live simultaneously "in an Age so remote" (p. 81). These ancient
wits whore and swear and flirt, visit coffeehouses, and wear

the shoulder knots of modern Restoration beaux, although they do slay "certain Dragons" (p. 74) and live in the once-upon-a-time world of primitive fairy tale and myth. In one place, the author informs us somberly that "Fashions [were] perpetually altering in that Age" (p. 89)—delightfully implying that modern ages know not the crush of fashions, tailors, and name-dropping, of courtship and schism; implying that modernity has delivered itself from the shackles of mutability and has slain the blatant beast *la mode*.

The same kind of confusion is generated when the modern persona advises his readers to distinguish "Differences of Persons and of Times"—to distinguish, in fact, antiquity from modernity. Of course, his illustration immediately following contradicts his general rule: "*Cicero* understood this [difference of persons and times] very well, when writing to a Friend in *England*, with a Caution, among other Matters, to beware of being cheated by our Hackney-Coachmen (who, it seems, in those days, were as arrant Rascals as they are now)" (p. 168).[55]

Such an example illustrates well the primary directive of Swift's hypothetical world: a *reductio ad absurdum* honoring modernity. Herein is the single and powerful *fiat* that draws the *Tale of a Tub* along, as by a chain. Swift, the alert, literal-minded, and skeptical satirist, has postulated a "world" that is uniformly timeless, a world confined to motile, perennial, and inescapable modernity.

[55] See *Tale*, p. 168, n. 1. Swift juggles the contents of two of Cicero's *Epistolae ad Familiares* (vii.6, vii.10), addressed to Trebatius, who intended to go to England but never did, and who was mortally fearful of the painted British savages. The "Hackney-Coachmen" are the hardly modern *essedarii*, drivers of war chariots.

As a result, the *Tale of a Tub*'s world accommodates an infinite expansion of the instantaneous, the contemporary, the impromptu, and the momentary. Its world bears witness to the victory of the modern instant, to the utter defeat of all time. In its realm, the modern and the extempore swell and bulge until they become, in a fine *reductio*, all things to all men—until they become *in saecula saeculorum*.

4. *Moderni* Mimesis in the *Tale's* Creation

Hail Horrours, hail
Infernal world, and thou profoundest Hell
Receive thy new Possessor: One who brings
A mind not to be chang'd by Place or Time.
The mind is its own place, and in it self
Can make a Heav'n of Hell, a Hell of Heav'n.
—Milton

Swift has responded fully to arguments of modern writers in the *querelle*. "Let there be modernity" is the *fiat lux* of his creation. And in the beginning, *modernity* is the satirist's "Word." Thereafter, in quick succession follow three further satiric commandments. These constitute the vital "unnatural laws" governing *A Tale of a Tub*'s new world.

I

Let there be no duration. In our examination earlier of conflict in the *Tale*, we emphasized the schizophrenic nature of the modern persona—the pattern of his Icarian flights upward that turn into descent, his changeable tones, the regularity of his contradictions. Critics in the past have remarked such qualities in the modern, of course. Martin Price comments that "the blindness of the Tale Teller emerges in a tissue of verbal contretemps; he is the victim of his own wit, which escapes his control and carries him

along, a helpless rider, in a direction he does not intend." [1]
Carried away he is—usually at a gallop; in fact, one of the
Modern's striking features is, as Kathleen Williams notes,
his sheer "breathless, aimless eagerness of manner." [2] Nor
does his wit permit repose; Ronald Paulson has studied the
Modern's repeated attempts to employ words in new ways,
noting that such words constantly reassert their normative
meanings, subjecting the Modern's wit to speedy over-
throw. "The modern's words do not stay posted long
enough for anyone to read them." [3]

It is certainly true that, like dramatic personae in a number of Puritan and anti-Puritan satires, the *Tale*'s modern
author is sprightly and precipitate, venerating "the things
of the moment." Yet the *Tale of a Tub* is unlike these
other works; its vivacity, speed, and spontaneity are not
simply local, rhetorical, or comic devices; they serve to
dramatize, rather, the work's central point. In the world of
the *Tale*, as the persona proudly avers, moderns have reduced all wit "to the Circumstances of Time, Place and
Person." Such wit is absolutely fettered to the immediate
and the local—to Covent Garden, to Hyde Park Corner,
and pertinent merely "*to day*, . . . or *in this place*, or *at
eight a clock*, . . . or *spoke by Mr*. What d'y'call'm, or *in
a Summer's Morning*" (p. 47). In contrast to God the

[1] *Swift's Rhetorical Art* (New Haven: Yale University Press,
1953), p. 86. John M. Bullitt, in *Jonathan Swift and the Anatomy
of Satire* (Cambridge, Mass.: Harvard University Press, 1953), p.
148, discusses the Modern's "converting imagination," as leading
him repeatedly to "an elaborate and artificial missing of the point."

[2] *Jonathan Swift and the Age of Compromise* (Lawrence: University of Kansas Press, 1958), p. 17. She explores such speed in
chap. vi, "Giddy Circumstance," pp. 118–154.

[3] *Theme and Structure in Swift's "Tale of a Tub"* (New Haven:
Yale University Press, 1960), p. 137; and see especially pp. 52–65.

Father's Will, which is "fitted to all Times, Places and Circumstances" (p. 73), the modern persona's philosophy endorses the singular and the momentary. He cannot help being aware of "the transitory State of all sublunary Things" (p. 66), for it is by the sublunary and the transitory that he is enthralled.

Total concern for the present moment prompts the persona frequently and precisely to date his work: his dedication is marked "Decemb. 1697" (p. 38); his wit is "calculated for this present Month of August, 1697" (p. 44); and he exactly locates himself in his garret as he is writing (pp. 44, 169). He affirms that Dryden, Tate, Durfey, Dennis, and the like are alive *now* and takes an oath "that what I . . . say is literally true this Minute I am writing" (p. 36). He is pleased with his age's acquirements—meaning the acquirements of "these last three Years" (p. 129); he alludes to Sir Humphrey Edwin, the Lord Mayor, who was elected in September, 1697 (p. 205), and mentions the tax on paper that was instituted in 1696 (p. 45). At one point, the Modern refers to "Times so turbulent and unquiet as these" (p. 208), and the bookseller's scholiast, himself as sequestered in the present as the Modern, needs to conjecture in a note that "This was writ before the Peace of Riswick" (p. 208)—that is, before September 20, 1697.

This overwhelming presentness gives the *Tale of a Tub* its atmosphere of impulsion and colors its modern author as well with a pervasive egotism. As if in haste, the Modern always speaks in the first person singular and always in the present tense, preferably in the progressive present: "I am now trying an Experiment" (p. 208); "I do here gladly embrace" (p. 175); "I am now advancing" (pp. 142, 163); "I do here humbly propose" (p. 185); "I proceed to refute"

(p. 96); "I do also advertise" (p. 106); "I go on boldly to pursue" (p. 104); "I do affirm" (p. 124); "I shall here pause a while till I find" (p. 210). Many verb phrases in the present tense employ the expletive auxiliary "do," a word normally used for emphasis but in the *Tale of a Tub* meaningless, commonplace, and redundant. The words "here" and "now" are likewise frequently a part of these constructions. Unconsciously, the reader comes to expect the literal and insistent presentness of physical time and space which all such usage reflects.

Similarly, the modern author regularly alludes to the immediately contemporary and is frequently in the act of arriving from an event or a place: he has "just come from perusing some hundreds of Prefaces" (p. 45); a "Grand Committee some Days ago" has just selected our author to write his *Tale* to "serve for an *Interim* of some Months" (pp. 40, 41); he has just come from being made a member of the "Illustrious Fraternity" of Grub Street (p. 63); his account of the three brothers assembles details only just now collected (p. 137); he writes "during the intervals of a long Peace" (p. 39); he imitates the method of "Acknowledgments" authors use "of late Years" (p. 181); and only "Yesterday" he ordered the anatomy of a beau (p. 173). Clearly the modern persona, like the three brothers he describes, is wholly dedicated to present "fashions."

The archetype of his habit of continuous verbal evacuation is the figure he employs to describe his own talk: "Since my *Vein* is once opened, I am content to exhaust it all at a Running" (p. 184)—a figure adequately representing his habit of attempting to commit immediate mental suicide. Another glorification of the extempore occurs in his recipe for the distilling of all knowledge: "You preserve only the first Running" (p. 128); or, again, criticism is best when "it is the very *first* Result of the *Critick*'s Mind" (p. 103).

Pope's Martinus Scriblerus praises modern usage, comparing it to the practice of sportsmen in the hunt: "Whenever you start a Metaphor, you must be sure to *run it down*, and pursue it as far as it can go." [4] The modern persona duly praises his contemporaries for this procedure when they seize upon the fashion "of deducing Similitudes, Allusions, and Applications, very Surprizing, Agreeable, and Apposite, from the *Pudenda* of either Sex." In spite of the fact that "this *Vein* hath bled so freely, all Endeavours have been used in the Power of Human Breath, to dilate, extend, and keep it open" (p. 147). Like Rabelais's inhabitants of the Isle of Ruach who live entirely on wind,[5] the modern "spirit" in the *Tale* lives on fashions, excitement, gossip of the day; modern talk is the wispy and diaphanous stuff of an everlasting moment.

It is not at all true, as the dedicatory epistle to Prince Posterity asserts (p. 31), that time is sworn enemy to the moderns. Rather, it is the other way round: moderns are contemptuous of time, of the durable, the lasting, of any process seeking continuity or completion. Martin is the least admired brother in the allegorical tale precisely because he demonstrates a "patience" in discarding—slowly —the quantities of fashionable clutter that he has over the years sewn upon his coat, a labor "prov[ing] to be a Work of Time" (p. 136). Martin is forthwith discarded by the

[4] "Peri Bathous, or, Of the Art of Sinking in Poetry," *The Works of Alexander Pope Esq. . . . ,* ed. William Warburton; VI: *Miscellaneous Pieces in Prose and Verse* (London, 1751), 230.

[5] François Rabelais, *Gargantua and Pantagruel, Quarte Livre,* chap. xliii.

modern historian in favor of Jack, whose more volatile nature endures neither patience nor any "Lecture in Morality." Jack is the more interesting because of his velocitous spirit, which regularly travels a "Flight-shot beyond his Patience" (p. 140). Hasty moderns naturally hold that "to enter the Palace of Learning at the *great Gate*, requires an Expence of Time and Forms; therefore Men of much Haste and Little Ceremony, are content to get in by the Back-Door" (p. 145).

Adoration of speed and immediacy is the reason the modern persona planned to include two additional works in an appendix to the *Tale*, but those have never progressed beyond the point of conception (p. 54). Precipitous optimism is the reason why eleven other works by the persona are represented as completed and to "be speedily published" but actually never appear. Speed is the reason why the three works in his volume—*A Tale of a Tub, The Battle of the Books*, and *The Mechanical Operation of the Spirit*—appear to be unrelated and to have been published simultaneously but to be incomplete. Hasty narration explains why we can never easily distinguish among the three brothers; like Peter at one point, they all seem permanently to dwell in the midst of "great Revolutions," during which everyone is so changed as to be unrecognizable (p. 105). Haste in fact accounts for the modern persona's preoccupation with fresh "Discoveries, Projects and Machines" (p. 105), with "Dress, and Dyet, and Diversions" (p. 206), with "*Indexes, . . . Compendiums* [and] *Quotations*" (p. 147).

In a world without continuity, without duration, the modern author, like jesting Pilate, cannot stay for an answer. He cannot conceive of cause followed by effect, of motivation and attendant response, of the will's control of action. For him, human behavior develops momentarily—in spurts, by accident, and by chance. For him, Peter merely "happened" to be book-learned (p. 83); and Martin, at the time of his reformation, appears to have made no decision, to be directed by no intentions: Martin merely "at this Time happened to be extremely flegmatick and sedate" (p. 139). And, if the author himself should "happen" to forget information, he must later interrupt the continuity of his narrative to insert it, out of place. To his mind, this forgetfulness is simply an event "as Fortune hath ordered" (p. 135).

In recounting his tale, the persona frequently accumulates mere swift summaries and lists: in town, he writes, the three brothers "Writ, and Raillyed, and Rhymed, and Sung, and Said, and said Nothing; They Drank, and Fought, and Whor'd, and Slept, and Swore, and took Snuff" (p. 74). In such listing there is no chronological, no ethical weighting; all activities are indiscriminately huddled together. The persona assures us that, as an author, he strives "to follow the Truth, step by step, whatever happens, or where-ever it may lead" (p. 133). But we conclude that his "history" and "truth" more accurately resemble disorderly fantasy and incredible fable. Gathered out of ancient authors, filled with stories of dragons, pickled houses, gold-consuming bulls, sibylline Aeolists, and dissenting musculous tongues—all is recounted with the naïve celerity of a fairy tale. Yet it is certainly true that the author follows his tale "whatever happens, or where-ever it may lead": he chases down dozens of digressive alleyways and byroads in telling the story.

The historical tale's progressions are likewise disrupted

by a swift narrative pace that refuses to amplify: "The three Brothers had acquired forty other Qualifications of the like Stamp, too tedious to recount" (p. 75). In fact, a host of devices recur which are at cross-purposes with the narrative. In a typical passage, the two brothers begin to revolt from Peter's sway; when he is away from home, they re-examine their Father's Will.

Whilst all this was in agitation, there enters a Sollicitor from *Newgate*, desiring *Lord Peter* would please to procure a *Pardon* for a *Thief* that was to be *hanged* to morrow. But the two Brothers told him, he was a Coxcomb to seek Pardons from a Fellow, who deserv'd to be hang'd much better than his Client; and discovered all the Method of that Imposture, in the same Form I delivered it a while ago, advising the Sollicitor to put his Friend upon obtaining *a Pardon from the King*. In the midst of all this Clutter and Revolution, in comes *Peter* with a File of Dragoons at his Heels, and gathering from all Hands what was in the Wind, He and his Gang, after several Millions of Scurrilities and Curses, not very important here to repeat, by main Force, very fairly kicks them both out of Doors, and would never let them come under his Roof from that Day to this [p 122].

Here is the modern historian's style: the insistent use of the present tense, the trot of long-winded sentences giving the impression of progress, the files of commas, the continual emphasis of capitals and italics. These sentences are confounded by the interruptions ("in the same Form I delivered it a while ago"; "not very important here to repeat"), the exaggerations (matters had *not* been in "agitation"; there were no "Clutter and Revolution," no "Millions of Scurrilities"), the awkward expressions ("all Hands . . . in the wind"), and the outrageously low diction, the bevy of clichés and slang expressions. All these are countered by the fairy-tale conclusion: Peter "would never let them come under his Roof from that Day to this." The passage's "ancient" allegorical story of the Protestant Reformation is countered by its "modern" setting, in a London filled with dragoons, Newgate prisoners, and Temple solicitors.

The passage is clearly not history. Nor do its complications and disruptions permit it to be a tale. Its style is ethically toneless; the historian expresses no emotions, is actuated to make no judgment of the events he recounts. All is equally weighted: the naming of "several Millions of Scurrilities" is mathematical only, concerned with measurement. The trite expressions, as well, contribute to undermine the making of distinctions and evaluations. The expression "very fairly kicks them both out of Doors" is typical; "very fairly" conveys no real meaning whatever. All these devices together give the impression of speed and vigor in the tale's unfolding, yet they forbid emphasis, progress, analysis. Such "history" is related as if it were just now unfolding, delivered from a limbo of the eternally momentary.

Indeed, all events and assertions encountered in the *Tale of a Tub* occur suddenly, swiftly, without the suggestion of transition, causality, or consequence. All happenings appear to be strokes of luck, chance, accident, or fate. In a world devoid of continuity, of construction, of relationship, there is no opportunity for "meaning" to emerge—no soil for motive or response, no haven for reason or incentive to responsibility. In the amazing montage of the *Tale of a Tub*'s various scenes, there is a continual jerkiness and speed reminiscent of the cinema of 1915, where on the screen a disjunctive and inconsequentially rapid story unfolds. Writers, projects, adventures, metaphors, and digressions race up, pass one by one before us with hapless singularity, and then, after playing their little distorting parts upon the scene, are swiftly whisked thence, are utterly put down, and, replaced by others, disappear from sight forever. The *Tale of a Tub*'s action epitomizes that cold, cosmic drama envisioned by Epicurus—the vapid, mechanical dance of faceless atoms in a void.

II

Let there be no past. Utter abolition of the past is the second fiat in Swift's literary creation, as we shall shortly see. At the conclusion of his lengthy treatise called *A Tale of a Tub*, the modern persona tells us candidly, "IN my Disposure of Employments of the Brain, I have thought fit to make *Invention* the *Master*, and to give *Method* and *Reason*, the Office of its Lacquays" (p. 209). Although invention is his goal, we have already learned that invention is precisely that capacity of which these latter ages have been deprived:

'Tis acknowledged, that were the Case the same among Us, as with the *Greeks* and *Romans*, when Learning was in its *Cradle*, to be reared and fed, and cloathed by *Invention;* it would be an easy Task to fill up Volumes upon particular Occasions, without farther exspatiating from the Subject, than by moderate Excursions, helping to advance or clear the main Design [p. 144].

Here is a central point: in this modern world, unlike the world of the past, there is no longer any "purpose," or "main Design." The reasons for this modern depletion and exhaustion—they entail some of the finer comic features of the *Tale*—require further examination.

Moderns, as we have noted, have initiated the "grave dispute, whether there have been ever any *Antients* or no" (p. 125). Neoterics hold either that antiquity in some awkward and backward time had a hazy existence or that antiquity never existed at all. By a complicated series of mental maneuvers, the *Tale*'s modern persona manages to endorse, and even to combine, both these views of antiquity's remoteness and nonexistence. For, although he is ready to pay lip service to the "Wisdom of our Ancestors" (p. 56), or to acknowledge that "some Remains of [Wit] were left us by the *Antients*" (p. 146), he asserts that ancient knowledge has not "been translated or compiled into systems for *Modern* Use. Therefore We may affirm, to our own Honor, that it has in some sort, been both invented, and brought to a Perfection by the same Hands" (pp. 146–147). Concerning classical writings, he is constrained, like William Wotton or posterity's "Governor," time, to "pretend it a demonstration that there never were any, because they are not then to be found" (p. 32). When the Modern has not encountered (or comprehended) particular ancient writings, or when he finds them inadequate for his present "use," his narcissism and "sufficiency" induce him to insist that he and his brother moderns "have proved beyond contradiction . . . that the noblest Discoveries those *Antients* ever made, of Art or of Nature, have all been produced by the transcending Genius of the present Age" (p. 97).

Indeed, moderns do not need the past; they are men in a hurry; their "Arts are all in a *flying* March" (p. 145). Such *moderni* naturally demand "a Shorter, and more prudent Method, to become *Scholars* and *Wits*, without the Fatigue of *Reading* or of *Thinking*" (pp. 144–145). Therefore, the Modern pays homage solely to modernity; for him,

> the Debate meerly lies between *Things past*, and *Things conceived;* and so the Question is only this; Whether Things that have Place in the *Imagination*, may not as properly be said to *Exist*, as those that are seated in the *Memory;* which may be justly held in the Affirmative, and very much to the Advantage of the former, since This is acknowledged to be the *Womb* of Things, and the other allowed to be no more than the *Grave* [p. 172].

The past is in the grave, dead and gone. In this sense antiquity has no existence whatever, and the modern persona can with justice claim that "former [Ages] have made no sort of Provision for ours" (p. 44).

Wearing a pair of blinders, the Modern sees in time no further than the moment, in space no further than his nose. Ironically, this nearsightedness is perfectly in order, for the modern pedant and virtuoso, dedicated as they are to the method of close observation and short views, positively require as their very *modus operandi*—if they are to study spelling and footnotes, flies and spittle—this elemental myopia.

There is an additional reason for this limiting vision that excludes the past: moderns are devoted to optimism, to an intractable theory of progress. They dare not "reckon upon the Infinity of Matter" (p. 147)—"matter" consisting either of mass or subject—because they intend to circumscribe the universe, to find the universe out. For them, "every Branch of Knowledge has received such wonderful Acquirements since [Homer's] Age, especially within these

last three Years" (p. 129). According to their thesis, progress, conceived as a rolling stone, far from being steady in
its acceleration, has in fact in the last moments phenome-
nally increased its speed. Because of this thesis' sudden elevation of modernity, the very latest modern, the modern
writing in "this present Month of *August,* 1697" (p. 44) or
better yet in "this Minute" (p. 36), will be the most
learned and progressive of all. As he is writing, the persona
of the *Tale* remains fixedly "confident to have included and
exhausted all that Human Imagination can *Rise* or *Fall* to"
(p. 129). He tells us frankly, "I here think fit to lay hold
on that great and honourable Privilege of being the *Last
Writer;* I claim an absolute Authority in Right, as the
freshest Modern, which gives me a Despotick Power over
all Authors before me" (p. 130).

The Modern's words are curiously poignant. From his
viewpoint, we witness a modernity stretched upon a very
strange time scale, where we discover a single line drawn
from the past (zero) to the very latest instant (infinity).
Here, at a stroke, the future is eliminated from consideration and even from existence. The past is questioned, perhaps is nonexistent—certainly, in any case, is of no interest.
All that remains is the *present moment,* wherein crouches
our solipsistic Modern, meditating upon his own "most finished and refined Systems of all Sciences and Arts" (p. 67).
Another moment can only bring us another modern (or the
same Modern in an appendix), together with more and nar-
rower "refining" paradoxically contained in grander and
more quixotic systems. We should not be surprised, given
this constricting compass, that the modern persona believes
all knowledge has "been both invented and brought to
Perfection by the same Hands" (p. 147). The elimination

of past and future, of course, represents the rigorous en-
forcement of the satirist's second commandment. It also
demonstrates the triumph of modernity's own vaulting ego-
mania.

It is appropriate and inevitable that the modern persona
is unconcerned with the "source" or "tradition" of any subject matter but dedicated only to its present state. He does
not care whether Jack or the "Original at *Delphos*" (p.
161) evolved the system of Aeolism, whether the works of
an author can be quoted when those works are entirely lost
(p. 102). In his hypersufficiency, the modern persona remains serene; for him the past is absent, but not at all
missed. In the *Tale of a Tub*'s usurping world, in fact, the
past somehow *is* the present: Homer has invented the compass, gunpowder, the circulation of the blood (p. 129);
Pausanias and Ctesias are precisely as allegorically dark and
Rosicrucian as the modern persona himself (pp. 96–100).

Upon the major scenes and characters of the *Tale* there
operates this same confounding of ancient and modern. Ir-
respective of time, place, or intention, every matter slips
and slides helplessly into that largest tub, the modern drain.
The ancient sect of Aeolists, in spite of the fact that materials about them are laboriously "gathered out of antient Records" (p. 151), metamorphose into contemporary British
Dissenters. The three wooden "Machines," created by the
"Wisdom of our Ancestors," transmogrify into a latter-day
Nonconformist pulpit, a modern British gallows, and a Restoration stage. The renowned clothes philosophy (pp.
76–81), "illustrated" by "the Authors of that [former]
Age" (p. 75), deviates into a cult of Parisian "Court-Fash-
ions" (p. 84)—all transmuted into Restoration customs of
moderns who "eat at *Locket*'s, loytered at *Will*'s" (p. 75),

"haunted the *Chocolate*-Houses" and "took Snuff" (p. 74). Every scene in the "tale" of the three brothers incorporates details of "Books [and] Dress, . . . Dyet, and Diversions" based on *"French* Modes . . . that Week in Vogue" (pp. 206–207). Everyone in the *Tale of a Tub*—the modern Grub Street persona, his rapacious bookseller, his commentators, the three brothers of the allegory—is a character native to the England of the Restoration and Age of Queen Anne.

Every object in the *Tale* is thus sunk in the timeless present; historical sense there is none. All knowledge is culled, with modernist uniformity, from the latest commonplace books, footnotes, indexes, and dedications. Just as the Modern himself never changes, remaining incessantly modern, so the characters of his tale never alter or progress; they simply vary their abodes, their modes and fashions of behavior. Unmoved, the brothers and the narrator alike continually experience in the present tense a miscellany of momentary actions and adventures. All ideas and events are studied with an immediate and toneless admiration. Living as they do without a past, without goals or judgment, these fops designate all events equally "wonderful to recount" (p. 112). They speak of "Pride, Projects, and Knavery" alike as "of most Benefit for Publick Imitation" (p. 114).

In such a hypothetical world, lacking traditions, devoid of historicity and futurity, these moderns employ no judgment, no moral discrimination, no system of values. Everything any character says or does, provided it occurs *now*, is of equal and trenchant interest. There can be, in the *Tale of a Tub*, no keeping to "the straitest and the commonest Road" and no arrival at any "Journey's End" (p. 188), simply because there is no common road or public highway. In this world, a Wotton or a Tom Durfey is exactly as important and as interesting as a Congreve, a Cervantes, or a Homer (pp. 207, 29, 127). In this world, troglodytes (naked cave dwellers of antiquity) somehow *are* "Philosophers" (p. 183). In this world, without continuity and with progress already achieved, the only tradition, progression, and direction are to be found obliquely—in digression.

Established upon such ground, all moderns are enabled to "refine" barbarism into culture, religious history into foppish tale, digression into progression, ancients into moderns. Moderns are great alchemists in their world, capable of transforming all baser metal into gold—and gold into baser metal. Nor can they be held responsible, for these moderns are akin to the vain and empty beloved addressed by Mauberley's "dumb-born" book of verses, the ignorant girl

> that goes
> With song upon her lips
> But sings not out the song, nor knows
> The maker of it.

For she inviolably

> sheds
> Such treasure in the air,
> Recking naught else but that her graces give
> Life to the moment.[6]

In the *Tale of a Tub*, the Moderns' "humor" and their predicament are like hers. It is a far cry from that central

---

[6] "Envoi (1919)," ll. 17–20, 8–11, Ezra Pound, *Personae: Collected Shorter Poems of Ezra Pound* (London: Faber and Faber, 1952), p. 207. Copyright 1926, by Ezra Pound. Reprinted by permission of New Directions Publishing Corporation and Faber and Faber Ltd.

tradition with which we are familiar, the tradition of the conscious *techné*, or maker, whose work is intended to last, the tradition asserting:

> Exegi monumentum aere perennius
> regalique situ pyramidum altius,
> quod non imber edax, non Aquilo impotens
> possit diruere aut innumerabilis
> annorum series et fuga temporum.[7]

This tradition in the West strives to endure beyond the broils of "sluttish time," laboring for permanent achievement, trusting that

> Not marble, nor the gilded monuments
> Of princes, shall outlive this powerful rime.[8]

The makers within the *Tale of a Tub* are alien to this tradition; they labor to a different end. Deprived of the past, moderns in the *Tale* cannot possibly construct traditions, laws, learning, art—or any of those cultural elements which literally coerce the shaping of order, judgment, value. Lacking all these, the *Tale of a Tub*'s world is set wholly adrift, loosed from gravity or control, in a formless limbo—a nameless and meaningless atom enveloped in the modern void.

III

Let there be no memory. At one point in his ramblings, the modern persona pauses to commend "a great Philoso-

---

[7] "I have erected a monument more lasting than bronze, and loftier than the royal site of the pyramids, which neither the devouring rainstorm nor the violent north wind nor the innumerable series of years and the flight of time can ever destroy" (Horace, *Odes* III.xxx.1–5).

[8] William Shakespeare, Sonnet LV, ll. 1–2.

pher's" attempt to create "an universal System in a small portable Volume" (p. 125). Particularly recommended is this philosopher's "Receipt" or "Nostrum" for the accomplishment of his grand design:

> You take fair correct Copies, well bound in Calfs Skin, and Lettered at the Back, of all Modern Bodies of Arts and Sciences whatsoever, and in what Language you please. These you distil in *balneo Mariae*, infusing *Quintessence of Poppy Q.S.* together with three Pints of *Lethe*. . . . You cleanse away carefully . . . , letting all that is volatile evaporate. You preserve only the first Running [p. 126].

As is frequent with the Modern's pronouncements, this recipe embodies an amusing paradox: in the modern world, out of opium will come lucidity; out of Lethe's forgetfulness will come forth knowledge. The conception of Lethe's power is particularly appropriate to the *Tale of a Tub;* for moderns who reject antiquity and deny the past are creatures without memory. What, after all, is mere memory but, as Hobbes had suggested, *"decaying sense"?* [9] Therefore, in modern society, let memory dissolve, be annihilated. This utterance is the foundation for the third and most important "unnatural law" governing the founding of the *Tale's* twisted great society: "Let there be no memory." Let us explore the effects of this law upon the *Tale's* modernity—modernity without a remembrance of things past.

The *Tale's* world is so overfull of writers waving pens that it is "hardly possible for a Man to travel, the very Air [is] so replete with Feathers" (p. 149). Such a "vast flour-

[9] *Leviathan*, I, ii, *The English Works of Thomas Hobbes of Malmesbury*, ed. Sir William Molesworth (London: John Bohn, 1839–1845), III, 4.

ıshing Body" (p. 31) of authors is prolific indeed. Their gross productions "hourly start up" (pp. 182–183), "yet are . . . hurryed so hastily off the Scene, that they escape our Memory, and delude our Sight" (p. 34). In the *Tale*, so rapidly falls the hoof of time that within "a very few Hours" from the inception of the newest works, they are dead, buried, wormed, forgotten—sunk into the abyss of the unrecollected and unknown: "The Memorial of them [is] lost among Men, their Place [is] no more to be found" (pp. 34–35). Although he complains to Prince Posterity of this infamous treatment, the modern persona himself cannot but agree with the result; for he is committed to preferring *"Things conceived"* to *"Things past"*:

And so the Question is only this; Whether Things that have Place in the *Imagination*, may not as properly be said to Exist, as those that are seated in the *Memory;* which may be justly held in the Affirmative, and very much to the Advantage of the former, since This is acknowledged to be the *Womb* of Things, and the other allowed to be no more than the *Grave* [p. 172].

Et erat.

Accordingly, from the very outset of the *Tale*, the Modern's own memory begins to falter. Even though he has "just come from perusing some hundreds of Prefaces," he can preserve only "a few Examples," to be set down "as near as my Memory has been able to retain them" (p. 45). The failure of his memory, with each complication as the *Tale of a Tub* approaches its catastrophe, grows and develops, becoming more apparent, more and more a general malaise. One of the Modern's earliest small digressions in the Preface occurs when, having avowed his love for panegyric and his utter incapacity to write satire, he commences for several pages to *satirize satire*. Then, suddenly, he catches himself up: "ʙᴜᴛ I forget that I am expatiating on a Subject, wherein I have no concern, having neither a Talent nor an Inclination for Satyr" (p. 53).

His first major digression (Section III), interrupting for the first time the hardly initiated "tale" of the three brothers, opens with the breathless announcement that "the unhappy shortness of [his] Memory" has led him to forget one of the most permanent of the latest modern rules, which requires performing "the due Discourses, Expostulatory, Supplicatory, or Deprecatory with my *good Lords* the *Criticks*" (p. 92). This error he must correct "immediately." And he does so—for thirteen copious pages.

Soon afterward, in Section VI, he confesses suddenly that in his tale he has forgotten, "about fifty Pages ago," to inform his readers that Peter, Martin, and Jack not only add one by one ornaments in the latest fashion to their coats, but also retain all past fashion tags, neglecting to remove a single one. He complacently excuses this "lapse":

The severe Reader may justly tax me as a Writer of short Memory, a Deficiency to which a true *Modern* cannot but of Necessity be a little subject: Because, *Memory* being an Employment of the Mind upon things past, is a Faculty, for which the Learned, in our Illustrious Age, have no manner of Occasion, who deal entirely with *Invention*, and strike all Things out of themselves, or at least, by Collision, from each other [pp. 134–135].

The friction and discord among modern writers and within each separate work are owing to just this egoistic spontaneity, to their mindless dedication to producing, always, "the very *first* Result of [their] Mind" (p. 103). Such hubris is appropriate for moderns in the *Tale*, since their forgetfulness of all other things more effectively permits them to concentrate upon themselves. While the Modern is securely at peace within, all outside is madly sounding the alarums of discord.

Yet the modern persona converts his weakness for creating discord to good account. Hobbes had identified *"good wit"* or *"good fancy"* with the ability to observe "similitudes" in all things and with *"celerity of imagining"*—all virtues which men perfect with "use," but "without method, culture or instruction." [10] Moderns have just such a fantastical ability to discover metaphysical metaphors in their imaginings—precisely without method, culture, or instruction. Thus, the Modern praises modernity and himself: "We think it highly Reasonable to produce our great Forgetfulness, as an Argument unanswerable for our great Wit" (p. 135). What would appear in some other "world" as disorder is here resolved into the neatness of planned haphazard. In spite of the fact that the modern persona had "forgot in due Place" the "material Circumstance" concerning the brothers' habit of amassing fashionable adornments one atop another upon their coats, this failure in memory occurs, he explains, "as good Fortune hath ordered" (p. 135).

Most important, near the *Tale*'s conclusion, the Modern discovers that he has had the "Unhappiness in losing, or mislaying among my Papers the remaining Part of these Memoirs," and, naturally, devoid of memory as he is, he must see his "memoirs" collapse, admitting that "with my utmost endeavours, I have been able only to retain a few of

[10] *Leviathan*, I, viii, *English Works*, III, 56, 57. The germ for this famous distinction between "judgment" and "fancy" may be found in Bacon's *Novum Organum*, I, lv.

the Heads" (pp. 203–204). In the modern manner, this considerable loss compels the abrupt cessation of the tale's retelling. Quite humorously, even the loss of these memoirs "which have now slid out of my Memory" and are "lost beyond all Hopes of Recovery" is itself an event treated as merely one more "Accident past Remedy" (p. 205).

Further, since this is a world that the satirist is creating, its natural laws may be expected to apply throughout the *Tale of a Tub*. It is not the modern persona alone who seizes the present instant in his vulgar embrace. His bookseller, too, is infected with the same malady. He, too, is stricken by the modern instant; the command "DETUR DIGNISSIMO" is to him an order to collect up-to-the-minute opinions about immediate greatness, ultimately resulting in a dedication of the *Tale* to John, Lord Somers, England's most notable figure *at the moment*.[11]

All moderns, as a matter of fact, ought to recognize the dilemma to which their devotion to the moment and their negation of memory expose them. Every modern must live hopelessly incarcerated in the immediate and local "present"; his failure of memory and lack of knowledge and responsibility defeat the very possibility of that "progress" to which he is dedicated. But moderns do not recognize this dilemma; although the modern persona attempts to remember and to follow all other *moderni* in their "fashions" and or-

[11] Somers had fallen from power as Whig Lord Chancellor in 1700 and had been impeached in April 1701 and acquitted. Under Queen Anne and the influence of her favorite, the Duchess of Marlborough, the stage was being set for the elimination of ruling high Tories from the ministry in April 1704. In 1704, then, Somers' star was again rising, and he ultimately became President of the Council, November 25, 1708 (*Dictionary of National Biography*, 1950, XVIII, 629–637).

thodoxies, his faltering memory causes him to fail to place all his digressions within the Preface. Rather, the digressions, insidiously exerting almost a life and will power of their own, escape everywhere into the body of his work, as when the lid had been knocked off Pandora's box. Escaped, the digressions fall like seed and take root at random among the fields of narrative, grow and prosper like wildweed, until they finally proliferate, advance, and ultimately confiscate all. At the last, progression ceases: in the final sections of the *Tale of a Tub*, digression manages a climax by strangling the whole of the narrative recital.[12]

At the outset of the *Tale*, the persona had commenced well (for a modern). In early sections the straightforward, businesslike tone employed in narrating the tale of the three brothers made that tale appear an utterly different work from the sections of digression. Moreover, sections of narrative tale and of digression were carefully kept separate. But the narrative tale cannot continue so nicely isolated. At the commencement of Section VI, the persona within a section of tale wanders widely from his story to analyze different types of authors but finally brings himself up short, promising that in the sections of narrative tale thereafter "I shall by no means forget my Character of an Historian" (p. 133).

But the modern persona inevitably *does* "forget": more

---

[12] Ricardo Quintana, in *The Mind and Art of Jonathan Swift* (London: Methuen, 1936), p. 91, recognizes that the two "themes" (i.e., abuses in religion and abuses in learning) ultimately merge: "The triumph of the work is the gradual approach of these groups to one another, until in the later sections—VIII, IX, XI—the enthusiasm of Jack the dissenter and all the forms of madness in the commonwealth of empire and learning are seen as one under the aspect of universal irrationality."

and more extensively in the later sections he interrupts his narration of the tale to praise projects, to remark upon the great "benefit" he is conferring upon his audience, and the like. In the *Tale of a Tub*'s most humorous and climactic revolutions in the later sections, it becomes impossible to distinguish tale from digression at all. The original policy of reserving odd-numbered sections for digressions and even-numbered sections for tale is finally obliterated: Section VIII's analysis and praise of Aeolism begin to appear to be, not the dry relation of historical tale that was intended and expected, but the persona's own project, his own digression. What is more, Section IX is merely a continuation in the digressive vein. Section X, correctly labeled *"Tale"* (p. 181), is nevertheless more digression still, wherein the Modern compliments his readers and gives advice about the reading of his dark and significant allegories (housed in earlier digressions). It is an unexpected reversal, then, when Section XI is *also* entitled *"Tale"* (p. 188); and —what is more unexpected still—for a time the prose does appear to unfold like many of the earlier passages of narrative, dealing as it does with the presentation of Jack and his projects. Nonetheless, in a manner that we have but latterly encountered, this narrative section is repeatedly interrupted with asides, commentaries, and analyses by the modern persona—not at all in his decorous "character" as a historian, but *in propria persona*, as the aimless, prolix, and ebullient Modern of the digressions.

In Section XI all coherence is gone. In a climax of sorts, tale and digression merge, become confounded.[13] The his-

---

[13] Jay Arnold Levine, in "The Design of 'A Tale of a Tub' (with a Digression on a Mad, Modern Critic)," *Journal of English Literary History*, XXXIII (1966), especially on pp. 206, 214–217,

torian disintegrates into a Grub Street animadverter and digresser and cannot even complete his telling of the little tale. Forgetting itself entirely, progression metamorphoses into digression. The failure of memory and control in the *Tale of a Tub* becomes complete.

traces as I do this progression of digression until it invests the entire work. But Levine rather unaccountably believes the tale a "travesty of the Bible" and the digressive critic one who overwhelms his own Bible that he is commenting upon (pp. 207, 209, 215, n. 33).

PART III

Theme: The Meaning of
the Satiric Fiction

5. The Decorum
of Modern Madness

My keepers knit the knot
  That youth did laugh to scorn,
Of me that clean shall be forgot
  As I had not been born.
            —THOMAS, LORD VAUX

By their rejection of custom, tradition, and the past, the moderns' horizon in the external world is ludicrously diminished. However, of the three disasters that befall the citizens of Swift's hypothetical world, the most far-reaching in its consequences is internal—the results of memory's destruction. The ancients had designated Memory the mother of the Muses for good reason: without memory, man is denied inspiration; without memory, he cannot develop custom, thought, history, or art. The capacity for retentiveness is in fact the very source of man's humanity; without memory, man loses altogether that sense of locus, of continuity, and of identity that constitute self.

For the treatment of madness ("a disorder in the imagination"), Locke had recommended that "having often recourse to one's memory, and tying down the mind strictly to the recollecting things past precisely as they were, may be a means to check those extravagant or towering flights of the imagination." [1] The point of course is that, lacking

[1] John Locke, "Miscellaneous Papers," in Peter (7th Baron) King, *The Life of John Locke, with Extracts from his Correspondence,*

memory, Swift's moderns are perpetual victims of the unchecked and soaring flight; they are helpless to restrain or to cure their madness.

All of Swift's personae in the *Tale of a Tub* must necessarily succumb to madness.

Locke had defined personal identity as an identity of consciousness through duration in time; the individual was in touch with his own continuing identity through memory of his past thoughts and actions. This location of the source of personal identity in the repertoire of its memories was continued by Hume: "Had we no memory, we never should have any notion of causation, nor consequently of that chain of causes and effects, which constitute our self or person." [2]

Herein lies the source of the *Tale of a Tub*'s telling contradiction: the *Tale*'s modern persona insists again and again upon his modernity, upon his locus, his identity, relying upon the local, the mechanical, and the concrete object and his own insistent personal self-assertion; yet simultaneously, deprived of memory, he is not modern at all; he lacks individuality and remains persistently mutable and lost. It is ironically appropriate that such a modern is left to us without even a name; he is deprived of personal identity, of distinctive self. The so-called modern is the cause and the effect of the contradictory conflict, the agon which abounds throughout his work—for that conflict originates in himself.

Journals, and Commonplace Books (London: Henry Colburn, 1829), pp. 328, 327.

[2] Ian Watt, *The Rise of the Novel* (Berkeley and Los Angeles: University of California Press, 1957), p. 21. See Locke's *Essay Concerning Human Understanding*, II, xxvii, 9–10, and David Hume's *A Treatise of Human Nature* . . . , I, iv, 6.

I

The better to understand the fountainhead of the Modern's internal conflict, it will be useful to examine the seventeenth-century notion of the nature of the human mind, attempting to discern what precise effects the loss of memory will have upon that mind. As Harold D. Kelling observes, Swift's conception of the mind's structure and operation was standard in his time, a conception in fact formulated in ancient Greece, handed down through the Middle Ages and the Renaissance to Bacon, Hobbes, and Locke. In the typical mind, newly obtained knowledge "lodged, according to the Aristotelian theory of faculty psychology, in the memory, which reason could consult."

And if the temptation to the same sin occurred, the impulse went through the senses to the imagination, and thence to the understanding or reason which interpreted the image in terms of the previously acquired knowledge of the folly and danger of the sin. The imagination thus presented a naked and deformed image to the appetites which directed the will to reject the temptation.

According to such a psychology the reason of the individual is, then, the result of his own experience. In strict terminology reason would be the faculty which enabled an individual to learn from experience . . . , an ability to relate a situation to a similar situation which caused pleasure or pain in the past either to the individual himself or some one he had observed.[3]

Precisely what effects a permanent failure of memory would have upon such an empirical mind and how these ef-

[3] "The Appeal to Reason: A Study of Jonathan Swift's Critical Theory and Its Relation to His Writings" (Ph.D. diss., Yale University, 1948), pp. 97–98; reprinted by permission of the author.

fects would have been commonly understood in Swift's day require consideration.

To appreciate the necessity of memory to the mind's normal functioning, it will be convenient to examine a typical "anatomy" of the mind. Robert Burton's description in *The Anatomy of Melancholy*, that standard encyclopedia of sciences in the seventeenth century, will serve our purpose.

ANATOMY OF THE MIND [4]

I. RATIONAL MIND: "the first substantial [part] of a . . . human . . . , by which a man lives, perceives, and understands, freely doing all things, and with election."
   A. UNDERSTANDING: "apprehends and judges; perceives universals" (includes *synteresis*, "the pure part of the conscience . . . , an innate habit, and doth signify a conversation of the knowledge of the law of God and Nature, to know good or evil").
      1. REASON: "perceives, knows, . . . judges, as well singulars as universals"; contains "innate notions."
      2. MEMORY: "remembers . . . singulars as [well as] universals."
   B. WILL: "covets or avoids such things as have been before judged and apprehended by the understanding."
II. SENSIBLE (ANIMAL) MIND: "hath sense, appetite, judgement, breath, and motion."
   A. APPREHENSIVE POWER (PERCEPTION):
      1. OUTWARD SENSE: the five senses
      2. INWARD SENSE:
         a. COMMON SENSE: rules the senses, differentiates, "perceives singularity."

[4] Compiled from Robert Burton, *The Anatomy of Melancholy*, ed. Floyd Dell and Paul Jordan-Smith (New York: Tudor, 1951), I, i, 2.5–11, pp. 135–148. A similar chart, assembled from the writings of Richard Hooker, may be found in Hiram Haydn, *The Counter-Renaissance* (New York: Scribner's, 1950), p. 318.

    b. PHANTASY (INVENTION or IMAGINATION): "doth more fully examine the species perceived by common sense, . . . recalling them to mind again, or making new of his own."

    c. MEMORY: "lays up . . . and records."

  B. MOVING POWER: contains the voluntary appetites; the capacity for locomotion.

III. VEGETAL MIND: contains the passions (or instincts); the source of drives to feed, reproduce the species, please the self.

The mind, as the seventeenth century conceived of it, has evolved through the ages and can be divided into three major functional sectors: the vegetal mind, the sensible mind, and the rational mind.[5] Plants, of course, possess only a vegetal mind, whereas, by the process of evolution, animals are equipped with both vegetal and sensible minds. Man is the only creature possessing the third mind, the rational, as well. We shall concern ourselves with man.

Observing the schema of the "Anatomy of Mind," we notice that the apprehensive power of the sensible mind collects the data of the five senses concerning the outside world—data arranged and controlled by the common sense. Once such materials are remembered and retained, fancy or invention may operate with confidence internally upon

[5] The view of the mind presented here is commonplace; consult Aristotle, *On the Soul, Parva Naturalia, On Breath,* ed. and trans. W. S. Hett, Loeb Classical Library (rev. ed.; London: William Heinemann, 1957), especially *De Anima* II–III, pp. 66–203, and "On Memory and Recollection," *Parva Naturalia,* pp. 288–313. A brief survey of the persistence of such ideas may be found in [George S.] Brett, *Brett's History of Psychology,* ed. and abr. R. S. Peters (London: George Allen and Unwin, 1953), especially pp. 105–115, 141–143, 207–211, 250, 355, 361, and 369.

such sensible information. Although the memory is normally situated by most authorities in the sensible mind,[6] we recall Hobbes's terse pronouncement upon the mind's creative process: "Time and Education beget experience; experience begets memory; memory begets judgment and fancy; judgment begets the strength and structure, and fancy begets the ornaments of a poem."[7] Burton also recognizes the importance of memory, to the extent that he includes it a second time—in the rational mind, under understanding. He does so because, although animals do display the ability to retain certain knowledge, man's rational mind relies heavily upon memory as well, for additional and higher purposes: "The power of thought depends upon the power of retention; in the flux of sensations nothing would remain were it not that memory holds the universal element given in the particular sensation."[8] In the sensible mind, the *sensus communis* remembers, deals with, and "only comprehends *singularities*," whereas in the rational mind, the understanding, which comprehends *"universalities,"* is likewise reliant upon memory.

Memory retains the impressions derived from the senses and from the fancy. Reason then judges and distinguishes among this mass of impressions and passes judgment. But after being judged and understood, such matter must be re-

---

[6] Consult Donald F. Bond, "The Neo-Classical Psychology of the Imagination," *Journal of English Literary History*, IV (1937), 245–264. See also Ricardo Quintana, *The Mind and Art of Jonathan Swift* (London: Methuen, 1936), pp. 49–69.

[7] "The Answer of Mr. Hobbes to Sir William Davenant's Preface Before *Gondibert*," *The English Works of Thomas Hobbes of Malmesbury*, ed. Sir William Molesworth (London: John Bohn, 1839–1845), IV, 449.

[8] Aristotle, *De Anima* II.viii, p. 112.

tained in the rational memory, if the will is regularly to control behavior according to the decisions of reason.

When all is functioning in the mind properly, we observe the typical human mind, with its rational mind controlling the operations of the senses and fancy. In such a mind, memory obviously plays a vital role:

Memory is the primary and fundamental power, without which there could be no other intellectual operation. Judgment and ratiocination suppose something already known, and draw their decisions only from experience. Imagination selects ideas from the treasures of remembrance, and produces novelty only in varied combinations. We do not even form conjectures of distant, or anticipations, [*sic*] of future events, but by concluding what is possible from what is past.[9]

Having secured this information about the mind, it is interesting to observe what befalls such a mind when thrust into Swift's forgetful modern world. We have seen that the memory aids the common sense in the sensible mind, while, in the rational mind, it is memory that preserves the stuff of the fancy and of the senses for reason to act upon. If memory is removed, annihilated, as in Swift's postulated case, the understanding suddenly has nothing to understand, and reason nothing to judge. At a stroke, the whole fabric of

[9] Samuel Johnson, *The Idler*, No. 44, in *The Rambler, The Idler, The Adventurer, The Connoisseur* (4 vols. bound as 1; London: Henry G. Bohn, 1863), II, 47. The idea is commonplace; *cf.* "For, though a man have understanding and judgement, which is one part of wisedom: yet wanting a remembraunce to apply things aptly, when time and place shal best require: he shall doe but small good with all his understanding" (Thomas Wilson, *Wilson's Arte of Rhetorique: 1560*, ed. G. H. Mair [Oxford: Clarendon Press, 1909], p. 209).

the rational mind falls to the ground. The sensible—or purely animal—mind is left to rule in its stead.

What happens in the sensible mind is that with no aid from the rational mind, the common sense can no longer mediate between the five senses and the fancy. These two opposing forces, the sensations and fancy, in the *Tale of a Tub*, wage war with each other. The senses, like modern virtuosi of the Royal Society, heed only experiments, surfaces, physical matter, the "superficies" of things, while the fancy, surfeited with visions, is empowered to soar randomly aloft, creating a host of allegorical figures, windy metaphors, metaphysical conceits, and mystical religious imaginings. The modern persona himself correctly describes this combat: "a Man's Fancy gets *astride* on his Reason, . . . Imagination is at Cuffs with the Senses, and common Understanding, as well as common Sense, is Kickt out of Doors" (p. 171). Then such a man is internally at war, is schizophrenic, is truly mad.

But that is hardly all. It is not simply in the memoryless cranium that fancy and sense are at war; more important, there is no longer present in the mind any means of distinguishing sense *from* fancy. Sensible facts are allegorized and rendered fanciful, just as, on the other hand, "converting Imaginations . . . can make *Shadows*, no thanks to the Sun; and then mold them into Substances, no thanks to Philosophy" (pp. 189–190). With the workings of fancy and sense indistinguishable, all images and ideas appear to arrive in the mind by accident, by luck, or by chance. Items of information from either realm course about aimlessly, so many atoms tumbling in a void. In Swift's postulated world, these two forces, the senses and the fancy, engage in aimless wandering; they are, like Hobbes's men in the state

of nature, irrevocably at war. And no mediator is any-
where at hand.

II

During the past several decades, a considerable amount
of criticism of the *Tale of a Tub* has been devoted to the
Tale's persona. A central problem for this criticism has
been to determine the nature and number of personae actually present in the sections of digression and of tale. But
among the authors of this body of literature there has been
little agreement.[10] Admittedly, the nature and number of
personae are difficult to determine. To be sure, only one
persona actually announces himself in the course of the
Tale; he claims to be a modern and a member of the Grub
Street "fraternity" (p. 63). He is very obviously present in
many sections of the digressions and in the clutter of pre-

---

[10] Much of this criticism has been concerned with Swift's manip-
ulation of his "masks"—some scholars maintaining that the mask in
the *Tale* is consistent, some maintaining that Swift "peeps" occasionally from behind this mask to offer comments *in propria
persona,* still others urging that there is no mask at all. A few
examples may serve: Ricardo Quintana, in *Swift: An Introduction*
(London: Oxford University Press, 1955), pp. 53–55, has distinguished six personae; Ronald Paulson, in *Theme and Structure in
Swift's "Tale of a Tub"* (New Haven: Yale University Press,
1960), pp. 28–30, 188–196, perceives but *one*—in the *Tale, The
Battle of the Books,* and the "Mechanical Operation of the Spirit,"
all together. Irvin Ehrenpreis, in *Swift: The Man, His Works, and
the Age,* I: *Mr Swift and His Contemporaries* (Cambridge, Mass.:
Harvard University Press, 1962), 197, finds the single persona, if
there is one, vague, inconsistent, unsubtle; elsewhere Ehrenpreis
actually denigrates the employment of any persona criticism whatever ("Personae," *Restoration and Eighteenth-Century Literature:
Essays in Honor of Alan Dugald McKillop* [Chicago: University
of Chicago Press, for Rice University, 1963], pp. 25–37).

faces. The difficulty is that he appears so vastly different in the sections containing narrative tale. Yet despite the different tone and style in these sections of tale, he never identifies himself in them as a distinct persona, but only as one who must not "forget [his] Character of an Historian" (p. 133)—which seems to indicate that the persona himself has occasionally adopted the mask of a truthful historian.

The impediments to understanding the nature of this speaker (or speakers) are owing to his great variety, to his protean changefulness. If at times he appears to be the historian, and at others the Grub Street hack, yet at still others he appears to be the dissenting enthusiast. Often he resembles the scholastic orator; often he seems the philosophical deducer of learned "systems" or the meticulous modern virtuoso conducting incisive anatomies. The considerable variety of his voices is not only confusing and misleading; it also becomes apparent that this variety is his only consistency.

Our examination of the nature of the satiric action in the *Tale of a Tub* should, however, take us some distance toward a comprehension of this persona. Study of the memoryless modern commentator, whose reason has been overthrown and whose imagination and senses conduct incessant combat, leading him ultimately to forget his "Character of an Historian" until he progresses only by temporizing digression, explains not only this character's nature but also his purpose in the aesthetic work as a whole. There is indeed present in the *Tale* a consistent and decorous single modern persona. That he is self-contradictory, engaged in civil warfare, bemusingly variable and forgetful, renders him an appropriate vehicle for the action imitated in the *Tale*. In an instantaneous and memoryless world of per-

fected modernity, the metamorphic persona generating in-
terruption, regression, and multiplication is strictly necessary.

Without time, tradition, knowledge, or memory, what
else can a modern do? It is all for the best in this best of all
modern worlds if he is happily inconsistent, brightly aware,
and yet maddeningly ignorant—in short, if he seems a perfect Whitmanesque, blandly and harmoniously appreciat-
ing his own discord:

> Do I contradict myself?
> Very well then I contradict myself,
> (I am large, I contain multitudes.) [11]

In Swift's hypothetical world, the Modern is without the
past, is nameless and without memory. Of necessity he cannot be consistent, or even recollect what he has been saying. He comes to us simply as a heritage, the archetype of a
broken modernity. But he is also the result of a perceptive
study of a schizophrenic mind—where rationality has fallen
to the ground, where imagination is at cuffs with the senses.

III

With a touch of irony, we might permit Thomas
Hobbes to suggest for us the full import of the probable
and necessary madness in *A Tale of a Tub:*

The truth is, that man is a creature of greater power than other
living creatures are, but his advantages do consist especially in
two things: whereof one is the use of speech, by which men
communicate one with another, and join their forces together,
and by which also they register their thoughts that they perish
not, but be reserved, and afterwards joined with other thoughts

[11] Walt Whitman, "Song of Myself," ll. 1324-1326.

to produce general rules for the direction of their actions. There be beasts that see better, others that hear better, and others that exceed mankind in other senses. *Man excelleth beasts only in making rules to himself, that is to say, in remembering*, and in reasoning aright upon that which he remembereth. They which do so, deserve an honour above brute beasts.[12]

This distinction of man from beast calls to our attention the great reversal engineered by Swift's satiric irony: his typical modern, who had aspired to be ancient as well as modern and all things else, instead begins a lesser translation, commencing to take on the features of a Gryllus or an Apeneck Sweeney before our eyes. The proud and progressive modern has succeeded, at the last, only to regress to primeval brute. "Icarus is the typical figure of satire, that is as a glass to concentrate the heat of the sun upon all those who attempt to rise on wings of wax."[13] The figure of Icarus, however, which we used in Chapter 2 to describe the modern's vain and fanciful flying, is no longer suitable. For Icarus, at least, was making an attempt that was serious and single-minded; it simply proved to be beyond the reach of his ability. The point is that Icarus, at least, was a man.

But in a series of bold strokes, Swift makes it clear that his hypothetical modern, on the contrary, is *not* a man. To him it is perhaps more fitting to apply that baser image of Matthew Prior's:

> . . . didst Thou never see
> ('Tis but by way of Simile;)

[12] "The Questions Concerning Liberty, Necessity, and Chance . . . ," *English Works*, V, 186; italics mine.
[13] Gilbert Cannan, *Satire* (London: Martin Secker, [1914]), pp. 12–13.

A SQUIRREL spend his little Rage,
In jumping round a rowling Cage?
The Cage, as either Side turn'd up,
Striking a Ring of Bells a-top—?
  Mov'd in the Orb; pleas'd with the Chimes;
  The foolish Creature thinks he climbs:
  But here or there, turn Wood or Wire,
  He never gets two Inches higher.[14]

It is poignant irony that the Modern, with all of his aggression, pride, and self-assertion, has merely won for himself a place—in the zoo. And there he may be seen, "tearing his Straw in piece-meal, Swearing and Blaspheming, biting his Grate, foaming at the Mouth" (p. 176). All of his hopes for progress and for noble sovereignty are reduced, in a final peripety, to a kind of mere barking, unrecollected tranquility. The first, in the *Tale of a Tub*, by a fine satiric magic, has become the very last.

As it happens, Swift's seemingly outrageous paradoxical reduction of the moderns has been given substance and point by subsequent history. Developments in Western culture since the eighteenth century have conferred upon Swift's highly comic postulates an aura of prophecy. Acceptance in the West of values of speed, modernity, and immediacy has lent to his work what Swift might have been pleased to call "a considerable point in the controversy."

The historical record reproduced by the daily "news" of our mass media of communication, though vastly extended in spatial coverage, is temporally confined to the immediate

---

[14] "A Simile," ll. 4–12, *The Literary Works of Matthew Prior*, ed. H. Bunker Wright and Monroe K. Spears (Oxford: Clarendon Press, 1959), I, 244–245; quoted by permission of the publisher.

present. Communication of news rarely serves to establish any "meaningful," or significant, relations between the events of one day and another, let alone one year and another; it rarely attempts to introduce any principle of organization, continuity, or structural relationship into the assemblage of isolated, cumulative facts considered newsworthy. News must be "hot," as we say, that is, of momentary appeal and significance, or it is not newsworthy. News must be "sensational," it must provide momentary excitement and titillation, or it does not sell. Again, what cannot be consumed now is worthless; and once it is consumed, it is worthless.[15]

The same paradox that Swift enacted—that the modern quest for progress cultivates regress—may be detected in present-day civilization's search for knowledge and experience.

The barriers of the past have been pushed back as never before; our knowledge of the history of man and the universe has been enlarged on a scale and to a degree not dreamed of by previous generations. At the same time, the sense of identity and continuity with the past, whether our own or history's, has gradually and steadily declined. Previous generations *knew* much less about the past than we do, but perhaps *felt* a much greater sense of identity and continuity with it because of the fixity, stability, and relative permanence of their social structure. Despite the enormous knowledge we have accumulated about

[15] Hans Meyerhoff, *Time in Literature* (Berkeley and Los Angeles: University of California Press, 1955), pp. 110–111. Erich Kahler stresses modern speed: the mass manufacture of news results in the "crowding of events in the domain of our vision and consciousness, an oppressive closeness and overwhelming shiftiness of events, an excess of details and complexities in every single event—in short, what I would call an *overpopulation of the surfaces*" (*The Tower and the Abyss* [New York: Braziller, 1957], pp. 95–96).

the past, the temporal perspective in the lives of individuals has become so foreshortened in our age as to condemn them to live in a perpetual present—not the experimental, qualitative co-presence of all the elements constituting their own past recaptured by memory, but the quantitative units of the present as defined by the consumption of goods, news, and the instrumental use of human beings themselves.[16]

Thus does modern melioration descend to atavism. By the irony of fate, what Swift hypothetically proposes, man in the twentieth century disposes.

[16] Meyerhoff, *Time in Literature*, pp. 109–110.

6. The Great Chain of Commentary

Let courtly wits to wits afford supply,
As hog to hog in huts of Westphaly:
If one, through nature's bounty, or his lord's,
Has what the frugal dirty soil affords,
From him the next receives it, thick or thin,
As pure a mess almost as it came in;
The blessed benefit, not there confined,
Drops to the third, who nuzzles close behind;
From tail to mouth they feed and they carouse;
The last full fairly gives it to the house.
—POPE

We have explored the commandments in the *Tale of a Tub* that serve to hoist the modern persona with his own petard. Moreover, we have grasped to a considerable extent the nature of "plot" in the *Tale:* a modern historian has set out to tell the simple-minded story of the three brothers, but his incipient habit of devising projects, his rampant, rambling modernity, and his failing memory increase in the course of the action until the historian and his tale are abandoned. The whole undertaking is scuttled with the triumph of digression and the loss of notes. Yet if we are to understand the *Tale*'s action more fully, we need to examine this modern persona and his intentions more closely.

I

If we wished to characterize the "voice" we regularly discern in the prefatory pieces and the digressions, we would have to identify it as the voice of a scholiast. If we sought, in Aristotelian terms, to describe the action of this commentator in the *Tale*, we should have to claim that he is attempting to retell, to "refine," and to annotate an ancient story. He is creating, in effect, that staple of Grub Street: a revised edition, an edited text, a fable "done into English" by an "eminent hand."

We remember that modern authors, represented in the *Tale*'s Introduction as being "more careful and curious in adorning [their works], than was altogether necessary" (p. 66), have so dazzled readers with the fulsome externals of their compositions that the virtues of the privy parts have remained secret and unknown. In order to remedy this defect, the Modern explains, "I have been prevailed on, . . . to travel in a compleat and laborious Dissertation upon the prime Productions of our Society" (p. 67). He has, in fact, already "finished . . . Annotations upon several Dozens" (p. 68). His commentaries have thus far been made upon such works as "*Tom Thumb*, Dr. *Faustus*, WHITTINGTON *and his Cat*, THE *Wise Men of* Gotham cum Appendice, and THE *Hind and Panther*" (pp. 68–69).[1] Throughout his treatise, he informs us, he has "closely followed the most applauded Originals" (p. 71).

---

[1] Consult John Ashton's collection, *Chap-Books of the Eighteenth Century* (London: Chatto and Windus, 1882), which contains the simple popular tales (i.e., "Faustus," "Dick Whittington," "The Wise Men of Gotham") to which Swift refers. Swift arranges that these childish stories are treated as significant "allegories" with medieval and scholastic pomp. He is poking fun at some facile allegorizing, as in the work of Dryden and L'Estrange. But classic authors often received such treatment; see Madeleine Doran, "Some Renaissance 'Ovids,'" *Literature and Society*, ed. Bernice Slote (Lincoln: University of Nebraska Press, 1964), pp. 44–62.

Is not this proceeding unusual—for a modern to follow *any* predecessor, for a militant contemporary slavishly to expound an ancient's text? Not at all. We should recall William Wotton's sober claim for modern scholars: that the making of commentary and the affixing of footnotes to ancient authors demonstrate more genius and learning than the classical authors being edited ever possessed. It is permissible, even preferable, for moderns to turn translators and expounders. Hence, Swift's Modern scrupulously pursues his applauded originals, making but a single, trifling "refinement" upon Wotton's pronouncement: his work is to be a modern commentary, not upon an ancient, but upon a *modern*, text.

Such an annotator is regularly apparent throughout the pages relating the allegorical tale. He is continually asserting, after the manner of medieval scribes, that he is "retelling" this "tale" of the three brothers. Like medieval scribes too, he repeatedly affirms that his tale offers "ensamples" *pro bono publico*. On the second page of his tale, he inserts "HERE the Story says" (p. 74), and continues placidly on his narrative course. Elsewhere he pauses to include "(says my Author)" (p. 115), and extols his own "Labour of collecting [and] Faithfulness in recounting" (p. 106) his story. He clearly thinks of himself, in such passages of the tale, as having assumed the "Character of an Historian" (p. 133), and so describes himself.

Yet he is not merely the subservient recorder or copyist. He is an explicator and commentator, as he says, whose duty is to ratify, to clarify, to elaborate, and to amend whenever occasion warrants. He intermits to explain at one point in the tale: "I must with the Reader's good Leave and Patience, have recourse to some Points of Weight, which the Authors of that Age have not sufficiently illustrated" (p. 75). Thereby, the modern scholiast grants himself carte blanche in dealing with his text. Later in the *Tale*, as we know, this potential authorization of illimitable invention and digression becomes an awful reality. In all, the modern annotator alludes to his "author" or the "undoubted tradition" from which he himself has been collecting at least nine times during these sections of allegorical tale.[2]

A number of critics have, to be sure, observed the foppish and soporific tone, meek and mild, of these sections of allegorical tale.[3] The pert modern commentator is retelling the oft-repeated story of Christianity, here bedecked in allegorical clothing that is rather thin and obvious. To the number of retellings of this shopworn story the digressive Modern blandly adds one more.

But as we have seen, the modern commentator's "action" is destined to be faulty. If it is his intention to re-edit a work, to annotate a tale, to elucidate a dark text for an enlightened future, his resolution wretchedly miscarries. As a modern, he is overcome by his ineluctable propensity for digression, improvisation, and forgetfulness. His scholarly labors falter and collapse, remaining forever undone. In the *Tale of a Tub*'s climax, the tides of amnesia and digression wash his plans away; his scrupulous pedantry devolves into fragmentation, hiatus, and disorder.

In the *Tale of a Tub*'s world, this resultant final disorder

----

[2] *Tale*, pp. 74, 75, 80, 106, 115, 133, 137, 151, 189.

[3] For instance: Henry Craik, *The Life of Jonathan Swift, Dean of St. Patrick's, Dublin*, 2 vols. (2d ed.; London: Macmillan, 1894), I, 140; G. Wilson Knight, *The Burning Oracle* (London: Oxford University Press, 1939), p. 117; and Martin Price, *Swift's Rhetorical Art* (New Haven: Yale University Press, 1953), p. 81.

is in order. For any modern who disclaims the past must face the consequences so plainly revealed in the dedication to Prince Posterity; if moderns ignore the past, urging such negligence as law, they themselves will as surely be ignored by succeeding hordes of future moderns: "Use the memory of thy predecessor fairly and tenderly; for if thou dost not, it is a debt will sure be paid when thou art gone." [4] Many a member of the "modern party" failed to grasp this maxim. A typical example of such missing of the point occurs in the writings of Francis Osborn:

All I seek is to find employment for a Spirit that would *break the Vessel*, had it nothing to work upon but it *Self*. Nor is it less true, That I might justly be *blamed* for *some things* here, had more time been imployed about them, than God in his *mercy*, or to *punish* my former *negligence*, hath afforded me liberty to spare. Who can be accountable to *Posterity* for nothing in this kind: being from my Birth uncapable to receive the rich *Talent* of *Learning*, looked upon as *the only key* of *Knowledge:* which if obtained, had been little advantage, since I want a *memory* wherein to hoord up what I had *stollen*.[5]

Osborn here writes a "Preface" to his readers; but if his readers had been as chary of reading, barren of learning, and feeble of memory as their author, they would never have read his work. Obviously, Osborn's own abstention from reading invites his audience to follow his example.

[4] "Of Great Place," *Essays or Counsels* . . . , in *The Works of Francis Bacon* . . . , ed. James Spedding, Robert Leslie Ellis, and Douglas Denon Heath (Boston: Taggard and Thompson, 1861–1864), XII, 115.

[5] Preface, *A Miscellany of Sundry Essaies, Paradoxes, and Problematical Discourses, Letters and Characters* . . . , in *The Works of Francis Osborn Esq.* . . . , (7th ed.; London: R. D., 1673), sigs. Qq^v–Qq2^r.

The modern persona of the *Tale* is at times more blissfully unaware than Osborn, and his assertions are a tissue of contradictions. As a modern, he would ignore the past—and yet he is editor of an ancient fable. As a modern, he is virtually without memory—and yet he wishes future generations to remember him. Thus, he dedicates his work to posterity (p. 30), expects later commentators to deal with his own text, presuming "that future Sons of Art, will return large Thanks to my Memory" (p. 114), and insists that all modern authors hold in common a "great Design of an everlasting Remembrance, and never-dying Fame" (p. 123).

However, at other times, the modern persona almost reverses this simplistic view:

Now, tho' it sometimes tenderly affects me to consider, that all the towardly Passages I shall deliver in the following Treatise, will grow quite out of date and relish with the first shifting of the present Scene: yet I must need subscribe to the Justice of this Proceeding: because, I cannot imagine why we should be at Expence to furnish Wit for succeeding Ages, when the former have made no sort of Provision for ours [pp. 43–44].

In his distorting way, the Modern recognizes with faint clarity the modernist dilemma and "the transitory State of all sublunary Things" (p. 66).

And surely, if the modern emendator expects his writings to pass by, to fall down, disappear, and become unintelligible with the first shifting of the present scene, he fully obtains his wish. In one of Swift's most creative jests, one central to the *Tale of a Tub*'s meaning, it happens that, since the Modern's *Tale* is published not in 1697, when it was so momentously composed, but in 1704, the Modern's own treatise has indeed become utterly out-of-date and all but incomprehensible. It too, in its turn, must be treated to a full set of notes, "refinements," and explications.

Here Swift has contrived a great ironic reversal, sweeping in its implications. It is obvious poetic justice that one who ignores the past will himself in a modern future be ignored. It is only fitting that, as if by chain reaction, the annotator must himself be annotated. And, finally, it is wonderful to behold how the persona's most modern work, appearing a few years later so heavily annotated, is metamorphosed into a work most ancient. Appearing as it does in 1704, together with two other fragments, with its title page badly torn (p. 71), its author unknown, its text filled with lacunae and "chasms," [6] it resembles the most hoary antique codex—and cries out for a key, for a variorum edition, for *apparatus criticus* and the full machinery of modern pedantry. Appearing again, in 1710, with its flamboyant apology and the footnotes of Wotton and the bookseller's scholiast, this ancient text is well on its way to becoming, like texts of a Heraclitus, a Sappho, or a Varro, fulsomely annotated. We might add that the *Tale of a Tub* has continued, over the centuries, to be edited and explained, assembling by accretion layer upon layer of modern notes—by John Hawkesworth, by John Nichols, by Sir Walter Scott, by A. C. Guthkelch, by D. N. Smith, by Emile Pons.

[6] See the asterisks and lacunae on pp. 62, 170, 179, 200; similar lacunae occur in *The Battle of the Books* (three on p. 244, two on p. 248, one each on pp. 247 and 250); *The Battle* in fact concludes with a hiatus and a *Desunt caetera* (p. 258). In *The Mechanical Operation of the Spirit* there is a large hiatus on p. 276; and smaller dashes and blanks occur on pp. 32, 85, 108, 176, 207, 287, and 288.

Confronted with this unknown text in 1710, the book-seller's scholiast has at times no idea what his author is talking about: "I do not well understand what the Author aims at here" (p. 159); and the annotator's ignorance and confusion about the meaning of his text are not confined to a single occasion: he is often forced to admit bafflement and incomprehension.[7] Of course, much of the commentator's confusion in 1710 simply stems from the thorny problems created by his author's ignorant use of dull allegory and private invention. But also pertinent and comic is the confusion engendered by this latest commentator's own weak memory; for he too is a modern—albeit of slightly later vintage. He finds it repeatedly necessary to "clarify" and to "restore" details for his own current covey of moderns— the momentarily contemporary audience of 1710. Thus, when Dryden is mentioned in the text as an author "now living," a footnote must judiciously clarify: Dryden the author *was* living, "*Viz in the Year* 1697" (p. 69).[8] When the Modern alludes to popish plots and meal tubs, this new annotator, stretching his memory, recalls vaguely and attempts to explain to later nescient moderns: "In King *Charles* the *II*. Time, there was an Account of a *Presbyterian* Plot, found in a Tub, which then made much Noise" (p. 70).[9]

[7] See the annotator's admissions of perplexity, pp. 84, 159, 179, 191, and 192.

[8] Guthkelch and Smith use "1698," the reading of the fourth and fifth editions; but Swift sustains the fiction of composition in 1696 and 1697; hence I restore the "1697" of editions 1–3.

[9] Like the modern persona, the annotator fumbles with his prose here; his "which" clause rather helplessly modifies "Tub": this meal tub, like the whalers' tubs and like the *Tale of a Tub* itself, is noisy.

Again, when in the text the modern persona refers to the *Anthroposophia Theomagica*, the new note maker, with some difficulty, recalls that this was "a Treatise written about fifty Years ago, by a Welsh Gentleman of Cambridge, his Name, as I remember, was Vaughan" (p. 127), but only poor Thomas Vaughan's surname is dredged up by recollection—and then only because he was mentioned (and refuted) by a later author. He has almost been forgotten. Likewise, when the modern persona in his text mentions Lord C—— and Sir J. W., the scholiast must cryptically, yet in all seriousness, append: "This shows the Time the Author writ, it being about fourteen Years since those two Persons were reckoned the fine Gentlemen of the Town" (p. 86).[10]

More overt still are the attempts the annotator makes to identify references and allusions to names now all but utterly gone from modern memory. The persona's veiled citation of a "Juno" and a "Venus" calls forth this densely lucid note: "*Juno* and *Venus* are Money and a Mistress, very powerful Bribes to a Judge, if Scandal says true. I reremember such Reflexions were cast about that time, but I cannot fix the Persons intended here" (p. 53).[11] Similarly,

[10] The jest of instantly identifying a dash and a pair of initials mocks Richard Bentley; Charles Boyle's group pretended to suppose Bentley capable of "restoring" a large marble inscription when only a few letters were legible. See William King, *Dialogues of the Dead* . . . , Dialogue VII, *Miscellanies in Prose and Verse* (London: B. Lintott and H. Clements, 1705?), p. 313.

[11] The *Tale* plays here with the famous story of Paris and the apple of discord, treating the ancient myth as a piece of modernity. The taking the names of Juno and Venus literally and the allusion to "scandal" are, I think, parodying Bentley, who in one place had introduced a "gossip's" tale: "A certain gossip of old, as the story goes, would needs tell her comrades what Jupiter once whispered

in a modern world of unremembered impermanence, when Will's Coffee House is mentioned, the latest scholiast knows well enough that he had better explain: "*Will's Coffee-House* was formerly the Place where the Poets usually met, which tho it be yet fresh in memory, yet in some Years may be forgot, and want this Explanation" (p. 64). Whatever else may happen to Will's Coffee House in the *Tale of a Tub*'s volatile world, it will certainly be forgotten. The *Tale*'s forgetful modern world is consistent and complete.

II

But is the *Tale* orderly and consistent, after all? Robert Martin Adams has recently questioned *A Tale of a Tub*'s very authorship. The recent acquisition by Cornell University's Olin Library of a copy of the 1704 edition of the *Tale of a Tub* heavily annotated in its margins by Thomas Swift has revived an old claim. Adams argues that it is very likely that Cousin Thomas Swift was author of 33 to 40 per cent of the *Tale*.[12] Adams urges, as Edmund Curll had done in 1710,[13] that Thomas was author of the entire allegorical "tale" of the three brothers—that is, of the *Tale*'s

---

to Juno in her ear. The company was inquisitive how she could know it then: but Mr. B[oyle] would have answered for her, *That they might as well ask her how she came to know his name was Jupiter? Fame, that told her the one, must tell her the other too*" ("Dissertations upon The Epistles of Phalaris . . ." [rev. ed., 1699], *The Works of Richard Bentley, D.D.*, ed. Rev. Alexander Dyce, 3 vols. [London: Francis MacPherson, 1836], I, 274).

[12] "Jonathan Swift, Thomas Swift, and the Authorship of *A Tale of a Tub*," *Modern Philology*, LXIV (1967), 196–232.

[13] Edmund Curll's *A Complete Key to the Tale of a Tub . . .* (1710), is reprinted in *Tale*, pp. 331–332.

Sections II, IV, VI, XI, and possibly VIII. A recent critical trend had already been inclined to separate portions of tale from those of digression. Miriam Starkman's book treats only the digressions; Phillip Harth's book deals solely with allegorical tale; and other critics have argued that these two different portions were composed at entirely different times —the tale early (c. 1685–1696), the digressions late (c. 1697–1704).[14] It is but a single step further to assign different authors to these separate parts. If such claims be true, how can one support the thesis, put forward in the present study, that the *Tale of a Tub* displays significant artistic coherence? To this question we must address ourselves here.

If Swift has pirated his cousin's writing and claimed it as his own, he is manifestly the literary thief. Is Swift generally, we want to know, such a plagiary? The answer is, I think, distinctly affirmative. R. S. Crane has recently made clear Swift's ingesting of the Porphyrian syllogism concerning horses, men, and the definition of *animal rationale*—and Swift's conversion of all into the mythos of Houyhnhnmland.[15] Likewise, Professor Landa has revealed Swift's metamorphosis of the economic maxim (concerning the people's

---

[14] See *Tale*, pp. xlvi–xlvii; Hermann Hofmann, *Swift's Tale of a Tub* (Leipzig-Reudnitz: August Hoffmann, 1911); George Hand, "Swift's First Thirty-six Years: A Study Preliminary to a Work Called *Irony and Jonathan Swift*" (Ph.D. diss., University of California, Berkeley, 1935), pp. 17–19, 148, 161–162, and *passim*; Phillip Harth, *Swift and Anglican Rationalism: The Religious Background of "A Tale of a Tub"* (Chicago: University of Chicago Press, 1961), chap. i.

[15] R. S. Crane, "The Houyhnhnms, the Yahoos, and the History of Ideas," *Reason and the Imagination: Studies in the History of Ideas, 1600–1800*, ed. J. A. Mazzeo (New York: Columbia University Press, 1962), pp. 231–253.

being the riches of a nation) into the "project" of his
Modest Proposal.[16] But that is hardly all; it is not merely
that Jonathan Swift often voraciously consumes maxims
and phrases. As virtually the almost perfect example of
ironic man, Swift is capable of donning the full face of a
generalized character—of the backsliding Christian of the
Argument against Abolishing Christianity or the ephemeral
Marcus Brutus, "Drapier," [17] or the supposed trimmer of
the *Examiner* papers. Moreover, he has appropriated the
very manner and occupation of particular men—reproducing the attitudinizing and assurance of Partridge the as-
trologer, plundering the pious platitudes of Robert Boyle
the preacher,[18] counterfeiting precisely a "dying-speech"
of the horse thief Ebenezor Elliston.[19]

Still better known are Swift's confiscation, in *Gulliver's
Travels*, of the lengthy paragraph of nautical terminology
and description of a storm at sea from Sturmy's *Compleat
Mariner* [20] and his pilfering, for use in *Gulliver's Travels*

---

[16] Louis A. Landa, "*A Modest Proposal* and Populousness," *Modern Philology*, XL (1942), 161–170, and "Swift's Economic Views
and Mercantilism," *Journal of English Literary History*, X (1943),
310–335. See also F. V. Bernard, "Swift's Maxim on Populousness:
A Possible Source, *Notes and Queries*, n.s., XII (1965), 18.

[17] Consult Jack Glenn Gilbert's "The Drapier's Initials," *Notes
and Queries*, CCVIII (1963), 217–218, and his "Knaves, Fools, and
Heroes: Jonathan Swift's Ethics" (Ph.D. diss., University of Texas,
1962), p. 115.

[18] "A Meditation upon a Broom-Stick . . ." (1703), *The Prose
Works of Jonathan Swift*, ed. Herbert Davis, 14 vols. (Oxford:
Basil Blackwell, 1939–1968), I, 239–240.

[19] Consult George P. Mayhew, "Jonathan Swift's Hoax of 1722
upon Ebenezor Elliston," *Bulletin of the John Rylands Library*,
XLIV (1962), 360–380.

[20] The paragraph is in Part II, chap. i, of *Gulliver's Travels*, in
Prose Works, XI, 68. See E. H. Knowles, "Dean Swift," *Notes and*

and in the *Tale of a Tub*, of a number of Royal Society experiments.[21] And nothing could be more comically brazen than Swift's abduction of sentences and paragraphs from William Wotton's *A Defense of the Reflections upon Ancient and Modern Learning . . . with Observations upon The Tale of a Tub* (1705) and his transplanting them as "footnotes" in the 1710 edition of his *Tale*. Less well known, but typically blatant, was Swift's tactic of plundering clichés and popular repartee from any available source to fill up his *Complete Collection of Polite Conversation* (1738).[22]

In spite of Swift's exalted claim, in the verses on his death, that he "To steal a Hint was never known, / But

Queries, ser. 4 (1868), 223, identifying the passage from Samuel Sturmy's *The Mariner's Magazine; or, Sturmy's Mathematical and practical arts . . .* (London: E. Cotes, 1669).

[21] See M. H. Nicolson and Norma Mohler, "The Scientific Background of Swift's Voyage to Laputa" and "Swift's 'Flying Island' in the Voyage to Laputa," *Annals of Science*, II (1937), 299–334, 405–430; and R. C. Olson, "Swift's Use of the Philosophical Transactions in Section V of *A Tale of a Tub*," *Studies in Philology*, XLIX (1952), 459–467.

[22] Mackie Langham Jarrell, in "Swift's 'Peculiar Vein of Humour'" (Ph.D. diss., University of Texas, 1954), pp. 281–283, 316, 393–411, and in "The Proverbs in Swift's *Polite Conversation*," *Huntington Library Quarterly*, XX (1956), 15–38, claims that all the proverbs were cribbed from John Ray's *Collection of English Proverbs* (1670, 1678). Actually, there is little evidence for this claim; see David Hamilton, "Swift, Wagstaff, and the Composition of *Polite Conversation*," *Huntington Library Quarterly*, XXX (1967), 281–295. Swift did at least pirate blunders and illogicalities and clichés from his friends' conversations; see George P. Mayhew, "Swift's Games with Language in Rylands English MS. 659," *Bulletin of the John Rylands Library*, XXXVI (1953–1954), 427, and "Some Dramatizations of Swift's *Polite Conversation* (1738)," *Philological Quarterly*, XLIV (1965), 63–64.

what he writ was all his own" [23]—the lines themselves
were plucked from Denham's verse [24]—we must conclude
that Jonathan Swift could and did very earnestly steal hints
—whenever it suited his purposes to do so. He may not
have been "known" to steal—his hand was not, in other
words, detected in another's pocket—but that is a tub of a
different metal. Swift was a distinguished, an inspired, plagiary.

But this is not to assert that Swift is guilty of forgery or
fraud. Swift's thefts are never manipulated for personal
gain; in every case, his thefts partake of literary jesting—in
parodies, imitations, mimes. Most frequently, it is not Swift
at all who pirates and prevaricates, but his personae. It is a
narcissistic Gulliver who preens himself on his nautical precision; it is Simon Wagstaff who would canonize himself
for scholarship in collecting "genteel" conversation for
thirty years; it is the money-hungry bookseller of the *Tale*
who searches for notes and "keys"—for any excuse to
launch a new edition. Even the speaker in the "Verses on
the Death of Dr. Swift" is not Swift himself, but a clubman
at the Rose engaged in presenting an encomium upon the
late Dr. Swift to suit his own ends; as he perorates (and
cribs from Denham), he exemplifies La Rochefoucauld's
egoist: the speaker comes not to praise Swift, but to bury
him—and to impress his auditors with his oratory.

[23] "Verses on the Death of Dr. Swift, D.S.P.D.," ll. 317–318, *The
Poems of Jonathan Swift*, ed. Harold Williams (2d ed.; Oxford:
Clarendon Press, 1958), II, 565.

[24] "To him no Author was unknown, / Yet what he wrote was
all his own," from "On Mr Abraham Cowley: His Death and
Burial Amongst the Ancient Poets," ll. 29–30, *The Poetical Works
of Sir John Denham*, ed. T. H. Banks, Jr. (New Haven: Yale University Press, 1928), p. 150; quoted by permission of the publisher.

For such reasons one cannot accept the thesis that Jonathan Swift is, as Adams has suggested, Thomas Swift's "collaborator" in the creation of the *Tale of a Tub*. It is not Swift's custom to participate, but to manipulate and to pillage. Professor Adams simply does not produce enough evidence to support his claim. Thomas may be coauthor; or he may not. Ultimately, we may accept either assertion. One practice of Thomas calls the probability of his authorship into question: he appears to have been compliant to the point of self-seeking zeal in his willingness to manufacture and generously circulate in well-to-do society copies of the *Tale* with notes superscribed in his own hand.[25] Nevertheless, Adams has made a real point: there is no irrefutable evidence that Jonathan Swift is sole author of a work that all his life he was careful never to own. It should not be possible for critics to dismiss Thomas Swift as airily and easily as they have in the past. Harold Williams' assertion in 1963 that, although Curll's *Key* had "attributed the composition of *A Tale* to Thomas Swift and Jonathan Swift conjointly, [and even] the more important part to the former . . . , this worthless story has long been disproved," [26] can no longer be made with such matter-of-fact assurance.

[25] In addition to the Cornell copy and an incomplete copy at Columbia, there is the so-called Lady Betty Germain copy in Thomas Swift's hand, also a 1704 edition (*Tale*, p. xvii); and Harold Williams has reported that the Duke of Buckingham's copy was similarly marked, and that he himself possessed a 1710 edition of the *Tale* which included Thomas Swift's notes ("Swift's 'Tale of a Tub,'" *Times Literary Supplement*, Sept. 30, 1926, p. 654).

[26] *The Correspondence of Jonathan Swift*, ed. Harold Williams (Oxford: Clarendon Press, 1963–1965), I, 165, n. 3. Williams' opinion has not changed in forty years; in 1926 he wrote: "It need not be stated that [Thomas Swift's] claim to authorship of any part of

Yet Adams has gone too far himself; the bold announcement that the "new edition of the *Tale* which he plans to edit some time in the next four or five years, will have a title page bearing the names of two authors: Jonathan Swift and Thomas Swift" [27] takes too much for granted; Adams appears to be convinced that he has established Thomas' rights as an author of the *Tale*—but he has done no such thing. Irvin Ehrenpreis, making no other mention of R. M. Adams whatsoever, disposes of his proposition in a curt and satiric footnote: "Professor Robert M. Adams has produced evidence corroborating Swift's suspicion that his cousin Thomas claimed to have a hand in writing *A Tale of a Tub*." [28] And Ehrenpreis is right: there is simply too little evidence favoring either side to allow one to settle the issue. Nor do I believe that sophisticated computer tests of style in sections of the *Tale* attributed to Thomas will solve the problem.[29] I should merely like to suggest here that Swift is surely capable of such a theft. But whether Swift is sole or partial author, the *Tale of a Tub* appears to this writer a masterful achievement.

the book is without substance" (*Times Literary Supplement*, Sept. 30, 1926, p. 654).

[27] Mrs. Tommie Bryant, "Who Wrote 'A Tale of the [*sic*] Tub'?" *Cornell Alumni News*, LXX (July 1967), 13.

[28] *Swift: The Man, His Works, and the Age; II: Dr. Swift* (Cambridge, Mass.: Harvard University Press, 1967), 338, n. 6.

[29] See Louis Tonko Milic's "Unconscious Ordering in the Prose of Swift," *The Computer and Literary Style*, ed. Jacob Leed (Kent, Ohio: Kent State University Press, 1966), pp. 79–106, and his inconclusive computer analysis of "A Letter of Advice to a Young Poet," in his *A Quantitative Approach to the Style of Jonathan Swift* (The Hague: Mouton, 1967). I believe the sections of "tale," if not Swift's own, have nevertheless been subjected to so many layers of Swift's additions and revisions that it would be difficult for any scientific testing apparatus to separate several styles.

For if Thomas Swift *had* devised an allegorical tale of the three brothers, we know that it would have been composed in 1696 and 1697; Thomas himself admits in his marginal notes in the 1704 edition at Cornell that his manuscript had indeed been out of his hands for at least seven years.[30] During that interval, I maintain, Swift had heavily reworked these materials. And, if Thomas was the author of such a tale, we might well consider taking the modern persona literally at his word: he everywhere admits, even aggressively asserts, that he has been annotating and recounting a "story" out of an older author; it would simply have happened that the "nearest Account [this commentator has] been able to collect" (p. 137) is the account of poor Tom Swift. In such case, Swift's comic genius would be manifest in his kidnapping a modern, soporific tale and submitting it to the annotations and reworkings of his distorted modern scholiast. At a stroke, the string of moderns and their commentators is further extended toward the horizon. Thomas has taken and retold the tale of the Reformation; Swift's modern annotator retells this twice-told tale yet once more; then, in 1710, William Wotton, B.D., and other more recent modern scholiasts rework these materials yet again.

Whether Swift has purloined pieces of his cousin's early work or whether he has invented his own childish tale, he has managed to render a modern world of the hasty, the

---

[30] Thomas Swift, in the Cornell copy of the *Tale of a Tub* . . . (London: John Nutt, 1704), sig. A₃4^r, inscribes "exactly true" where the bookseller asserts that these papers were composed seven years earlier, in 1697. Elsewhere, on p. 280 (otherwise blank), Thomas Swift reiterates: he recalls giving some suggestions about the composing of *The Battle of the Books*, "but It being seven years agoe I do remember ye less of ye particulars."

momentary, the traditionless, and the memoryless that is consistent, decorous, and complete. Within the *Tale of a Tub*'s boundaries, the laws of modernity are everywhere obeyed. Creating a full-bodied satiric modernity, such laws should be recognized as the very internal principles of plot that we have been seeking, principles which shape and control the *Tale*'s formal structure. It is this structure, with or without the contribution of other hands, that is Swift's own.

Perhaps most witty and amusing in all this creation is Swift's identification of Restoration beaux tacking and patching layer upon layer of fashionable patches onto their coats with generations of scholars nuzzling texts and affixing to them layer upon layer of annotations. His vision of editor upon editor, of file upon file of commentators—each author of the present moment fixing upon the last author's work with an intractable scholarly voracity—is witty in the extreme. What is more, Swift was to behold this vision of a distorted chain of being again. In one of his poems, he contrives the same handsome image:

> The Vermin only teaze and pinch
> Their Foes superior by an Inch.
> So, Nat'ralists observe, a Flea
> Hath smaller Fleas that on him prey,
> And these have smaller Fleas to bite 'em,
> And so proceed *ad infinitum:*
> Thus ev'ry Poet in his Kind,
> Is bit by him that comes behind;
> Who, tho' too little to be seen,
> Can teaze, and gall, and give the Spleen.[31]

---

[31] "On Poetry: A Rapsody," ll. 335–344, *Poems*, II, 651.

Very possibly, modern readers, in their turn, are destined to be "bit." For Swift, in his infinity of wit and jest, can tease and gall and give vexation. But he also gives much more: brilliant modern form and striking satiric fiction.

7. Paradox: The Dotage
of the Modern World

The thing that hath been, it is that which shall be;
and that which is done is that which shall be done:
and there is no new thing under the sun.
Is there any thing whereof it may be said,
See, this is new?
it hath been already of old time, which was before us.
There is no remembrance of former things;
neither shall there be any remembrance of things
that are to come with those that shall come after.

—ECCLESIASTES

We have remarked some of the telling reversals of intention that the modern persona endures and have suggested
how such reversals give point to the *Tale of a Tub*. The
very assertive and progressive Modern, planning the conquest of all knowledge, never manages to complete a single
work. The hypersensitively contemporary Modern, insist-
ing always upon his individuality and self-sufficiency, nonetheless manages to appear to us as one nameless—not an individual at all, but a collection of fragmented and disparate
personalities. The Modern, in spite of his ambition to embody at once a high point of ancient *and* modern progress
and learning in himself, succeeds instead in accomplishing a
considerable retrogression; in place of the *Ubermensch* that
he seeks to become, his madness transforms him into a primitive beast. And the modern explicator must himself be
submitted to the toils of explication.

Since it is these paradoxical reversals that constitute the

satiric reduction in *A Tale of a Tub*, revealing much of the work's artistry and meaning, this concluding chapter will explore the most important of these paradoxes. We shall attempt to name such paradoxes, observing how they serve in the *Tale* to convey artistic meaning.

I

The modern persona certainly does suffer a series of reversals—achieving the opposite of what he intends. For this very reason, it is all the more paradoxical to note that the Modern very consciously seeks to be paradoxical. He is, to the very core, the maker of paradoxes. He declares his ability to write "On Nothing" (p. 208); he argues that where his own writing is incomprehensible, "it shall be concluded, that something very useful and profound is couch't underneath" (p. 46). He praises destructive criticism (Section III), extols digressions (Section VII), lauds madness (Section IX). He finds the Restoration stage and the dissenting pulpit identical with the gallows (pp. 56–60) and finds Popish Peter precisely as interesting as Dissenting Jack (Sections IV, XI), further arguing that, although the one dresses in laces and the other in rags, they are very like—even indistinguishable (pp. 199–200). This insistence upon maintaining the identity of nonsense and significance, of beggar and beau—this yoking of opposites violently together—epitomizes the workings of paradox. For paradox reasonably argues the unreasonable, firmly clasps the untenable, establishing kinship and contiguity between principles that are distinct, alien, and disjunct.

The modern persona goes further still, framing local paradoxes at numerous points. He urges that the end of literature and ethics is the "Reader's *Repose*" (p. 140); that

"*Labor* is the Seed of *Idleness*" (p. 146); that the purpose of a good meal is to encourage men "only to *doze*, or to *sleep* out the rest of the Day" (p. 208); that "*Night* being the universal Mother of Things, wise Philosophers hold all writings to be *fruitful* in the Proportion they are *dark*" (p. 186). Finally, just as Aeolists had discovered the identity of carnal and spiritual "Extasie" (p. 157), the persona maintains that the human mind eventually discovers "how near the Frontiers of Height and Depth" (pp. 157–158). Like the projector in *The Mechanical Operation of the Spirit*, he claims that moderns "have discovered a gross Ignorance in the Natures of Good and Evil, and most horribly confounded the Frontiers of both" (p. 274).

A prototype for this confusing of frontiers is in the account of one Bedlam student's subsistence: "The best Part of his Diet, is the Reversion of his own Ordure, which exspiring into steams, whirls perpetually about, and at last reinfunds" (p. 178). The modern persona's chief paradox confusing borders, as we have seen, is the deliberate confounding of the frontiers of antiquity and modernity. The Modern is regularly and intentionally paradoxical, and his unflagging praise of modernity is his seminal paradox. Of course, he wishes to be paradoxical in the best and most acceptable "modern" manner.

For, pray Gentlemen, was ever any thing so *Modern* as the *Spider* in his Air, his Turns, and his Paradoxes? He argues in the Behalf of *You* his Brethren, and Himself, with many Boastings of his native Stock, and great Genius; that he Spins and Spits wholly from himself, and scorns to own any Obligation or Assistance from without [p. 234.]

Paradoxical or no, the persona must suffer one more reversal. He may seek to be paradoxical in the modern manner, yet investigation teaches us that he is paradoxical in an old and traditional way. Whether he hates tradition or not, the modern persona lies squarely in the seventeenth-century "line of wit," [1] which had been everywhere paradoxical. "In Philosophy," said Sir Thomas Browne with some satisfaction, "where Truth seems double-fac'd, there is no man more Paradoxical than my self." [2] Indeed, the first work in Greek to be translated by an Englishman was Synesius' paradox, the "Praise of Baldness." [3] By the end of the sixteenth century, a number of terse, witty, and ingenious modes of expression had become popular in England —the dialogue, the epigram, the essay, the "character," the problem, and the paradox.[4] All these forms accommodated balance, antithesis, chiasmus, catachresis, surprising subject matter, facetious manner, brazen metaphor, zeugma, and oxymoron. The very essence of seventeenth-century poetic wit has been described as

the power of creating emotional surprise by the unexpected combination or contrast of generally diverse ideas or images, especially of incompatibles or contraries. It is often the exploitation of a latent resemblance between incompatibles which capitalizes on the contrast (catachresis) or a reconciliation of

[1] See F. R. Leavis, *Revaluation: Tradition and Development in English Poetry* (New York: Stewart, 1947), pp. 10–41, esp. p. 29. Swift's *Tale* is placed in this tradition by Herbert Davis, in *The Satire of Jonathan Swift* (New York: Macmillan, 1947), pp. 14, 28–29.

[2] *Religio Medici, The Works of Sir Thomas Browne*, ed. Geoffrey Keynes (London: Faber and Gwyer, 1928–1931), I, 10.

[3] John Free translated Synesius' work into Latin about 1461; see G. K. Hunter, *John Lyly* (Cambridge, Mass.: Harvard University Press, 1962), p. 34 and p. 353, n. 54.

[4] William Garrett Crane, *Wit and Rhetoric in the Renaissance . . .* (New York: Columbia University Press, 1937), p. 12.

contraries which capitalizes on the union (paradox). Both can produce emotional surprise and express mixed feelings.[5]

To be sure, paradox may be found earlier, in the poetry of Marino and Gongora at the end of the sixteenth century as well as in medieval lyrics; an old and continuing Christian tradition employed paradox.[6] The chief source of its influence, however, is in Greco-Roman tradition.

The term *paradox* (from the Greek, "contrary to common opinion") even in classical antiquity bore a variety of meanings. In one sense, *paradox* designates nothing more than a rhetorical figure, a brief verbal device akin to *ironia* or oxymoron. Cicero and Puttenham in discussing tropes treat of paradox in this narrow rhetorical sense.[7] Employed as a figure of speech, paradox has been popular in oratory for centuries. In another, more important sense, the paradox inherits a greater distinction in serious and philosophical history. The oration that is paradoxical in its entirety, the sophistic paradoxical encomium, has been popular since its use by Gorgias in fifth-century Athens; such sophistic oratory was adopted as a favorite by the rhetorical schools.[8] Moreover, this sophistic rhetorical tool was em-

[5] George Williamson, *The Proper Wit of Poetry* (London: Faber and Faber, 1961), p. 25.

[6] For examples of Christ's and Paul's use of paradox, see Matt. 5:39, 10:39, 12:10, 19:30; Luke 15:1–32; John 12:24; 1 Cor. 1:20–21; 2 Cor. 6:9–10; and Eph. 3:8. Consult A. J. Jenkinson, "Paradox," *A Dictionary of Christ and the Gospels*, ed. James Hastings (New York: Scribner's, 1907–1908), II, 319.

[7] Cicero, *De oratore* II.lxv.263; George Puttenham, *The Arte of English Poesie* (1589), ed. G. D. Willcock and Alice Walker (Cambridge: Cambridge University Press, 1936), p. 225.

[8] Arthur S. Pease, "Things without Honor," *Classical Philology*, XXI (1926), 29; Theodore C. Burgess, *Epideictic Literature* (Chicago: University of Chicago Press, 1902), pp. 157–166.

ployed as the weapon of philosophical schools in logical controversies. The Skeptical paradox has been used devastatingly since the time of Timon of Phlius (c. 315–275 B.C.); [9] and the witty logical paradox wielded by Cynics and then by Stoics has been used since the time of Zeno (c. 333–262 B.C.). [10] Sophists, Skeptics, and Stoics alike utilized the paradox to attract audiences to their public lectures; here, frequently, the paradox became the very form and substance of a speech. Used so, paradox constituted the "thesis" of an oration. In using it, such philosophers sought to gain attention, to provoke thought, to win the public away from complacency and outmoded or unexamined custom.

Traditions of paradoxical argumentation continued popular in the Middle Ages, perhaps too much under the sway of sophistic rhetoric. The influence is noticeable in the host of philosophical questions, the *débat*, the *jeu parti*, the riddle, and the love question popular in the twelfth and thirteenth centuries. [11] In the Renaissance, education in rhetoric guaranteed the considerable proliferation of sophistic

[9] Louis I. Bredvold, "The Traditions of Skepticism," *The Intellectual Milieu of John Dryden* (Ann Arbor: University of Michigan Press, 1934), pp. 16–46; Pierre Villey, *Les Sources et l'évolution des "Essais" de Montaigne* (2d ed.; Paris: Librarie Hachette, 1933), II, 153–171.

[10] Consult André Oltramare, *Les Origines de la diatribe romaine* (Geneva: Imprimeries Populaires, 1926), and George Converse Fiske, *Lucilius and Horace*, University of Wisconsin Studies in Language and Literature, VII (Madison: University of Wisconsin Press, 1920), pp. 143–218.

[11] See Archer Taylor's "Paradoxes," in *A Bibliography of Riddles* (Helsinki: Suomalainen Tiedeakatemia Academia Scientiarum Fenniga, 1939), pp. 145–148.

paradoxes; but Christian paradoxes also acquired a certain vogue,[12] as did skeptical and stoic paradoxes.[13] In addition, perhaps motivated by the Aristotelian *Problems* and Sextus Empiricus, a whole new species of popular scientific paradoxes, problems, and *physica curiosa* became fashionable.[14]

In form, these types of paradox are unlike the paradox that is a mere figure of speech frequently consisting of but a striking sentence or two. Rather, these more extensive paradoxes, like Cicero's *Paradoxa Stoicorum* or Donne's *Paradoxes and Problems,* tend to assume the form of the full-bodied argumentative essay. Therein, a general assertion is defended by a succession of illustrations and confirmations. In this oratorical form, the paradox naturally employed, as it had even among the early Sophists, the stand-

[12] As in Francis Bacon's (?) "The Characters of a Believing Christian, in Paradoxes and Seeming Contradictions," *The Works of Francis Bacon* . . . , ed. James Spedding, Robert Leslie Ellis, and Douglas Denon Heath (Boston: Taggard and Thompson, 1861–1864), XIV, 143–151; and Ralph Venning's *Orthodox Paradoxes, Theoretical and Experimental, or a Believer Clearing Truth By Seeming Contradictions* (London: John Rothwell and L. Chapman, 1652).

[13] Louis I. Bredvold, "The Naturalism of Donne in Relation to Some Renaissance Traditions," *Journal of English and Germanic Philology,* XXII (1923), 471–502; Robert Hoopes, *Right Reason in the English Renaissance* (Cambridge, Mass.: Harvard University Press, 1962), pp. 33–45 and *passim.*

[14] Consult R. L. Colie, "Some Paradoxes in the Language of Things," *Reason and the Imagination: Studies in the History of Ideas,* ed. J. A. Mazzeo (New York: Columbia University Press, 1962), especially pp. 109–126; and Robert Ellrodt, "Scientific Curiosity and Metaphysical Poetry in the Seventeenth Century," *Modern Philology,* LXI (1964), 180–197.

ard structure of the declamation, as it was called in the schools.[15] Such set pieces argued or defended a simple "thesis." When employed as school exercises, as they were for more than two thousand years, the set speeches too often defended or praised some insignificant or unworthy subject; and this class of display oratory came to be termed "adoxography" or "paradoxical encomium." [16] This genre of rhetorical paradox may be exemplified by Lucian's *Laus Muscae*, Libanius' "Encomium of Thersites," Synesius' *Calvitii encomium*, and by Ortensio Lando's collection of *Paradossi*.

Their very popularity as school exercises rendered such paradoxes numerous, facetious, and facile. Rhetoricians had long ago "pointed out that in *vituperatio*, the ninth form [for students writing orations], one used exactly the same heads as in *laus*, for one could vituperate anything he could praise." [17] Any subject could be argued *pro* or *contra*, and students for centuries did formally debate innumerable questions.[18] The training was distinctly sophistic and amo-

[15] I refer to the traditional parts of speeches: *exordium, narratio, partitio, argumentatio,* and *peroratio.* On the origins and evolution of the *declamatio,* see Charles Sears Baldwin, *Ancient Rhetoric and Poetic* (New York: Macmillan, 1924), pp. 87–101.

[16] Throughout this discussion I am indebted to Henry Knight Miller, "The Paradoxical Encomium, with Special Reference to Its Vogue in England, 1600–1800," *Modern Philology,* LIII (1956), 145–178.

[17] T. W. Baldwin, *William Shakspere's Small Latine and Lesse Greeke* (Urbana: University of Illinois Press, 1944), II, 331.

[18] Carneades of Cyrene (214–129 B.C.) is a skeptic famous for delivering in Rome on successive days orations for and against justice. Examples of works in the Renaissance which argue both sides of a topic include Christoph Hegendorfer's "Encomium Sobrietatis" and "Encomium Ebrietatis" (1519); Milton's "L'Allegro" and "Il Penseroso"; Tom Brown's "A Declamation in Praise

ral, emphasizing purely mechanical skills, as many thinkers over the centuries have complained. Like Schoolmen, Locke felt, students of such rhetoric "obstinately . . . maintain that side of the question they have chosen, whether true or false, to the last extremity; even after conviction." [19]

The seventeenth century embraced sophistic paradoxical rhetoric wholeheartedly, employing it jocularly and seriously in every kind of writing.[20] The practice in fact merely subserved the century's devotion to baroque mannerism. In his handbook of oratory, John Newton makes clear that

such is the Curiosity of this age in which we live, as that it is grown weary of these plain and ordinary waies, & requireth or expecteth in the very style something more than ordinary; insomuch that now a daies he is not worthy the name of an *Orator*, that knowes not how to brandish an Oration, by some sharp & witty flourishes.

By sharpness and wit Newton means ingenuity; and ingenuity at its best "is that which is called *unnatural*, because it begetteth great admiration." He designates such ingenuity *"disagreeing concord,"* or *"agreeing discord."* [21] The

of Hereditary Quality and Wealth" and "A Declamation against Wealth and Quality, in Praise of Poverty"; and Thomas Parnell's "A Night-Piece on Death" and "A Hymn to Contentment." Consult as well Milton's extant school exercises, in *Milton: Private Correspondence and Academic Exercises*, trans. Phyllis B. Tillyard (Cambridge: Cambridge University Press, 1932), pp. 53–120.

[19] *Essay Concerning Human Understanding*, IV,vii,11.

[20] For study of almost every kind of paradox, refer to Rosalie L. Colie, *Paradoxia Epidemica: The Renaissance Tradition of Paradox* (Princeton: Princeton University Press, 1966).

[21] *An Introduction to the Art of Rhetorick* . . . (London: Thomas Passenger, 1671), pp. 28–32.

literature of the period is full, in verse and prose, of pieces like the praises of dishonor, ignorance, and cuckoldry in Shakespeare's plays, the paradoxes in Sidney's *Arcadia*, Donne's "The Will," "The Indifferent," and his more formal paradoxes and problems, Jonson's "Fit of Rime against Rime," Herrick's "Delight in Disorder," Suckling's "Sermon on Malt," and, in the latter half of the century, Henry King's poetic paradoxes, Cowley's second ode ("That a pleasant Poverty is to be preferred before discontented Riches"), Rochester's "Of Nothing" and "Satyr against Mankind," and the maxims of La Rochefoucauld.[22] A poet in the Restoration period could hardly venture forth in rhyme without the powders and periwigs of paradox; Edmund Waller on love bears sufficient witness:

> So like the chances are of love and war,
> That they alone in this distinguished are,
> In love the victors from the vanquished fly;
> They fly that wound, and they pursue that die.[23]

[22] Consult Alfred Harbage, "Paradoxes," *As They Liked It* (New York: Macmillan, 1947), pp. 73–82; Alexander H. Sackton, "The Paradoxical Encomium in Elizabethan Drama," *University of Texas Studies in English*, XXVIII (1949), 83–104; George Walter Hallam, Jr., "Functional Paradox in Sidney's Revised *Arcadia*" (Ph.D. diss., University of Florida, 1959); A. C. Hamilton, "Sidney and Agrippa," *Review of English Studies*, n.s., VII (1956), 151–157; and Harold E. Pagliaro, "Paradox in the Aphorisms of La Rochefoucauld and Some Representative English Followers," *PMLA*, LXXIX (1964), 42–50.

[23] "To A Friend, on the different success of their Loves," ll. 25–28, *The Poetical Works of Edmund Waller*, ed. Robert Bell (London: Charles Griffin, 18——), p. 129. That suave rake Dorimant admires these lines in Sir George Etherege's *Man of Mode*, III.iii.44–45.

Such paradoxes had, in fact, established their popularity in the sixteenth century, when humanists lauded "Smoke and Shadow, Blindness and Deafness, Gout and Ague."

It was a fashion easily adopted, and before the [sixteenth] century was over the learned world was deluged with the sonorous praise not merely of negations or vacuities such as these, but of ridiculous or loathsome things, asses, owls, geese, vermin, and dung.[24]

As the seventeenth century progressed, so popular did paradoxical display pieces become, that Grub Street publications were distended with trite and fantastic propositions: "The Mirrour of Madness; or a Paradoxe maintaining Madness to be most excellent"; the "Prayse of Nothing"; a "Declamation: For the ignorant"; "The Praise, Antiquity, and Commoditie of Beggerie, Beggars, And Begging"; an argument "That Inconstancy is more commendable than Constancie"; "That all Sciences may be profitably reduc'd to one"; "That Ignorance is better than Knowledg, and Fools more happy than wise Men"; the postulate of "A Paradox Against Liberty"; a piece *"In Praise of a* PRISON, *call'd by its* Prisoners *their* College; *and written there"*; and even a paradox "In Praise of a Paradox." [25]

---

[24] Charles H. Herford, *Studies in the Literary Relations of England and Germany in the Sixteenth Century* (Cambridge: Cambridge University Press, 1886), pp. 381–382. See also Sister M. Geraldine, C.S.J., "Erasmus and the Tradition of Paradox," *Studies in Philology*, LXI (1964), 41–63.

[25] The similarity of the topics in these paradoxes to those in *A Tale of a Tub* should be obvious. The paradoxes named are, respectively, (1) a translation from the French by James Sanford (London, 1576); (2) a piece by Edward Dyer (1585); (3) the third declamation in *The Defence of Contraries . . .* , trans. A[nthony]

This abuse of the paradox naturally enticed the satirists' jesting barbs:

> 'Tis strange how some men's Tempers suit
> (Like *Bawd* and *Brandee*) with Dispute,
> That for their own *Opinions* stand fast,
> Only to have them claw'd and canvast.
> That kept their *Consciences* in Cases,
> As Fidlers do their *Crowds* and *Bases*,
> Ne'er to be us'd but when they're bent
> To play a fit for *Argument.*
> Make *true* and *false*, *unjust* and *just*,
> Of no use but to be discust.
> Dispute and set a *Paradox,*
> Like a strait Boot upon the Stocks,
> And stretch it more unmercifully,
> Than *Helmont, Mountaign, White,* or *Tully.*[26]

Indeed the reaction to the excesses of farfetched paradox by the end of the seventeenth century was considerable; the mass of such trite paradoxes served to denigrate the very term "wit," as is pointed out in Sir Richard Blackmore's attack in *A Satire against Wit* (1700) and in Addi-

M[unday] (London, 1593); an English version of Charles Estienne's French version of Ortensio Lando's *Paradossi;* (4) a piece by John Taylor (1621); (5) the fourth paradox of Cornwallis (c. 1600), in R. E. Bennett, "Four Paradoxes by Sir William Cornwallis, the Younger," *Harvard Studies and Notes in Philology and Literature,* XIII (1931), 219–240; (6) John Dunton's *Athenian Sport* (London, 1707), No. 118; (7) *Athenian Sport,* No. 78; (8) an anonymous poem (1679); (9) anonymous (1704); (10) *Athenian Sport,* No. 1.

[26] Samuel Butler, *Hudibras,* II,ii,1–14. Line 14 alludes to such paradoxers as Jan Baptista Van Helmont, Montaigne, Thomas White (the Catholic controversialist), and Cicero (noted for the *Paradoxa Stoicorum*).

son's renowned *Spectator* papers deriding "Mixt" and "False Wit" (nos. 58–63). Lee Ustick and Hoyt Hudson, surveying wit in the poetry of the seventeenth century, trace the decline in popularity of the paradoxical conceit:

First, we have seen how thoroughly, here and there, the epigram (and the emblem, a related form) had permeated the writing of other types of poetry. Second, we have seen that the "conceit" in its worst forms, based upon a theory of wit which emphasized novelty, surprise, verbal ingenuity, and the linking of apparently incongruous ideas, was actually cultivated in the grammar schools of the sixteenth and seventeenth centuries. Third, we have seen that this theory of wit had some, if not much, critical support. . . . Fourth, we have seen that . . . sane writers of the eighteenth century [largely] threw overboard this false and mixed wit, with its progeny of conceits.[27]

Precisely the same blossoming and decline attended the vogue of the formal rhetorical paradox. E. N. S. Thompson believes that the paradox as a form passed through three phases in its popular history. In the first phase, as in the case of Parmenides' paradoxes, Aristotle's *Problems*, Plato's dialogues, the Stoic diatribes, and the *essais* of the skeptical Montaigne, the paradox was put to serious use. In the second phase, during the sixteenth century, partly as a result of the influence of Erasmus' *Praise of Folly*, elements of irony, of appeal to popularity, of *jeu d'esprit* developed in the paradox. "The upholding of . . . heterodox ideas became more and more a diversion for clever men. The paradox then advanced to its third stage, when seriousness en-

[27] "Wit, 'Mixt Wit,' and the Bee in Amber," *Huntington Library Bulletin*, VIII (1935), 129–130.

tirely disappeared, and the author pursued his fantastic argument simply to display intellectual adroitness."[28]

Consequently, although the modern persona in the *Tale of a Tub* claims to be wholly modern and "new," "strik[ing] all Things out of [himself]" (p. 135), his "many Strains of Wit, and pretty Paradoxes to divert the Reader," as Swift once scornfully referred to them,[29] are in actuality stale and trite epideictic and forensic paradoxes in a long and tired tradition. Thus, while the modern persona is himself consciously paradoxical, one of the finest ironic reversals that Swift engineers in the *Tale of a Tub* is his own accomplishment, at the Modern's expense, of a greater series of paradoxes. Swift presents to us a Modern who, intending to be original, paradoxically is traditional, a Modern somehow caught employing ancient rhetorical paradoxes—in sum, a Modern who beats "the dirty paths where vulgar feet have trod," [30] writing at best "in an old beaten trivial Manner upon Topicks wholly new." [31] In fact, novelty and innovation in *A Tale of a Tub*'s "modern" paradoxical arguments are simply not to be found.

II

In sharp contrast to his persona, Swift himself was certainly not the maker of trite paradoxes. He had no taste for

[28] *The Seventeenth-Century English Essay* (Iowa City: University of Iowa Press, 1926), pp. 94–96.

[29] *The Examiner*, No. 34, *The Prose Works of Jonathan Swift*, ed. Herbert Davis, 14 vols. (Oxford: Basil Blackwell, 1939–1968), III, 118.

[30] "To Mr. Congreve," l. 205, *The Poems of Jonathan Swift*, ed. Harold Williams (2d ed.; Oxford: Clarendon Press, 1958), I, 49.

[31] Swift, "Remarks upon a Book, intitled, The Rights of the Christian Church Asserted . . . ," *Prose Works*, II, 69.

the modern persona's species of wit—clichés and bombast arrogantly parading as perspicuous originality. Rather, Swift in his satires regularly created inflated and pretentious personae whom he sought to expose; their every utterance exhibited "that self-assertion which piques itself on originality because it knows no rule [and generated a scorn which] lay at the very root of Swift's literary, as it did of his religious and moral, judgment." [32] Truly, "Swift despised the trope of paradox as a species of modern vulgarity: his 'paradoxes' lead straight to the heart of his irony—and to its absolute distinctions of value." [33] Swift despised the formal paradoxes of the schools because they were habitually taught and mechanically and tritely repeated and because they elevated display, decoration, and diction (*verba*) above content (*res*). The rhetorical device is ostentatious and capricious, appealing not to the reason but to the passions. It is "a perfect Cheat, to stir up Men's Passions against Truth and Justice, for the Service of a Faction, to put false Colours upon Things, and by an Amusement of agreeable Words, make the worse Reason appear to be the better." [34] Such paradoxical rhetoric is unethical, "where Men can argue with Plausibility on both Sides of a Question." [35] Its method is predictable and commonplace;

[32] Henry Craik, *The Life of Jonathan Swift, Dean of St. Patrick's, Dublin,* 2 vols. (2d ed.; London, Macmillan, 1894), I, 92.

[33] John Traugott, "A Voyage to Nowhere with Thomas More and Jonathan Swift: *Utopia* & *The Voyage to the Houyhnhnms,*" *Sewanee Review,* LXIX (1961), 534.

[34] Swift, "Sermon: Upon Sleeping in Church," *Prose Works,* IX, 214. Consult Charles Peake, "Swift and the Passions," *Modern Language Review,* LV (1960), especially pp. 171–175; and A. C. Howell, "*Res et Verba:* Words and Things," *Journal of English Literary History,* XIII (1946), 131–142.

[35] Swift, *Gulliver's Travels,* IV,viii, *Prose Works,* XI, 267.

like fashions in clothes, such rhetorical paradoxes are of a piece—"All of old Cut with a new Dye." [36]

Yet in spite of his antipathy to the tiresome and flippant paradox, Swift in his satires was himself a very considerable maker of paradoxes. "The secret of [Swift's] success, here [in *Gulliver's Travels*] as elsewhere, is [his] marvellous imperturbability in paradox, his teeming imagination and his rigid logic." [37] But Swift's paradoxes differ sharply from those of his Modern. The modern paradoxer, like the freethinking Tindal, "hath somewhere heard, that it is a Point of Wit to advance Paradoxes, and the bolder the better. But the Wit lies in maintaining them, which he neglecteth, and formeth imaginary Conclusions from them, as if they were true and uncontested." [38] Swift *has* the wit to "maintain" his paradoxes. Unlike the modern persona, who unconsciously follows an old and shopworn tradition of the paradox, Swift consciously follows another, venerable tradition—of the satiric paradox.

An examination of the satiric paradox can find no more appropriate place to begin than the classic drama of fifth-century Athens. When we turn to Aristophanes' plays, one of the recurrent tactics to strike our attention is paradox. Professor Burgess records the following paradoxes of this type in the plays: (1) Philocleon praises the litigious dicasts

[36] Swift, "Ode to the Athenian Society," l. 227, *Poems*, I, 23.

[37] Richard Garnett and Thomas Seccombe, "Swift," *Encyclopaedia Britannica* (11th ed.; Cambridge: Cambridge University Press, 1910–1911), XXVI, 229.

[38] Swift, "Remarks upon a Book, intitled, The Rights of the Christian Church . . . ," *Prose Works*, II, 101. Joseph Addison, agreeing with Boileau and Pope, makes the same point: "that Wit and fine Writing doth not consist so much in advancing Things that are new, as in giving things that are known an agreeable Turn" (*The Spectator*, No. 253).

(*The Wasps*, ll. 548–631); (2) the chorus of wasps (parodying the formal political speech) praise Athens (*The Wasps*, ll. 1071–1090); (3) Poverty delivers a formal celebration of poverty (*Plutus*, ll. 507–592); (4) the chorus of women eulogize women (*The Thesmophoriazusae*, ll. 785–846); (5) Praxagora, chief among the feminine revolutionaries, praises women (*The Ecclesiazusae*, ll. 214–240); (6) the chorus of knights praise themselves (*The Knights*, ll. 595–610); and (7) the chorus of knights, with more vigor and contortion, again celebrate themselves (*The Knights*, ll. 1264–1315).³⁹ Burgess is quite right in stressing the importance of paradox in these plays.

Furthermore, more important than these particular paradoxes in Aristophanes' plays is the paradoxical nature of the plots themselves. Wrong Logic's encomium upon herself and her triumph in an agon over Right Logic (*The Clouds*, ll. 1031–1104) is the initial action that later in the play compels the victory of faulty logic, at play's end, in every walk of life. Similarly, in *The Birds,* the Hoopoe sophistically argues with the birds that one can learn most, benefit most handsomely, from an enemy (ll. 366–430), and the Athenian entrepreneur Pisthetaerus then addresses to the birds a speech in praise of birds, demonstrating their power and antiquity, eventually arguing their superiority to men and gods alike (ll. 465–626). Subsequently in the play, the birds *do* subjugate the human and divine, conquering, in fact, the universe. So it is in Aristophanes' other plays, where one regularly discovers the triumphs of madness, demagoguery—and women.

Nevertheless, at the center of the Aristophanic plays

³⁹ Theodore C. Burgess, *Epideictic Literature* (Chicago: University of Chicago, Press, 1902), pp. 162–163.

stands the satiric paradox in the agon. Where in actual life the politician and the sophist employ the topics and form of the classical oration, cunningly inserting the rhetorical paradox, Aristophanes in literary practice parodies the formal oration, salting his confection with outrageous metaphor and sharp paradox. It is one thing for the housewife to dote upon her own cooking, for the tyrant to extol tyranny, or for the patriot to praise chauvinism; it is paradoxical, yet it happens often enough. But it is something else for the satirist, who reduces such paradoxes to absurdity, permitting a man to celebrate aviary patriotism (*The Birds*), a sophist to endorse criminal nihilism (*The Clouds*), and Athenian women (politically little better than helots) to consort with the enemy in wartime, to barricade the holy shrines on the Acropolis, and to seize absolute control of the state (*Lysistrata*).

If the standard sophistic paradox enlivens and surprises, the satiric paradox partakes of double surprise. Just as tragedy "brings in the opposite," with tragic irony yielding the audience a great synthetic experience,[40] so the ironic paradox renders harmony from discord. It affords the satirist opportunity to explore and to display his abilities within a trite rhetorical convention at the same time that it permits him to undermine, to disparage, and to transcend that selfsame form.

Of such satiric paradox there has been a long tradition: of paradox doubly employed, for serious as well as for comic purposes (the terms *joco-seriae* and *spoudaiogeloion* are commonly invoked). Plato utilizes satiric paradox frequently in his dialogues—in the funeral oration in the *Me-*

---

[40] I. A. Richards, *Principles of Literary Criticism* (New York: Harcourt, Brace, n.d.), p. 250.

nexenus, in the defeat inflicted upon the poor rhapsode in the *Ion*, in the debate of Socrates and Thrasymachus at the outset of the *Republic*, in the *Protagoras*, and especially in the *Parmenides*—all of which dramatize men's firm convictions tumbling into logical absurdity or comic impasse. Cicero in the *Paradoxa Stoicorum* treats the self-evident principles of ethics as shocking paradoxes, implying that a depraved Roman society is ignorant of the most elementary morality. Juvenal frequently bases the action in his works upon satiric paradox; [41] and Lucian, particularly in "The Parasite," exerts extensive influence upon later authors.[42]

In the Renaissance, this satiric tradition continued vigorously to flourish,[43] many of its paradoxes arguing satirical theses similar to those encountered in Aristophanes' plays —praising ignorance, madness, tyranny, and the rule of women. In like manner, Henry Cornelius Agrippa, straitly adhering (for once) to Christian doctrine in the *De incertitudine et vanitate scientiarum* (1530), learnedly dispraises learning. Erasmus commends folly in his famed *Encomium moriae* (1509); Wilibald Pirkheimer's *Apologia seu Podagrae laus* (1521) applauds the gout; Rabelais incorporates numerous mock encomia in his paradoxical *Gargantua et Pantagruel* (1532–1552); and Heinrich Bebel's *Triumphus*

[41] See William S. Anderson, "Studies in Book I of Juvenal," *Yale Classical Studies*, XV, ed. Harry M. Hubbell (New Haven: Yale University Press, 1957), 31–90.

[42] Consult C. A. Mayer, "Rabelais' Satirical Eulogy: The Praise of Borrowing," *François Rabelais: Ouvrage publié pour le quatrième centenaire de sa mort, 1553–1953*, Travaux d'humanisme et Renaissance, VII (Geneva: Librairie E. Droz, 1953), 147–155.

[43] See Adolf Hauffen, "Zur Litteratur der ironischen Enkomien," *Vierteljahreschrift fur Literaturgeschichte*, VI (1893), 161–185; and J. B. Heidler, "Praise of Folly and Related Satirical Literature," *Methodist Quarterly Review*, LXXVI (1927), 607–614.

Veneris (1509?) savagely praises carnal love. The *Epistolae obscurorum virorum* (1516–1517) satirically contrives a collection of letters in which utterly unknown scholastic dunces praise their Magister Ortwin Gratius. Friedrich Dedekind's *Grobianus* (1549) is a learned "manual" of conduct (after the manner of *Il Cortegiano*), giving scrupulous instruction in the refined art of slovenliness. The Calvinist Henri Estienne, in his *Apology for Herodotus* (1567), indirectly exposes modern Catholic credulity by undertaking "to prove the credibility of the wildest fables of the ancient Greeks by assembling a selection of the even more grotesque miracle stories and fairy tales which the priests of his time had imposed on a credulous people." [44] And Montaigne's renowned "Apologie de Raimond Sebond" (1580) offered to prove, at a time when disastrous religious civil war benumbed France with violence and unreason, the reasonableness of Sebond's rational theology by appealing to man's inherent unreason. The influence of this satiric tradition was broad and continuous: Swift, for instance, was familiar with these very satiric paradoxes we have been describing. [45]

[44] Herbert Luethy, "Montaigne, or the Art of Being Truthful," *Encounter*, I (1953), 42.

[45] Michel de Montaigne, *Essais*, II, xii. In 1715 Swift owned every satire and paradox discussed, except only those by Bebel and Pirkheimer. Swift also possessed Heinsius' *Laus Asini*, More's *Utopia*, Erasmus' *Colloquies*, Cervantes' *Don Quixote*, and standard editions of the Greek and Roman satirists. Consult T. P. Le Fanu, "Catalogue of Dean Swift's Library in 1715, with an Inventory of His Personal Property in 1742," *Proceedings of the Royal Irish Academy*, XXXVII, Sec. C (London: Williams and Norgate, 1927), 263–275. By 1744, Swift had acquired copies of Rabelais, the *Satyre Ménippée*, and Charles Cotton's *Virgile Travestie* (re-

It should be clear, then, that the satiric paradox—unlike its more pert, scholastic kin, the rhetorical paradox—sustains a manifold seriousness; it argues a thesis that is shocking or untenable, exposing faulty logic and simplistic opinion. Its function is akin to that of Aristophanes' chorus of deific clouds:

> Such is our plan. We find a man
>   On evil thoughts intent,
>   Guide him along to shame and wrong,
>   Then leave him to repent.[46]

The ironic paradoxer endorses sin so that he may be quit of it. As satirist, he cannot praise a fugitive and cloistered virtue; rather, he endorses experience, deliberately courts the descent into hell. His prescription is homeopathic, administering poison to immunize the patient.

This is precisely the explanation that a number of authors give for their employment of paradoxes. Charles Estienne explains.

Thus I have presented to you in this book the debate of several propositions, which the ancients termed paradoxes: that is, contradictions of the opinion of most men. I have done so in order that, by their presentation, their exact opposite, the truth, may be made more lucid and apparent to you in future. Moreover, I sought to stir you into debate about matters which compel you diligently and laboriously to seek reasons, proofs, authorities, histories, and memoirs quite esoteric and diverse.

ported in Harold Williams, *Dean Swift's Library* . . . [Cambridge: Cambridge University Press, 1932]).

[46] *The Clouds*, ll. 1458–1461; reprinted by permission of the publishers and THE LOEB CLASSICAL LIBRARY, from *Aristophanes*, trans. Benjamin Bickley Rogers, 3 vols. (London: William Heinemann; Cambridge, Mass.: Harvard University Press, 1950), I, 397.

But Estienne does not merely wish to provoke thought; paradoxically, he seeks to substantiate the very common opinions he attacks:

In this, however, I would not wish you to to become so shocked at what I assert or conclude that you believe anything other than the common opinion. But remember, diversity delights men's minds the more when it ever and again leads them to recognize what is common and customary among men.[47]

In an epilogue to his "Satire against Vertue," John Oldham likewise explains his intent:

> Pardon whate'er [my Muse] hath too boldly said,
> She only acted here in Masquerade.
> For the slight Arguments she did produce,
> Were not to flatter Vice, but to traduce.[48]

Satiric "traduction" of folly and vice is the point, and Swift is *primus inter pares* among traducers.

In the *Tale of a Tub*, while the modern persona contrives his series of traditional rhetorical paradoxes, Swift himself, behind the scene, succeeds in converting these into the more meaningful paradoxes of satiric tradition. The

[47] Introduction to *Paradoxes, ce sont propos contre le commune opinion: Dabatus, en forme de declamations forēses;* quoted in Warner G. Rice, "The *Paradossi* of Ortensio Lando," *Essays and Studies in English and Comparative Literature* (Ann Arbor: University of Michigan Press, 1932), p. 67. For further consideration of the serious intention of such paradoxes, see A. E. Malloch, "The Techniques & Function of the Renaissance Paradox," *Studies in Philology*, LIII (1956), 191–203.

[48] "A Satire against Vertue: A Pindaric Ode," *The Works of Mr. John Oldham Together with his Remains*, 2 vols. (London, 1722), I, 94.

play in the *Tale of a Tub* of such a series of double ironies, where the Modern posits a paradox and Swift counters with one more telling still, reversing the Modern's intention, constitutes the work's brilliant and witty traductive center.

III

Of major concern to the *Tale of a Tub* was the *querelle* of antiquity and modernity. (See Chapter 3, above.) It should not be surprising, therefore, that the best examples of paradoxes and reversals are based upon this quarrel. On this subject, the modern persona repeatedly elects to be paradoxical: he is "the *Last Writer*" and "*freshest Modern*" (p. 130) at the same time that he is the paternal exemplar of "Orthodox" (p. 44) and "establish'd Custom" (p. 132). At select moments these roles coalesce, and he becomes ancient *and* modern; then he urges that all machinery and knowledge have "in some sort, been both invented, and brought to a Perfection by the same Hands" (p. 147).

Swift counters by forging paradoxes that exceed the Modern's, revealing the modern persona now as ancient, now as modern, in ways the persona never suspects or intends. Swift intensifies the ambiguities of youth and age, of antiquity and modernity, that the persona had attempted to insist upon, until the persona, like Perillos, is pent in his own brazen bull. "Youth" and "age," as Swift well knew, are terms that may be variously interpreted. He plays wickedly upon the meanings of these words. Freshness, spontaneity, and youth, for instance, need not inspire euphoria. When Falstaff asks what time it is, Hal wonders, "What a devil hast thou to do with the time of day?" (*I Henry IV*, I.ii.7), and one critic justly comments:

Not to know the time of day is to be governed, like animals and children, by the immediate mood of the self. To know the time of day, to structure the passage of time, is to submit the self to the ego which takes purposive decision with a view to attaining some future good; it signifies that a person is conscious of a vocation, of the kind of person he intends to become.[49]

Understood in this light, the *Tale of a Tub*'s persona, asserting youthful modernity, is in reality most ancient, a pristine child of aboriginal time, his ignorance of the past rendering him devoid of memory, experience, knowledge. Cicero offers a reflection that has become a commonplace: "To be ignorant of what occurred before you were born is to remain always a child. For what is the worth of human life, unless it is woven into the life of our ancestors by the records of history?" [50] Deprived of history, of authority, of values, Swift's Modern is just such a *bête innocente*, an infant in time. Though he is a hoary and decrepit modern, "depraved in these latter sinful Ages of the World" and "vitiated by the Rust of Time" (p. 111), he is yet simultaneously a swaddling savage, indentured to primitive times when the world was young.

Such paradoxical juxtapositioning constitutes the central comic maneuver of the *Tale*. It would be well to examine an important instance in which the persona employs a mod-

[49] W. H. Auden, "Notes on the Comic," *Thought*, XXVII (1952), 69.

[50] *Orator* xxxiv.20, trans. H. M. Hubbell, *Brutus and Orator*, Loeb Classical Library (Cambridge, Mass.: Harvard University Press, 1952), p. 395. On the paradoxical mixing and interchanging of youth and age as a classical commonplace, see E. R. Curtius, *European Literature and the Latin Middle Ages*, trans. Willard R. Trask (N.Y.: Pantheon, 1953), pp. 98–105.

ern paradox, then to observe how Swift alters and deepens the paradox, causing it to expose the persona himself. Perhaps the most common paradox to emerge from the modern revolution commencing in the sixteenth century was the one that challenged the "common opinion" reverencing classical antiquity. Arguing their case for inductive science and the contemporaneous event, moderns arraigned all traditional authority, praising their own king, their own nation, their own century. Francis Bacon first popularized what was to become in the seventeenth century the moderns' most oft-repeated paradox. "Antiquitas saeculi juventus mundi," Bacon had argued: the ancients had actually lived in the infancy of time, whereas moderns live in the world's latter ages.[51] The moderns are therefore the true ancients, elders both in historical time and in the quantity of experience accumulated over the ages.

As R. F. Jones has explained, "wide currency" in the sixteenth century of the idea that in its latter ages the world had grown old and decrepit, nearing death and decay—argued forcefully for instance, in Dr. Godfrey Goodman's *The Fall of Man, or the Corruption of Nature Proved by Natural Reason* (1616)—fostered among most men despair or passive resignation, allaying the spark of ambition.[52] It was necessary (and just) to controvert this pessimism, and Bacon's efforts were directed to this end.

Nevertheless, the paradox itself, asserting that modern

[51] *The Advancement of Learning*, I, *Works*, VI, 130; for similar passages, see I, 290–291, II, 136–137, VII, 131–132, and VIII, 116.

[52] Richard Foster Jones, "The Background of the *Battle of the Books*," *Washington University Studies*, Humanistic Series, VII, ii (1920), esp. pp. 104–106. For a thorough study of the evolution of the idea of nature's decay, see Victor Harris, *All Coherence Gone* (Chicago: University of Chicago Press, 1949).

ages are the truly ancient, was clearly superficial. It became
still more so, for in the course of the seventeenth century it
recurs in the writings of George Hakewill, Hobbes, Descartes, Nicolas de Malebranche, John Wilkins, Pascal, Joseph Glanvill, and Butler, until, tattered with overuse, it
came to rest in the facile hands of Bernard de Fontenelle,
Charles Perrault, Thomas Pope Blount, John Dennis, and
even John Dunton.[53] At last, in *The Battle of the Books*,
when a single aged tome quietly attempts to defend classical antiquity, the bevy of modern books are ready with
their trite reply: "These [modern books] denied the Premises, and seemed very much to wonder, how the *Antients*
could pretend to insist upon their Antiquity, when it was
so plain (if they went to that) the *Moderns* were much the
more *Antient* of the two" (p. 227). The marginal note in
all editions of *The Battle* bluntly comments: "According to

[53] *Tale*, p. 227, n. 2, cites passages where the paradox appears in
Bacon, Hobbes, Collier, Fontenelle, and Perrault. Foster E. Guyer,
in " 'C'est nous qui sommes les anciens,' " *Modern Language Notes*,
XXXVI (1921), 257–264, cites passages in Pascal, Descartes, and
Malebranche. See also George Hakewill, *An Apologie or Declara-
tion of the Power & Providence of God . . .* (3d ed., rev.; London,
1635), p. 27; *The Mathematical & Philosophical Works of the
Right Rev. John Wilkins* (London, 1802), II, 138; Joseph Glanvill,
The Vanity of Dogmatizing . . . (facsimile of 1661 ed.; New York:
Columbia University Press, 1931), pp. 141, 240; Samuel Butler,
Characters and Passages from Note-Books, ed. A. R. Waller
(Cambridge: Cambridge University Press, 1908), pp. 43, 439, 451;
Sir Thomas Pope Blount's Essays on Several Subjects (London,
1697), pp. 124–126, 144–145; John Dennis, "Reflections upon a
Late Rhapsody called an Essay upon Criticism" (1711), *Critical
Essays of the Eighteenth Century, 1700–1725*, ed. Willard Higley
Durham (New Haven: Yale University Press, 1915), p. 231; and
John Dunton, *Athenian Sport: or Two Thousand Paradoxes Mer-
rily Argued, To Amuse and Divert the Age . . .* (London, 1707),
p. 327.

the Modern paradox." This very paradox inspires the modern volumes to make their rash decision: "As for any Obligations they owed to the *Antients*, they renounced them all" (p. 227).

We can appreciate why the modern persona of the *Tale* is similarly attracted to Bacon's prostituted trope. Feebly searching for originality and surprising wit in his attempt to denigrate the ancients, the dull modern persona naturally would embrace such a paradox. *Antiquitas saeculi juventus mundi* becomes the axiom of the modern's thinking: he *is* ancient, learned, and sedate, while the ancients are childish, inexperienced, and uninformed. Time is literally inverted: ancients lived "when Learning was in its *Cradle*" (p. 144) whereas moderns are the "Fathers of Learning" (p. 145). Everywhere in the *Tale* the modern paradox is rigorously applied. Repeatedly it is asserted that "the very finest Things delivered of old, have been long since invented, and brought to Light by much later Pens" (p. 96). Uneasily, we come to accept the logic that considers Restoration beaux to have lived "in an Age so remote" (p. 81) or that chastises a "modern" Homer for his ignorance of "ancient" writers like Sendivogious, Jacob Boehme, or Thomas Vaughan (p. 127). So implacably is this logic pursued that the modern persona ultimately sees himself as "the *Last Writer*" (p. 130), whereas there is "grave Dispute, whether there have been ever any *Antients* or no" (p. 125).

Moreover, the modern persona implicitly utilizes the Baconian paradox as a general assumption operating throughout the *Tale of a Tub*. In order to comprehend the modern persona's procedure, it will be profitable to examine the *locus classicus* of the paradox in Bacon's *Advancement of Learning* (1605) more closely. One of the most serious "peccant humours" causing the modern "disease of learning," Bacon explained, was excessive reverence for antiquity:

Antiquity deserveth that reverence, that men should make a stand thereupon, and discover what is the best way; but when the discovery is well taken, then to make progression. And to speak truly, *Antiquitas saeculi juventus mundi.* These times are the ancient times, when the world is ancient, and not those which we account ancient *ordine retrogrado,* by a computation backward from ourselves.[54]

It is not simply that we encounter here a new and "modern" notion of "time," where time considered as "a hierarchy of values" is replaced by the conception of it as a "system of magnitudes," so many distances to be measured —although this change does take place—or that "value, in the doctrine of progress, was reduced to a time-calculation: value was in fact *movement in time.* To be old-fashioned or to be 'out of date' was to lack value. Progress was the equivalent in history of mechanical motion through space." [55] What is more important in Bacon's praise of modernity is the seed of a grand sufficiency. Although Bacon explains that we must not calculate events *ordine retrogrado,* from ourselves, Bacon's and the moderns' revolutionary practice consisted precisely in the calculation of all things backward, from themselves. This Baconian and modern scientific point of view emphasizing *ego* is solitary and particular; the modern single self at the latest instant becomes the sole curator and final arbiter of all history.

[54] *Works*, VI, 129–130; Bacon echoes and alters Jeremiah 6:16 here.

[55] Lewis Mumford, *Technics and Civilization* (New York: Harcourt, Brace, 1934), pp. 20, 183–184.

Still more absurdly, such a proud position implies that the particular observer and the latest moment are somehow situated at the "end" of history and time, when in fact any specific momentary modern stands, not at the end of history, but in the midst of its broiling stream. Obviously, any modern occupies a relative position in space-time, although his hubris may induce him not to know it. The logical weakness of his position, as Pope was to urge in the *Essay on Man*, is that, since he does not stand outside the object (time, history, God's creation) he wishes to measure and survey, he remains incapable of obtaining valid conclusions. Nonetheless, this proud assumption of an absolute position in time and history becomes a fallacy to which leading thinkers of the eighteenth, nineteenth, and twentieth centuries have been eminently subject.

In the same way as the progress of a living being is knowable only if it is considered when it has reached a full-grown and perfect state, so likewise knowledge of the progress of the mind is possible only if its history is complete and terminated; this is why the history of philosophy in Comte and Hegel (and the same characteristic is to be found in much later historians) is an inverted history, which really begins at the end, and disposes all its content in time according to its view of the issue of the process.[56]

Swift recognizes very clearly the sufficiency and patent illogic requisite for the attempt to compute *ordine retro-*

---

[56] Emile Bréhier, "The Formation of Our History of Philosophy," trans. Mary Morris, *Philosophy & History: Essays Presented to Ernst Cassirer*, ed. Raymond Klibansky and H. J. Paton (Oxford: Clarendon Press, 1936), p. 168. This point is made throughout in Herbert Butterfield's *The Whig Interpretation of History* (London: G. Bell, 1931).

grado, from the self. But his modern persona does not. Indeed, the persona's habit of assuming that he is an ancient in time, of calculating *ordine retrogrado,* from himself, is his means of placing himself at the top of history. "WHOEVER hath an Ambition to be heard in a Crowd, must press, and squeeze, and thrust, and climb with indefatigable Pains, till he has exalted himself to a certain Degree of Altitude above them" (p. 55). His determination to stand at the "end" of history and to calculate *ordine retrogrado,* from himself, constitutes his crucial *"Edifice in the Air"* (p. 56), or elevation of the ego. Such exaltation of the self is the mighty engine of the modern persona's devising that operates throughout *A Tale of a Tub.*

Moreover, the machinery of sufficiency governs all of Swift's moderns. The modern projector of the *Mechanical Operation of the Spirit* determines all matters backward from himself. Moderns, he observes,

because Antiquity is to be traced *backwards,* do therefore, like *Jews,* begin their Books at the wrong End, as if Learning were a sort of *Conjuring.* These are the Men, who pretend to understand a Book, by scouting thro' the *Index,* as if a Traveller should go about to describe a *Palace,* when he had seen nothing but the *Privy;* or like certain Fortune-tellers in *Northern America,* who have a Way of reading a Man's Destiny, by peeping in his *Breech* [pp. 283–284].

The Modern of the *Tale* obviously endorses backward measurement and inverted progression:

The whole Course of Things being thus entirely changed between *Us* and the *Antients;* and the *Moderns* wisely sensible of it, we of this Age have discovered a shorter, and more

prudent Method, to become *Scholars* and *Wits,* without the
Fatigue of *Reading* or of *Thinking.* The most accomplisht Way
of using Books at present is twofold: Either first, to serve them
as some Men do *Lords,* learn their *Titles* exactly, and then
brag of their Acquaintance. Or Secondly, which is indeed the
choicer, the profounder, and politer Method, to get a thorough Insight into the *Index,* by which the whole Book is governed and turned, like *Fishes* by the *Tail.* For, to enter the
Palace of Learning at the *great Gate,* requires an Expence of
Time and Forms; therefore Men of much Haste and little Ceremony, are content to get in by the *Back-Door.* For, the Arts
are all in a *flying* March, and therefore more easily subdued
by attacking them in the *Rear.* Thus Physicians discover the
State of the whole Body, by consulting only what comes from
Behind. Thus Men catch Knowledge by throwing their *Wit*
on the *Posteriors* of a book, as Boys do Sparrows with fling-
ing *Salt* upon their *Tails.* Thus Human Life is best understood
by the wise man's Rule of *Regarding the End.* Thus are the
Sciences found like Hercules's Oxen, by *tracing them Backwards.* Thus are old Sciences unravelled like *old Stockings,* by
beginning at the *Foot* [pp. 144–145].

The Modern's adoration of the present moment and his inflexible position at the terminus of history render him identical with the madman; each "conceive[s] it in his Power,
to reduce the Notions of all Mankind, exactly to the same
Length, and Breadth, and Height of his own" (p. 166).

Moreover, Swift's own superlative "converting imagination" assimilates from Bacon another popular figure. Bacon
was fond of arguing that the quantity of knowledge coming down from antiquity was slight. In spite of the fact that
he had elsewhere argued that truth is the daughter of time
and the product of slow maturation, he frequently mini-

mized contemporary "vulgar and received opinions" accepted from antiquity, since "time seemeth to be of the nature of a river or flood, that bringeth down to us that which is light and blown up, and sinketh and drowneth that which is solid and grave." [57] It is not simply that Swift plays with this idea, as when he causes his modern persona to argue that modern productions should not be lost from sight or "sunk in the Abyss of Things," since " 'tis certain, that in their own Nature they were *light* enough to swim upon the Surface for all Eternity" (p. 32). More important, the Modern metaphysically equates the "last moment" with the "surface" of time's stream, with the "surface" of any physical object, and with "superficies" generally. The modern instant sits lumpishly upon time's tip. And in the *Tale of a Tub* all subject matter is converted and refined to suit this imagery of the surface. Thus, Parisian fashions and clothes, settled as they are upon the outward *surface* of men, acquire the first importance. And an appropriate religious sect is accordingly founded, which reduces man to the inessential and worships his clothing as if it were a rational being (p. 78). Allegory, too, is granted crucial importance, since allegorical meanings sit upon the *surface* of the merely literal. Decorously too, commentaries and notes are settled upon the surface of the text. Digressions regularly perch upon the surface of the fable. Such digressions acquire the further substantial justification of being modish; their sudden appearance here and there has a certain right-

<hr/>

[57] *Filum Labyrinthi* . . . , *Works*, VI, 426. Bacon is fond of this figure; see I, 202; VI, 42, 131; VIII, 29, 103, 108; and XII, 259. Logically, of course, it is a mere play upon words; see the incisive critique by John Stuart Mill, *A System of Logic Ratiocinative and Inductive* . . . , 2 vols. (8th ed.; London: Longmans, Green, Reader, and Dyer, 1872), II, 378–379.

ness, since *at the moment* of their conception they lie uppermost in the author's mind.[58]

The very words "surface" and "superficies" play a dominant role in the *Tale*. The persona claims to have contrived his allegories so that meaning lies "near the Surface" (p. 100). The exalted tailor, a veritable deity of superficial fashions, is conceived as an idol "placed in the highest Parts of the House," and his seat upon the raised altar is a "superficies" (p. 76). Madness itself is defined as delight in the surface (p. 173), and the madman described as contented "with the *Films* and *Images* that fly off upon his Senses from the *Superficies* of Things" (p. 174). Ultimately, madness is reduced to vapors which rise to the top of a man, establishing a residence in the brain. All madness by definition finally emerges as the "Redundancy of *Vapour*" (p. 174). Similarly, critics are comprehended as those who delight "to nibble at the Superfluities and Excrescencies of Books" (p. 98). And the essence of all brazen modern superficiality is reflected in modern critics and modern mirrors. In both, *"Brass* is an Emblem of Duration, and when it is skilfully burnished, will cast *Reflections* from its own *Superficies*, without any Assistance of *Mercury* from behind" (p. 103). In such a quotation, Swift's puns and plays upon words achieve monumental proportions.

Naturally, in this climate, the *Tale*'s very substance is dramatized as cloth of superficial cut. Witty lines are at moments hurried and huddled incongruously; narrative

---

[58] Swift was fond of treating time spatially, with emphasis upon surfaces; thus Gulliver claims to know very well "that Writers of Travels, like *Dictionary*-Makers, are sunk into Oblivion by the Weight and Bulk of those who come last, and therefore lie uppermost" (*Prose Works*, XI, 276).

seams are tacked together haphazardly. Moreover, the image of the tailor's linsey-woolsey is supplemented by the metaphor of the chef's decoctions; devious appearance is reinforced by bad taste. Jack's humor, like the brothers' bedecked coats, is "Meddly" (pp. 135, 137)—so much sauce (p. 50). Soups, olios, sauces (p. 143)—the surfaces and decorative edges of nutriment—are the *Tale*'s staple and steady diet. For books are no better than they should be, "like Dress, and Dyet, and Diversions" (p. 206).

Perhaps one of the most noteworthy endorsements in the *Tale* of the surface occurs when the persona attempts to account for the increasing number of modern writings that hourly start up. He appeals to the "Troglodyte Philosopher," who explains:

'Tis certain . . . some Grains of Folly are of course annexed, as Part of the Composition of Human Nature, only the Choice is left us, whether we please to wear them *Inlaid* or *Embossed;* And we need not go very far to seek how that is usually determined, when we remember it, it is with Human Faculties as with Liquors, the lightest will be ever at the Top [p. 183].

It is typical that a cryptic—and trite—expression should be made to come from the lips of a "philosopher," just as it is suitable in the *Tale*'s perverted world that an ancient barbarian should be the source of modern philosophical wisdom and that the *surface* should be underwritten by the inhabitant of a *cave.*[59]

---

[59] The original troglodytes (cave dwellers) were identified in classical times as naked savages, swift animal-like runners dwelling in Sinus Arabia, along the Red Sea. See Herodotus, *Histories* IV.-183; Aristotle, *History of Animals* VIII.12; and Pliny, *Natural History* VI.xxxiii.168–xxxiv.170, VI.xxxv.189. Restoration and Louis le Grand satirists took pleasure in referring to savages as if they

We have seen the modern persona wielding the trite paradox and Swift's subsequent infinite playfulness with terms like "superficiality" that buffet and overturn the modern wit. It remains to comment upon Swift's management of his most skillful paradoxical reversal, utilizing the worn *antiquitas saeculi juventus mundi* and bringing it tellingly to bear upon the modern persona himself. Since the Modern's work is published, not in 1697 when it was so momentously written, but in 1704, it has obviously fallen, as I note in Chapter 6, into the irretrievable past. Out of fashion and out of date, the Modern and his work, in an unanticipated application of Bacon's paradox, have literally become antiquities.[60] The author is unknown and unnamed; his work has become an antiquity. Like an Egyptian scroll or

were learned men, e.g., as Lapland and Persian magi, gymnosophists, Scythians, Iroquois virtuosi, literati of Tobinambou.

[60] Though not an author to repeat himself, Swift nevertheless again inverts antiquity and modernity in a minor *jeu d'esprit:* "A Discourse to Prove the Antiquity of the English Tongue, Shewing, from various Instances, that HEBREW, GREEK, and LATIN, were derived from the ENGLISH" (*Prose Works*, IV, 231–239). Scholars have neglected Swift's use of the Baconian paradox in the *Tale*. Indeed, Emile Pons actually laments Swift's failure to employ this type of paradox in his satire: "We cannot prevent ourselves from expressing the idle regret that Swift [Pons is speaking particularly of *The Battle of the Books*], confronting this empty debate concerning the relative superiority of different ages, had not himself taken into account this idea expressed in turn by Giordano Bruno, Bacon, Descartes, Pascal, Perrault, Fontenelle, Malebranche, and others, and which appears to be characteristic of all times, since one finds it already in the Old Testament—that it is the ancients who represent humanity's infancy, while the moderns are its antiquity." Thereupon, Pons takes an imaginative flight, considering how Swift *might* have employed the paradox—to denigrate the ancients (*Swift: Les Années de Jeunesse et Le "Conte du Tonneau"* [Paris: Librairie Istra, 1925], p. 285).

a wizened medieval manuscript, the "Modern tale" can barely be deciphered or comprehended; it will be adorned with a full course of footnotes and explanations, will submit to edition and "restoration." As a barren manuscript from the distant past (of 1697), it demands the acquisition of scholarly superficies, refinements, and polite elegancies of the modern world (of 1704). The gateway to the work must be sown with dedications, cultivated with prefaces, and chaffed with a bookseller's meditations. Its simplistic tale must be stuffed with digressions and supplied with morals. The manuscript's lacunae must be plugged with conjectures and stuffed with notes.

Yet these niceties serve a modern edition for 1704 only. By 1710, with the enormous lapse of time, the work again is antique, again requires resurfacing, puffing, and resurrection. And so it will ever be. Swift's satiric fiction marvelously dramatizes the paradox of modernity: an insistent modernity is the perennial of fashion and the fool of time. In short, modernity *is* antiquity. Moderns had sought to be considered ancients; the fine paradoxical stroke of the satirist's fiction has fully granted them their wish.

IV

We have not, with the discussion of the comic transformation coercing Swift's moderns to become flatulent antiquities, completed the analysis of Swift's ineluctable ability to play endlessly upon words like "antiquity" and "modernity" and to vary the metamorphosis of classical antiquity into Queen Anne modernity. One further series of paradoxical inversions in the *Tale of Tub* deserves examination. For Swift reveals, in one more paradoxical way, that the modern persona cannot possibly be, in spite of himself, a modern at all.

In new ways the persona is repeatedly dislodged from modernity and cast back into the past. Thus, for instance, although the Modern claims to be the most up-to-the-minute modern, "just come from" his initiation into the *"Grub Street* Brotherhood" (pp. 63–64), we immediately afterward learn that the Grub Street fraternity is *not* the most modern organization. Lately the "Societies of *Gresham* and of *Will's*" have seceded from their "Parent" Grub Street Society and have become the stronger organizations, made up of "revolted and new-fangled Writers" (p. 65). In a trice, the Modern has become out-of-date; instead of being the freshest and most youthful, he has become parental, reactionary, a member of an older and largely supplanted generation.

Again, as "Historian," the Modern attempts to strengthen his repeated assertion that he is recounting a "true" story by a series of appeals to earlier texts. He regularly alludes to his own "Labour of collection [and] the Faithfulness in recounting" (p. 106) the tale of the three brothers. At times he specifically cites "my Author" (p. 115), as if scrupulously retelling an ancient tale. Such practices—making little distinction between "story" and "history," rigorously retaining bookish tradition by adhering strictly to earlier texts, and repeatedly citing one's sources and authors—are all, as C. S. Lewis reminds us, eminently characteristic of medieval historiography.[61] Once more,

---

[61] *The Discarded Image: An Introduction to Medieval and Renaissance Literature* (Cambridge: Cambridge University Press, 1964), pp. 5, 178–185.

the modern persona is translated backward in time, becoming medieval man.

Most often in the *Tale*, however, the Modern is propelled still further backward in time. Repeatedly the Modern is discovered to be an ancient in earnest. The *Tale*'s most telling paradoxical reversal proves, by means of the Modern and his tale, despite his endeavor absolutely to reject the past, that there is no new thing under the sun. Again and again the poor modern persona produces nothing but knowledge long ago propounded. Despite his insistent attempts at "Innovation" and "Invention," his undertaking to "Spin and Spit wholly from himself," he can manufacture nothing but "ancient" wisdom. With supremely comic helplessness, the modern persona in his postulates is revealed to be as ancient as the aegis, Panpipes, and urn.

Accordingly, when he wishes to defend his modern work on grounds of its "depth" (pp. 185–187), he appeals, for justification, to the threadbare habit of allegorizing and to the critical search for hidden meanings inaugurated in late antiquity, repeatedly employed in the Middle Ages, and sustained even in the seventeenth century. Similarly, the Modern's dissertation upon Aeolism leads him back to the oracular founder, "the Original at *Delphos*" (p. 161). His learned postulate that "vapors" cause madness (Section IX) merely confirms the theory of humors accepted since the time of Hippocrates and Empedocles. Likewise, when, in attempting to account for madmen's acquiring followers, he conjectures that there is "a peculiar *String* in the Harmony of Human Understanding, which in several individuals is exactly of the same Tuning" (p. 167), and an inevitable "Sympathy" created among those whose "Tuning" is at the same "Pitch," he is embracing a concept distinctly Pythagorean.[62]

Doubtless the finest examples of this unsuspected resurrection of the past in the *Tale of a Tub* are represented by an undercurrent of allusions to Horace's *Ars Poetica*.[63] Admittedly, the persona's attempt to be most modern, most divorced from antiquity, triumphantly succeeds. His amnesia and his work's vast digressiveness and its incompleteness clearly mark his composition as the very antithesis of a "classic." Unlike a classic, his *Tale* is "unnatural"; his work is kin to every creation that strives for monstrous innovation; he "is like a painter adding a dolphin to the woods, a boar to the waves." [64] Unlike the classical author, the Modern displays no "maturity of *mind*," no "maturity of *manners*," no "maturity of language" whatever. His work could not be further removed from the traditional order and restraint that he himself, in dismissing, had called the

---

[62] See Aristotle, *Politics* VIII.v.10; and Plato, *Phaedo* 93. See also Phillip Harth, *Swift and Anglican Rationalism: The Religious Background of "A Tale of a Tub"* (Chicago: University of Chicago Press, 1961), pp. 119–120; and Edward W. Rosenheim, Jr., *Swift and the Satirist's Art* (Chicago: University of Chicago Press, 1963), p. 194, n. 13.

[63] The *Ars Poetica* was widely admired and imitated in the Restoration; see George Sherburn, *A Literary History of England*, ed. Albert C. Baugh (New York: Appleton-Century-Crofts, 1948), p. 721; and Caroline Goad, *Horace in the English Literature of the Eighteenth Century* (New Haven: Yale University Press, 1918), especially p. 10.

[64] *Ars Poetica* 29–30; reprinted by permission of the publishers and THE LOEB CLASSICAL LIBRARY from Horace, *Satires, Epistles, Ars Poetica*, ed. and trans. H. Rushton Fairclough (London: William Heinemann; Cambridge, Mass.: Harvard University Press, 1929), p. 453.

"common Forms" (p. 171). Clearly, his work adheres to no "generally accepted standard." Most important, he is barren of what is possibly most requisite for the classic, "the consciousness of history." [65] Without memory or discipline, he has no sense at all of "chronology," no historical sense.

> Of History in general Chronology is the very Quintescence; the rest without it is but a Rope of Sand, a Tale of a Tub: where any Writer has failed in it, his whole Book has been condemn'd; and where any Speaker is not guided by it, his Discourse will not be minded.[66]

Lacking chronology, the Modern's creation *is* "a Tale of a Tub."

Consequently, his work cannot be farther removed from the precepts of the *Ars Poetica* and Horace's injunctions to avoid the unnatural (*invita Minerva*, l. 385), to "keep to the type," observing probability or universality (ll. 23, 41, 152, 195, 242), and to maintain decorum and consistency (ll. 92, 119, 127, 157). Indeed, as Pope was later to suggest, every insistently modern author runs directly counter to Horace's recommendations, becoming "Grotesque." The modern's "works would be spoiled by an imitation of nature, or uniformity of design."

He is to mingle bits of the most various, or discordant kinds, landscape, history, portraits, animals, and connect them with a great deal of flourishing, by heads or tails, as it shall please his imagination, and contribute to his principal end, which is

---

[65] T. S. Eliot, *What Is a Classic?* (London: Faber and Faber, 1945), pp. 12, 16, 13, 19.

[66] Matthew Prior, "Heads for a Treatise upon Learning" (1721), *The Literary Works of Matthew Prior*, ed. H. Bunker Wright and Monroe K. Spears (Oxford: Clarendon Press, 1959), I, 581.

to glare by strong oppositions of colours, and surprize by contrariety of images

Serpentes avibus geminentur, tigribus agni.

Hor.

His design ought to be like a labyrinth, out of which no body can get clear but himself. And since the great Art of all Poetry is to mix Truth with Fiction, in order to join the *Credible* with the *Surprizing;* our author shall produce the Credible, by painting nature in her lowest simplicity; and the Surprizing, by contradicting common opinion.[67]

Certainly, Swift's persona's composition violates every Horatian injunction. Yet by a remarkable circumvolution, the Modern simultaneously not only repeats in his "discoveries" many of the *Ars Poetica's* famous dicta, but also obeys them. By means of Swift's magic art, the banished past is again recaptured.

Horace had praised the moderns of his own day (ll. 285–291), and the modern persona lavishly follows. Horace had recommended that the poet rigorously revise his work, employing the file (ll. 291, 390, 441, 448); in the *Tale* moderns are so heavily addicted to such "refining" (pp. 44, 67, 101, 143, 166, 174, 181, 190, 206) that there is reason to doubt whether any modern topic is left (p. 146); hence moderns will be reduced to writing *"upon Nothing"* (p. 208). Horace had advocated the observance of *decorum personae,* whereby each character in a fiction is self-consistent and acts according to his age, class, and changing

---

[67] "Peri Bathous, or, Of the Art of Sinking in Poetry," *The Works of Alexander Pope Esq. . . . ,* ed. William Warburton; VI: *Miscellaneous Pieces in Prose and Verse* (London, 1751), 206–207. For classic instances of Pope's imitation of the grotesque, see *The Dunciad,* I, 69–78, and Moral Essay IV, ll. 119–126.

nature (ll. 119, 127, 157, 316); Swift's Modern seriously attempts to maintain in sections of tale his "Character of an Historian" (p. 133), although increasingly unable to do so.

Most humorous are those passages in which the Modern articulates "new" pieces of wisdom. Where Horace had recommended that the poet study Greek models both day and night—*vos exemplaria Graeca / nocturna versate manu, versate diurna* (ll. 268–269)—the Modern describes himself as one educated "but thro' the Assistance of our Noble *Moderns;* whose most edifying Volumes I turn indefatigably over Night and Day, for the Improvement of my Mind, and the good of my Country" (p. 96). The *Ars Poetica*'s most renowned passage occurs where Horace advises that the poet's goal should be *aut prodesse aut delectare* (l. 333), to teach and to delight his audience. He adds that the greatest success is realized by those poets who blend teaching with pleasure (*qui miscuit utile dulci*—l. 343). In a grand anticlimax, Swift's modern author formulates anew this selfsame knowledge. After great labor and study, he tells us, "I do affirm, that having carefully cut up *Humane Nature,* I have found a very strange, new, and important Discovery; That the Publick Good of Mankind is performed by two Ways, *Instruction,* and *Diversion*" (p. 124). Blandly, he informs us that he has attempted to knead "up both together with a *Layer* of *Utile* and a *Layer* of *Dulce*" (p. 124).

The most striking repetition of Horace to be found in *A Tale of a Tub* vitally concerns a classic Horatian mandate:

> . . . si quid tamen olim
> scripseris, in Maeci descendat iudicis auris
> et patris et nostras, *nonumque prematur in annum,*

membranis intus positis: delere licebit
quod non edideris; nescit vox missa reverti

[*A.P.*, ll. 386–390—italics mine].

"Do not hasten to publish," Horace had counseled: *"keep your work beside you for nine years,* polishing it and correcting." [68] The Modern, it is true, wholly fails to refine his work, even mislaying his papers entirely after composing portions in 1696 and 1697; ever after, "the Author came to be without his *papers*" (p. 16), so that the work lay at the printers untouched for years, a manuscript "which he could have easily corrected with a very few Blots, had he been Master of his Papers for a Year or two before their Publication" (p. 4). Thus, by a seeming accident, the Modern's unrevised, incomplete, and hasty work, filled with "chasms," is, as it were, "rushed" into print *in the ninth year* after it was written. The Modern has ignored Horace's advice that the artist exercise patience,

[68] Horace's playful advice that one should keep one's "conception" for nine years before giving it birth was widely popular. It did not originate with Horace. See Catullus, *Carmina* XCV; Suetonius, *De Grammaticis* 18; Quintilian's Dedication to Trypho, 2, *Institutio Oratoria* I; Erasmus, *The Praise of Folly*, ed. and trans. Hoyt H. Hudson (New York: Modern Library, 1941), p. 74; Pope's "Epistle to Dr. Arbuthnot," l. 40; and Johnson's *The Idler*, No. 60, and *The Rambler*, No. 169. Caroline Goad, in *Horace in the English Literature of the Eighteenth Century*, cites a number of other places in Prior, Richardson, Walpole, Johnson. Swift's own persona, the pedantic and curious collector Simon Wagstaff, claims to have gathered his materials for twelve years and to have refined them for sixteen more: "Herein, I resolved to exceed the Advice of *Horace*, a *Roman* Poet, (which I have read in Mr. *Creech's* admirable Translation) that an Author should keep his Works nine Years in his Closet, before he ventured to publish them" ("A Complete Collection of Genteel and Ingenious Conversation . . . ," *Prose Works*, IV, 101).

labor, and time; yet he has *obeyed* Horace's exhortation by waiting those prescribed nine years—although he has done so for the wrong reasons. His treatise, appearing in 1704, is not only incomplete and precipitate; it is inscrutable and antique as well.

Finally, Horace, at the conclusion of his epistle, had related a tale of the frenzied and impetuous poet who, filled with inspiration of the moment like the lunatic (*iracunda Diana*), roams the streets aimlessly eructing his own verses, until he falls, unawares, into a pit, where he is laughed at by children and feared by the crowd. What is the cause, Horace had wondered, of such frenzy? Is such a one pursued by nemesis? Has he, perhaps, defiled ancestral ashes (*utrum / minxerit in patrios cineres*—ll. 470–471)? He is, in any case, enclosed like the madman, in a cage. Swift's modern persona likewise tells the story of enthusiastic Brother Jack's wandering wildly through the streets, laughed at by children and feared by the crowd, and of his fall into a kennel (pp. 192–195).

There had been an application of a moral to the tale in Horace: in poetry there is no middle ground; if it fails of sublimity, the poem sinks to the very lowest depths (*si paulum summo decessit, vergit ad imum*—l. 378). In his fall, Jack is kin to the fancy of the *Tale*'s famous simile, which rises, wavers, and subsequently, like a "dead Bird of Paradise," falls to the ground (pp. 157–158). Jack is kin, as well, to the modern persona himself, likewise mad, who again and again in the course of his thinking travels the vain arc of an Icarian flight. Like all these others, the modern persona seeks an Empedoclean fate: to "descend to the very *bottom* of all the *Sublime*" (p. 44).

In all such flights, Swift's modern persona unwittingly

retraces the very course that fanciful madness plods in the *Ars Poetica,* and against which Horace had given warning. Yet, as Swift well knew, "no Preacher is listened to, but Time; which gives us the same Train and Turn of Thought, that elder People have tried in vain to put into our Heads before." [69] It is so; but the ancient Modern, cast by his amnesiac ignorance into the youth of the world, is condemned forever to live exiled from the munificence of time.

As a result, Swift's persona is revealed to have broken every rule, both ancient and modern. He himself is ancient and modern; for he has, despite Horace's caveat against it, managed to confuse the demeanor and the speech of the "ripe old man [and] one still in the flower and fervour of youth," assigning "a youth the part of age, or a boy that of manhood" (*A.P.,* ll. 115–116, 176–177). Swift has created a modern and a modern world in the *Tale of a Tub* that are decorous and complete in their inversions, a world where youth and age, story and digression, sanity and bedlam shuffle, collide, and interchange. And what is the source of such violent transpositions? The answer is simple: Swift's moderns have run mad out of pride; like Horace's frenzied poet, *utrum minxerit in patrios cineres,* they have defiled and abolished the past; they have violated the ashes of their ancestors. In so doing, according to Swift's brazen and inflexible irony, they have, although they do not know it, fouled their own little nest.

v

As a matter of fact, "Moderns" of every period assert that they need not rely upon ancient knowledge, that if an-

[69] Swift, "Thoughts on *Various* Subjects," *Prose Works,* I, 241.

cient wisdom were entirely lost, ingenious moderns would rediscover it. In our own century, John Herman Randall has assured us that the classics would not have been missed:

> If the manuscripts of Greece and Rome had perished every one beneath the monk's missal, the outcome would not have been essentially different. Men would still have turned to man and nature, and if the modern world might not so soon have come into being, it is quite possible that men would not have wandered down so many blind alleys. Of a truth the Renaissance discovered the humanities, but it found them in Florence or Augsburg or Paris, not in ancient books.[70]

Fontenelle, that avid seventeenth-century modern, was pleased to urge the same point:

> If a man who has made a good start in science and letters develops an illness which makes him forget them, will that mean that he has been incapacitated? No: he can acquire such knowledge again whenever he wishes, by beginning once more with the first elements. If some remedy suddenly restored his memory, this would hardly be a difficulty; he would discover himself knowing all that he had known, and, in order to continue, he would merely have to pick up again where he had left off. The reading of the ancients has dispelled ignorance and barbarism in previous centuries. I know it well. It restores to us all at once ideas of truth and beauty which we would have been long in recovering—but which we would have grasped ultimately, without the help of the Greeks and Romans.[71]

[70] *The Making of the Modern Mind* . . . (Boston: Houghton Mifflin, 1926), p. 115.

[71] [Bernard Le Bovier de] Fontenelle, "Digression sur les anciens et les modernes," *Entretiens sur la pluralité des mondes, Digression sur les anciens et les modernes,* ed. Robert Shackleton (Oxford: Clarendon Press, 1955), p. 171.

Swift's answer is the satirist's *fiat lux*, creating *A Tale of a Tub*. In the book resides just such a forgetful modern as Fontenelle had envisioned. The *Tale* is the mathematician's solution to the equation, the satirist's hypothetical "test case," empirically studying a memoryless modern set adrift in a traditionless world. It remains for us, the observers of the satirist's experiment, to draw conclusions. Swift's modern persona flatly rejects the past—and yet dedicates his work "To Posterity" (pp. 30–38), "for the Universal Improvement of Mankind" (p. 1). Edmund Burke challenges the ambivalence of such revolutionaries: "A spirit of innovation is generally the result of a selfish temper and confined views. People will not look forward to posterity, who never look backward to their ancestors." [72] Referring to Swift's fictional creation, we

[72] *Reflections on the Revolution in France* (London: Dent, 1960), p. 31. Moderns normally contradict Burke, claiming it *is* possible to serve posterity while ignoring the past. Thus R. V. Sampson argues that moderns choose to serve posterity solely from the psychological urgings of "present emotional needs" (*Progress in the Age of Reason: The Seventeenth Century to the Present Day* [Cambridge, Mass.: Harvard University Press, 1956], p. 128). But where, we might ask, do these present needs come from? Is not the "present" boasting of one's motives but another instance of gratifying one's conscience at the moment? Present-day moderns still play with such "modern" paradoxes—without supporting them. Carl L. Becker, in *The Heavenly City of the Eighteenth-Century Philosophers* (New Haven: Yale University Press, 1932), p. 131, propounds such a paradox: The Humanists "missed the simple fact (and there are still many who refuse to see it) that the true way to imitate the Greeks is not to imitate them, since the Greeks themselves imitated no one." But surely Becker is merely playing with words, restricting the word "imitate" to the imitation of literary models. We can as easily claim that to ignore the Greeks would be to imitate them, since they ignored us. Most telling, however, is the fact that Becker's modern paradox is very, very old; it

must answer two questions: Will a man who rejects his ancestry labor for his progeny? Will a man who has lost the past be able to retrieve it? The answer to the first leaves no doubt. The modern persona's private concern with his own garret, his own projects and curiosities, utterly prevents him from serving commonwealth or mankind. Rather, his crass interest in sales, in fashions, in patronage, in projects leads him to serve only himself. We have seen that his private vices lead not to public benefits, nor even to public detriment, but instead to public bewilderment. Swift's great irony simply reveals that the modern of the instant will in a few short years grow out of date and obscure; Swift's modern persona—like the Struldbruggs of *Gulliver's Travels*—will not serve the future, because future generations will not comprehend his antique language and his wizened text.

To the second question—will the Modern as a "single man" be able to recapture the vanished past of tradition?—the answer is equally negative. The very considerable irony

was used by Thomas Sprat, in *The History of the Royal Society of London, For the Improving of Natural Knowledge* (3d ed.; London, 1722), pp. 49–50, and used still earlier by Giordano Bruno, in *Eroici Furori* (cited in Giacinto Margiotta, *Le Origini Italiane de la Querelle des Anciens et des Modernes* [Rome: Editrice Studium, 1953], p. 140). It is so hoary as to have been employed by Horace (*Epistles* II.i.90–92). The great irony—and Swift perceived it clearly—is that "moderns," though professing novelty, continually rely upon age-old tradition. Wotton, too, imitates the past while arguing for modernity; in the structure and the content of his *Reflections*, "Wotton depended entirely upon Glanvill, and chapters fourteen to twenty-six are definitely modelled upon the *Plus Ultra*, which, in turn, had been patterned, though not so closely, upon Hakewill's book" (R. F. Jones, "The Background of the *Battle of the Books*," p. 150).

of such an answer lies in the fact that the modern persona, despite his remarkable singularity and his distance from the classical past and all its wisdom, does manage to echo—repeatedly—ancient preachment and ancient practice. Yet the wisdom of the ancients that he recovers is wisdom broken, accidental, and obscure. Without memory, the Modern can never construct coherent tradition: he will forget the very pieces of ancient lore that he has accidentally, only a moment ago, reclaimed.

The most substantial irony of the *Tale of a Tub* reveals the modern persona, herald of infinite progress, reproducing only imperfect and stunted caricatures of hoary tradition. After laboring mightily at original conception, after waiting nine years for gestation, the Modern ultimately gives birth—in snippets from Pythagoras, Isocrates, Hippocrates, Theophrastus, Galen, Horace—to his own ancestors. Santayana renders Swift's point explicitly:

Progress, far from consisting in change, depends on retentiveness. When change is absolute there remains no being to improve and no direction to set for possible improvement: and when experience is not retained, as among savages, infancy is perpetual. Those who cannot remember the past are condemned to repeat it.[73]

"Those who cannot remember the past are condemned to repeat it." *Et erat.* The *Tale*'s aspiring modern persona, in a way he never suspected, *is* the past; his modernity *is* antiquity, and with a vengeance: Swift's finest paradox converts modern victory into defeat. According to *A Tale of a*

[73] George Santayana, *The Life of Reason, or the Phases of Human Progress*, rev. and abr. by Santayana and Daniel Cory (New York: Scribner's, 1954), p. 82.

Tub's comic vision, *Antiquitas capta ferum victorem cepit:* antiquity at last has captured her captor.[74]

Rejecting his predecessors, the Modern has rejected the future. Rejecting memory, the Modern has rejected mind. Rejecting the past, he has somehow managed to echo that past, but faintly.

> If there be nothing new, but that which is
> Hath been before, how are our brains beguil'd,
> Which, labouring for invention, bear amiss
> The second burden of a former child! [75]

In the *Tale of a Tub* that very forgetful miscarriage which nonetheless redelivers the rejected past is Jonathan Swift's central artistic action. And Swift has accomplished this action with probability, with decorum, with extensive "modern" inventiveness, while yet adhering to classic satiric tradition. That he has generated all this variety of creation from his single theme is demonstration enough of Swift's brilliant, brazen, and memorable art.

[74] To suit my context, I have adapted Horace's witty paradox in *Epistles* II.i.156.

[75] William Shakespeare, Sonnet LIX, ll. 1–4.

Index

[231]